GREAT GIG MEMORIES
FROM PUNKS AND FRIENDS

COMPILED BY NIALL McGUIRK AND MICHAEL MURPHY

HOPE PUBLICATIONS

In memory of Kathlyn Murphy and Joe McGuirk

Hope Publications, Dublin 2020
All contributions © 2020 the authors.

ISBN 978-0-9955475-2-0

Design, layout, vision: Russ Bestley
Photography, front cover: Steve Averill
Editor, proof-reader: John Fleming
Compiled by Niall McGuirk and Michael Murphy
Printed by www.rotatorpm.com, a subsidiary of www.rotatorvinyl.com, specialist vinyl and CD production and packing experts

www.hopecollectiveireland.com
Hope Publications: 31 Hazel Road, Donnycarney, Dublin 9
E-mail: Niall@thumped.com

CONTENTS

We list the contributors with the names of some of *our* favourite bands that they were in. So it's not a complete list by any means.

INTRODUCTION

This book is the sound of our record collections talking.

We wrote to people from our favourite bands, and to some of the great behind-the-scenes people in music. We asked them to write about a memorable gig. They did. You can read the results here. It's a celebration of music, people, community, spirit, creativity and do-it-yourself action.

This is a scrappy scrap-book eye-witness history of punk. It's also a good reminder that most musicians are fans at heart. Some of the people you stand beside at gigs will form bands you love. Creativity inspires creativity. Is there any better reason for creating something?

This is a sequel to the book we released in 2017 which raised over £5,000 for the Irish Red Cross Syrian Refugee appeal. But why would two punk rockers from Dublin compile a book of gig memories to raise funds for the NHS Charities Together Covid-19 appeal? For the same reason that the people in this book wrote gig memories. To do something. To try something positive. To reflect on just how much music has given to us. To remember the front-line people who look after us when we need them.

This book was a collaborative effort, and the punky community made it possible. Special thanks to everyone who helped. Russ Bestley made it look beautiful and put us in touch with some of our favourite music people. John Fleming went way above and beyond too. He reached out to some incredible people and then volunteered to proof-read the book. Steve Averill donated the powerful image of The Clash for the cover. Peter Jones answered countless questions about printing after he opened up his address book and asked loads of his friends to write something. The book also benefited from incredible work by Dave Linehan, Jude Carr, Tom Crossley, Elvera Butler, Dave Bason, Chris Haskett, Catherine McRae, Eugene Lee, Mike Dines, Catonia Whalen, Terry O'Neill, Drew Stone, Ron Burman, Russell Mills, Neville Farmer, Garry Bushell, Steve Lindsey, Tadanoshin and Andy 'Blackpool' Higgins. Beth Alice Edelstein deserves special thanks for all her work. Thank you to Miriam McGuirk and Jo Scott. You are all incredible people and you are living proof that community works.

Niall McGuirk and Michael Murphy

PUNK AND COMMUNITY

Does community mean anything to you? It means the world to me. Whether community is the area you live, the sport you play, the people you work with or the music you listen to, it is an essential bond for living.

I am a member of many communities, but it is the punk rock one that I hold dear. Whenever times are tough, I reach to my record collection and allow the memories of each slab of vinyl to come through. They in turn trigger different memories, of times when I listened to records with other people or of journeys to gigs to see the band.

My first bond with music came when I borrowed Elvis Costello's "Armed Forces" album from a school mate. I had been listening to my brother's record collection until then but this one gave me my identity. Something they hadn't already got. I got The Skids' "Days In Europa" as a Christmas present in 1979 and it took off from there. Really it was The Clash that changed it all though. The Clash made me want to play in a band. A few Christmases after "Days in Europa" I got a bass and a small amp and started playing Clash songs. After that, the politics of Crass and Flux of Pink Indians showed me I didn't have to wait for others to do things for me. I could do it myself. So when we needed to play a gig the obvious route was to put it on ourselves. When we wanted a band like The Membranes, and then Fugazi, to come to Ireland we asked them over and suggested they play here.

I saw Paranoid Visions play and their sense of belonging and community stuck with me ever since I went up and said hello that first night. They were always ready to help others. I saw The Pleasure Cell play and struck up a lifelong friendship with Michael. People who went to see these bands weren't consumers, we were almost an extension of the band. Everyone knew each other and gigs were family occasions. It was this sense of community that stuck with me when trying to put on gigs as part of Hope Promotions and then the Hope Collective.

I look back and dream of sets from bands like Fugazi, The Ex, The Clash, Against Me, Menstrual Cramps, Pleasure Cell, Chumbawamba, Damien Dempsey, M(h)aol, Latterman, A Page of Punk and so many more. Nights when bodies were crushed together, our hands in the air dreaming of a brighter future. This wasn't quite the future we hoped for, so we have turned back to the community to help. It's what we do in times of trouble.

Niall McGuirk

A NOTE ON EARLY PUNK IN IRELAND

The punk songs of Northern Ireland are some of the most celebrated and memorable sounds in the history of punk. You probably already know them, if you don't there's a treat in store for you.

But south of the Border, in Ireland, punk had a completely different history. If some of the bands in this book are unfamiliar to you, it's not because they weren't brilliant, it's because of that different history. While the first punks in most countries and scenes encountered hostility and scorn, in Ireland early punk's reputation was absolutely poisoned when its brightest moment became its darkest hour.

In June 1977, an extraordinary gig was organised with some of the best bands from both sides of the Border, including The Radiators from Space and The Undertones. Tragically, at the gig Patrick Coultry, who was just a teenager, was stabbed to death. Irish punk made the cover of the NME for all the wrong reasons. Venues wouldn't touch punk and it was forced underground. That meant that in 1976-1978 the scene never produced bands that closely followed the path of The Sex Pistols or The Clash.

In a better world The Radiators from Space *might* have done that. In fact, for some of their early shows they were sort of like "a Clash-fronted-by-a-Jello Biafra". But after Patrick Coultry's death they rushed their debut album and became exiles in London. It was Dublin's great loss. The Boomtown Rats who emerged just after The Radiators, also emigrated, although they were always on their own path towards the type of Dr Feelgood-fuelled explosive pop that made the pop charts so enjoyable at the time.

There was a real irony about Ireland being cut off from punk across the water. The prototype London punk label, Chiswick, had Irish founders, Ted Carroll and Roger Armstrong, while one of Stiff Records' co-founders was Dave Robinson, a Dubliner. The great early supporter of punk, Paul Charles, the booking agent who found live work for bands including Buzzcocks and The Undertones, was also Irish.

The young bands left in Ireland absorbed the great bands of punk and new wave. Musically, they drew from The Stranglers, The Skids, XTC and especially The Jam. Ireland's power-pop had arrived, and it was *sensational*, although the bands generally couldn't afford the quality of studios available across the water. They were a world away from the British charts. With hindsight, as one of them wrote, they didn't have a "ghost of a chance".

That's why it's such a thrill to have input in this book from: Revolver, The Strougers, The Atrix, DC Nien, The Blades, The Vipers, The Threat, Chant! Chant! Chant! and early electronic pioneers like Steve Averill, The Fountainhead, Stano and Zerra One.

For the small number of music fans in Ireland who were hungry for something new, exciting, dynamic and original, they were the soundtrack of our young lives. Soon, but maybe not soon enough, a wave of bands did emerge in Ireland who were influenced by John Lydon's Pistols, and even more by his Public Image Ltd. These bands didn't have a unifying sound, but they did have a unifying sensibility that drew from Crass and Flux as well as PIL. They were like lo-fi Killing Jokes, with Paranoid Visions being the longest-lasting. They were attention-grabbers, statement-makers, instigators, dark nursery-rhymers but never happy-ever-afters. While The Virgin Prunes and, later, My Bloody Valentine, were the best-known, and nothing like most of their contemporaries, the bands of the era were haunted and cryptic, they were theatre *and* hate.

The Irish bands could also be brilliantly funny and simply brilliant, even with a sense of the shadow. Above all, they could be entertaining. You'll find Microdisney, Five Go Down To The Sea, Into Paradise, The Golden Horde, Bad Karma Beckons, The Stars of Heaven, The Babysnakes and The Sultans of Ping FC in this book too. They represented many of the highlights of innovative Irish rock and pop in their day. While so many Irish bands of the 1980s and 1990s sounded like they were chasing acclaim and the charts, the best of Irish rock was off the chart. Those bands didn't chase trends, they made them.

So, while the Irish bands of the era never got the attention they deserved overseas, they meant so much to their local scene, small and unviable as it was. That lack of overseas success may have fostered the defiance of the Irish underground DIY scene. There, big (in terms of sales) didn't mean better. What it did mean was: if we don't get the entertainment that we want from overseas, we'll do it ourselves.

Michael Murphy

BLACK FLAG AND THE NHS, LONDON

Black Flag played a big gig at the Rainbow ballroom in London. During it the vocalist smashed me in the face with his elbow. I came up briefly blinded by blood streaming out of a gash in my brow. I finished the show and went to the hospital for some stitches. In the US it would have cost around $1,000 and been an administrative nightmare. That on top of taking all night instead of an hour. Britain's NHS rules. I wish we had something like it. Nice and friendly.

Chuck Dukowski, Black Flag

JIMI HENDRIX, LONDON 1967

The best gig I ever saw was in 1967, and it was Jimi Hendrix upstairs at the Manor House pub, right by Manor House tube station in Seven Sisters Road, north London. I think I was at Watford School of Art then and had come with a couple of friends as we'd seen Jimi doing "Hey Joe" on Top of the Pops, and had heard "Purple Haze" etc.

It was quite a small venue and Jimi was quite late coming on stage. I would have noticed this as I was living in Bushey, near Watford, and would have to rush after the gig to get the train back home. I think I and maybe everyone at the gig standing around waiting for Jimi were preparing for a bit of a disappointment when he came on. I guess Jimi had been playing somewhere else earlier in the evening as I think he did lots of gigs around that time. His roadies brought the gear onto the stage (I'm not sure there actually was one), set it up and then Jimi and the band came on. I think he apologised for being late and then they suddenly exploded, playing the intro to "Purple Haze" and my God it was incredible! It was really loud and intense and almost unbelievable! It was really great. Further on into the set he introduced one, saying "This is one written by my friend Bobby Dylan" and played "All Along the Watchtower". His stage announcements weren't that good but of course his guitar playing was unbelievable. I can't remember if he played the guitar with his teeth because in all honesty the few opening chords to "Purple Haze" had totally fried my brain!!

Knox, The Vibrators

JIMI HENDRIX, LONDON 1967

I had got tickets for my girlfriend and myself to see the Mothers of Invention at the Royal Albert Hall. I went to Hammersmith where she lived – we met in the pub by Hammy Pally where everyone meets for concerts there. Caroline had brought a couple of her girlfriends. We had a pint or three and jumped into a taxi to South Kensington.

We found our seats to be a few rows back (the stage was on our left) and steeply banked. Three of us went to the bar. We had more beers and brought some back. As we got to our seats, we found that Jimi Hendrix was seated behind us.

I can't remember the year, it must have been mid-1960s, I can remember Zappa playing an amazing solo. When the concert was over I stood up and said hello to Jimi and asked him if I could have his autograph. I put the bottom of my buckskin jacket across his knee and, with one of my art pens, he wrote a fine Jimi Hendrix.

Later down at the bar, we met again and chatted. I had been to his first show at the Flamingo Club – there were 30 people there in a little room.

Then I was at the Marquee also in Wardour Street, Soho. There were 300 people with mouths open in disbelief. He finished the number and announced that he would just play the next song for Jesus (a character who was at every show in the 1960s). He called the rest of us lame fuckers. I did introduce myself beforehand, while we were chatting. He more or less said, "Never mind the small talk Charlie, could you introduce me to your friend?". He pointed to Val. I did. I think she was in shock. It would be nice to think that they lived happily ever after.

Charlie Harper, UK Subs

GRANNY'S INTENTIONS, DUBLIN 1967

First gig I ever went to. We were about 14, went with my friends Michele Walsh and Sylvia Mahon. Jammed right up at the front of the stage. It was thrilling. (They had a hit at the time, "Sandy's on the Phone Again", and my dad had come home with the single one day.) All I could think of, though, was *I want to be doing that too.*

Barbara Gogan, The Passions

BERT JANSCH, BRISTOL 1968

Summer 1968.

When I first saw Bert Jansch, he was already something of a star, although you might not have noticed from his appearance. The cult of Jansch was gaining ground, driven as much by electric guitarists as folkies; Neil Young, Jimmy Page, Paul Simon, Rory Gallagher, all saw something unique in Bert's laconic style.

Expecting a decent turnout, the Bristol show's organisers had put him on in a big, plain meeting room. No stage. They'd lashed together two refectory tables and balanced a wooden chair on top. A precarious, rickety set-up – I can think of few platforms less welcoming or more exposed – but Bert didn't seem bothered. In fact, he rarely seemed bothered much by anything. The most relaxed, the drunkest man I ever saw play a perfect set.

Eventually the room settled and up went Bert onto the rostrum. Several pints follow. A hush falls over the room. Bert sits down, picks up the guitar and starts going slowly through his pockets. Audience wait expectantly. Then something happens. Bert decides to go through his *trouser* pockets. Whatever he's looking for, he still hasn't found it. Eventually he speaks up. "Anyone got a pick?"

Bert was never overly bothered about presentation. If he felt like singing, he'd sing. If he didn't, he just played. If he got bored mid-song, he just stopped and played something else instead. He worked with his head down or his eyes closed yet he was riveting to watch, possessing a sort of anti-charisma every bit as potent as more orthodox varieties. I was used to Attack, Extroversion, Guitar Circus, bands making a Big Show. This was the first time I saw someone work the opposite strategy, slowing everything down, using silence to draw a crowd in. Dylan sometimes used the same technique, but I hadn't seen him. In any case, Bert wasn't *strategising* – he just couldn't find a pick.

Among 1968's guitarists Bert was near-unique. Davy Graham invented the British acoustic folk-blues style but built it from recognisable components. Jansch took it somewhere else entirely. And he developed so quickly. Hamish Imlach told a story of Bert, back in the early Edinburgh days, playing for an impressed Big Bill Broonzy. "How long you been playing?" asks Big Bill. "Six weeks," says Jansch.

Today, when everything's available and few things are mysteries, it's near impossible to convey how unique his playing was back then; how strange, how incomprehensible he seemed to audiences. Back then few people knew of alternative tunings – and those who did mostly played straight 12-bar blues – so Jansch appeared to be performing miracles on a plain acoustic guitar. And "plain" is the right word. He seemed to prefer "difficult" guitars. At folk clubs, half the audience brought their own guitars along; all Bert had to do was hitchhike to a venue, roll up to the bar, borrow a guitar and play. A "show" was little different from going down the pub. Sometimes he fashioned a thumb-pick by bending a teaspoon round his thumb, but his first thought was to get a drink.

The show I saw, a primitive sort of In Concert, was memorable. He played for about an hour and was just astonishing. I didn't know the songs he played, didn't know the genre. I wasn't a folkie, didn't have his records – but you didn't need to.

I last saw him play decades later, not long before he died in 2007, and spoke about the impression his early shows had made on me – but he wasn't particularly impressed. No longer a man whose days were spent in pubs, he thought for a moment then replied, "I prefer it these days, I can remember what I played."

John Perry, The Only Ones © John Perry 2020

BOB DYLAN, ISLE OF WIGHT 1969

I was 16 when I travelled to see Bob Dylan at the Isle of Wight Festival in 1969. It was my first festival. I got there early and walked through a wood with speakers hanging from trees into a clearing where long-haired men were setting up a stage. It was all new to me and I was in awe of every moment. All kinds of strange and wonderful people descended as musicians began sound-checking onstage. I walked around the back of the stage to get a closer look. Bonzo Dog Band and Donovan talking to George Harrison and other Beatles arriving and a lot of hugging stars. I didn't know half of them at the time, but I knew they were musicians and poets all together in some magic world and I was there too.

My heart was thumping as the first band took the stage. It was a two-day festival and this was the first day. The Who, Moody Blues, Joe Cocker, The Bonzo Dog Band and Free were just some of the act on that wonderful Saturday. On Sunday the word was that Bob Dylan was on his way and would be arriving by helicopter. Richie Havens, Tom Paxton, Julie Felix, Pentangle and the Third Ear Band would play that afternoon. I kept an eye to the stars as I listened out for Dylan. As twilight ended, Dylan descended on stage in a white suit, his backing band were The Band. After the first song, there was applause mixed with boos and whistles. There were a lot of "folkies" there who objected to electric Dylan. I didn't care. I was on the side of The Band. It was an incredible night.

When I got back home that September and returned to school, I was walking on air and already looking forward to seeing Jimi Hendrix, The Doors, Miles Davis, Joni Mitchell, Leonard Cohen, Sly and the Family Stone, Chicago, Jethro Tull, Free, Procol Harum, The Who, Emerson, Lake & Palmer, Ten Years After, Joan Baez and the Moody Blues at the Isle of Wright 1970 which I am glad to say I did.

Hugh Friel, The Atrix

TYRANNOSAURUS REX, LONDON 1970

Extravaganza Olympia Exhibition Hall.

My formative years were in London, settling in just off the now uber-trendy North End Road, Fulham. The daily market barrows adorned the full length of the road, selling everything from fruit and veg to clothing and my favourite – the record stall that was positioned just across from Woolworths.

The location was very close to many famous landmarks such as Earl's Court, where I remember going to the Motor Show of 1965 and Stamford Bridge, attending my first Chelsea game in 1967 losing 1-2 to Aston Villa. Both of these memorable events were attended with my father and younger brother Brian.

The first event I went to on my own was the Extravaganza 1970 festival which took place in the Olympia Exhibition Hall. It was a short bus ride away and took place from May 29th to June 6th. The week-long festival featured the pop groups in the afternoon sessions at 3pm and the more teen-orientated "album" groups in the evening sessions from 8pm.

I attended the first Saturday event on May 30th that featured cult underground duo Tyrannosaurus Rex featuring Marc Bolan and his newly installed replacement bandmate Mickey Finn as the 8pm headliners.

Although I had heard of them, I was unfamiliar with any of their music with the possible exception of "Deborah" from a couple of years previously. There were many other activities within the Olympia that day such as film shows, fashion show, stalls for clothes and food etc. I was almost ready to head home when

John Peel's voice suddenly came through the PA and, after a short introduction, welcomed Tyrannosaurus Rex to the stage. They looked sort of cool, so I decided to hang around. I became aware of the sudden surge of people within the hall to the main stage area to see this "cult" duo.

From the moment Marc Bolan spoke and flicked those curls aside, smiled and began singing in the most extraordinary way, I was hooked. The audience hung on his every word and movement as if he was playing just for us individually. He sat cross-legged at one stage as he became more engrossed in his own self-belief in the beauty of his words and music, with Mickey Finn providing the perfect yang to his ying.

He slowly rose and changed to electric guitar and proceeded to blow the mind of this 16 year old as they played key tracks from their album "A Beard of Stars". No one shouted "Judas".

The following week, I bought their current single "By the Light of a Magical Moon" and within a few months they had abbreviated their name to T.Rex and released "Ride a White Swan".

The rest they say is history

Pete Holidai, The Radiators From Space, Trouble Pilgrims

DISTANCE/SUICIDE/THE DOGS, NEW YORK 1973

Suicide? Yes everyone must watch though!

One of the strangest shows I've ever played was when I had a band called Distance. This was way before my band Testors that played CBGB and Max's Kansas City and before Liquid Diamonds. Early to mid-1970s we played a show in a huge concert room on St Mark's Place, NYC, with Suicide (Alan Vega and Martin Rev) and The Dogs from Detroit. Way before that fateful show, I would often see two mysterious-looking characters pushing gear down the street in a shopping cart. Didn't know who they were, but it definitely looked odd seeing them walking along the sidewalk on St Mark's Place or Canal Street pushing an A&P cart with a keyboard that had no protective case sticking out of the cart.

The first time I played a show with them was at a place called The Circus/Playwrights Workshop. It was originally called The Electric Circus where all the 1960s groups like Hendrix and The Doors played. Then a bit later, it was called

The Dom, and when I played with Moe Tucker and Sterling Morrison they told me they played there early on when it was briefly called The Balloon Farm, and also they did a lot of the Exploding Plastic Inevitable performances there when it was The Dom. I remember Andy telling me he rented the place sometime to put on his events. And recently Jimmy Recca and I were talking about his shows there with The Stooges. So it really was *the* hip place to play.

But unfortunately by the time I was on the scene with my band Distance, they changed the name of the venue back again to approximate the original name The Circus but the 1960s spirit was gone. No more dayglow paint on the stoops of St Mark's Place and basically no "scene". Distance and I wanted to play our music live, but we were presented with a sort of cold David Lynchian landscape to try to survive in. The truth was that bands like mine and Suicide were desperate to play anywhere, to somehow survive, so we got in there and organised a show. We were not aware that soon, we would be at the vanguard of a whole new scene, with our own wild and exciting presence. But at the time, even with the desolate terms before us, we were excited to be able to play on stage, with a big PA system. So we printed up a shitload of posters and flyers, stuck them all over Greenwich Village, and promoted our show. As I said, the bill was Distance, Suicide and The Dogs. The Dogs eventually gained the mighty status level of an MC5 for playing amazingly raw rock n roll, but these were early times for us all.

The Dogs had moved to NYC to try to get some exposure. I remember talking to them a couple of weeks before this show and they said they were all living in an apartment together surviving on a huge bag of potatoes. And it wasn't funny. I have to be honest when I first met them they looked like something from The Weathermen or Baader-Meinhof. They seemed way more serious than the left-over NY hippie/glam types. I'm gonna describe the action that day for you. We pulled up in our dilapidated station wagon, the Distance Mobile. It was some whacked-out Ford or Chevy we had to haul us anywhere we could play. We pull up in front of the venue at 23 St Mark's Place and, sure enough, at that very moment, coming down the sidewalk with their shopping cart were Alan Vega and Martin Rev of Suicide. They looked like fucking priests or something coming up the street. Now I knew who these characters were, those two shadowy figures walking around town were performers. As they got closer, they didn't look like priests at all but what were they? Alan had on a leather jacket with a very high collar. On the back of the jacket were these large metal studs spelling out S-u-i-c-i-d-e. It was very provocative and somehow shocking.

Remember these times were on the tail-end of the hippy days, rainbows, bubbles, lovey-dovey and this was light years before shocking names like The Dead Kennedys. The effect of the name alone at that point in time was somehow profound and confusing. They dragged their shopping cart up the long steps and went inside. We also began to load in our amps, guitars and drums into the cavernous cold, dark room. We all kind of stood before the stage with our gear in piles. Marty and Alan from Suicide came up to me and asked if they could borrow our drummer's cymbal, snare drum and one drumstick. I said, "Do you have a drummer who is gonna show up?" Alan said, "Nahh Marty will play the cymbal and snare while he plays the keyboard." This sounded strange to me, but we lent them our stuff and they set up on stage. It was obvious by now that this "drumming" wasn't going to have anything to do with Ringo Starr, Ginger Baker or Mitch Mitchell. Turns out by some unknown system of osmosis that they would be the first to do their sound check.

I watched Marty set up his organ and then connect a whole chain of LPB-1 distortion/power booster boxes to it. In other words, he connected around four or five distortion boxes together in a chain, and then put the output of the organ through all that. The sound in that huge place was otherworldly in its aggression and he only played two notes, 1,2,1,2 over and over. Then he placed the snare drum and the cymbal to the right side of the keyboard within his reach and the soundcheck began. This was before Marty used rhythm/drum machines. He made the "rhythm" with his right hand by whacking the snare and cymbal very hard and he played the organ with his left hand. The first song had the same two notes he had been warming up on and the second song had the same two notes reversed. As he played, he oscillated between the two droning keyboard notes and he robotically cracked the snare and crashed the cymbal. After this went on for five or eight minutes, Alan came out. He was screaming and moaning into the microphone with an ungodly amount of reverb. He must have told the soundman to turn the reverb full blast. He was making little yelp sounds like a lamb and then he would go "Ohhhh... Ohhhhhh" in a deep kind of horror-movie voice. Lamb yelps, deep grunts and more moaning. I was shocked and to be honest, sort of disgusted. What the fuck???

After their soundcheck I went up to Alan. "Listen man, we sent out postcards and stuff to around 30 record companies and told them to arrive early, I don't want you guys going on before us because they will all fucking leave and then all my work was for nothing." Alan said "Awwww maaaan, they ain't even gonna show up. They will be sitting home drinking beer and watching TV." Suffice to say, it turned out Alan was right, but in my naivety, I imagined dudes in business suits clamouring up to us, with briefcases full of contracts and millions of dollars and I really didn't want Suicide scaring them off. So, we made an agreement that the bill would be Distance first up, then Suicide and then The Dogs. We played and I remember the audience's clapping had an echo because the place was so empty. I think there was around 20 people there.

The whole room was pitch-dark except for the stage. I guess Hendrix's roadies or Moby Grape stole the colour light gels in the 1960s because all we had was blinding white light. Of course, we still played our music as if the existence of the world depended on us and also, even though we couldn't see them, I was sure there were two or even three record company representatives in suits waiting with those briefcases! Yup we played all our songs and had a good time. Next up was Suicide, and Martin had a joint hangin' out of his mouth as he came up and sat onstage alone before his keyboard. He then played his drone notes, crashing the cymbal and snare for about 10 minutes, non-stop. Right away, a few people left the building. Then Alan came on stage and gave some weak yelps into the mega-reverbed PA.

At the same time that Alan was making these sort of lamb-sounding yelps, he was standing in a stiff, still, contorted pose. This "song" didn't have any of the grunting, growling sounds, just the plaintive lamb yelps. Suddenly he grabbed a three-foot length of chain and began to beat himself across the face with it while yelping, faster and faster, yelping with blood all over his face. Marty was still droning louder and louder. And more people left. Then Alan jumped off the stage and approached a woman in the front-row area who seemed to be the only person in the place kind of "into it". He literally stood directly in front of her face and came closer and closer. He had the mic up to the side of his mouth and was eventually nose to nose, eye to eye with this woman and yelled, over and over again "I'm too fast for you! I'm too faaast for youuuu! I'm too faaaast for youuuuuu!" Right then, the woman jumped up and shook her hands frantically in front of her face and ran out of the building. The only thing missing was her hair was not on fire.

The Suicide show lasted around 15-20 minutes and all the audience left the room except for five people. By the time The Dogs came on, there were maybe nine or 10 people watching them because some folks came back in. In that moment, I thought that Suicide was the absolute worst crap, bullshit, ever. I went home and complained to anyone in the neighbourhood within earshot about this violent experience. But then something shifted in me, slowly, very slowly injecting my DNA, entering my consciousness from my subconscious. Like a new planet that takes time to traverse, off-course, the light years it takes to enter into a new solar system. I began to feel a change, a shift in my tectonic plates. I would ruminate on that event/show and the performance of Suicide. Eventually it hit me! It hit very viscerally and not intellectually. I was suddenly bowled over by the effect it had on me and the raw artistic power of Suicide. I began proselytising and encouraging everyone and anyone to go to their shows. A year or so later, I became friends with Alan and he invited me to play guitar on some Suicide recordings but in those days you were never "untrue" to your band. Never!

Sonny Vincent, Distance, Testors

ALICE COOPER, LIVERPOOL 1975

Liverpool Empire, September.

Pre-punk I only had two musical loves – Bowie and Alice Cooper – both of whom I followed with the obsessional fervour only a pre-teen boy without a girlfriend could have. With Bowie it was "Aladdin Sane" and Alice "Billion Dollar Babies" that got me. So in each case I dedicated my life to collecting their back catalogues, bootlegs and any rarity I could get my hands on. "Welcome to My Nightmare" had been released earlier in the year and I'd played it on the family stereogram so often that my big bro Colin would hide it to see my tears of anguish. I saw the gig advertised in NME and begged Getty to go with me, he had been a fan of both Bowie and Alice before me but had recently moved on to the New York Dolls having got "Too Much Too Soon" from his record club. It's hard to believe my parents had no qualms letting me, just turned 15, and Getty (only slightly older) travel on our own to Liverpool but hey it was a different time.

Finally, the day came. We flew that morning having first been held at the airport and our parents called in case we were runaways. We got to the theatre at about 2pm and waited with 30 older fans at the stage door. I still remember the magic of being with that group and the way they looked after the wee Belfast boys hoping for a glimpse of Alice. After a couple of hours a dirty transit van pulled up and out spilled the nearest thing to a punk band I was going to see for a few years. The Heavy Metal Kids with their torn clothes and Gary Holton's red Ziggy hair – they signed our programmes and made us promise to get to our seats early to see them. We saw their full set with Getty especially loving them, but at last the lights dimmed and the show started with the creepy prologue of the booming voice of Vincent Price. What followed was a ghoulish horror show featuring snakes, an execution, sliced up babies, dancing skeletons – and even better he interspersed the new album with his biggest hits, finally encoring with "School's Out". We were mesmerised by the huge spectacle of it all and so lucky to be there at an age untainted by cynicism when it really was the best thing we'd seen in our whole lives.

Greg Cowan, *The Outcasts*

LED ZEPPELIN, LONDON 1975

When I was asked to pick a memorable show, it seems fitting that I pick this event as 2020 marks the 45th anniversary of Zeppelin's series of historic gigs at Earl's Court.

At the time, I was an up-and-coming cub reporter at Sounds magazine and, due to the journalistic hierarchy, would usually get handed out the scraps at our weekly meeting. Rather than a sniff of the Stones, I would usually end up at the Marquee reviewing bands as instantly forgettable as Strider and Strife.

Not that I got the gig because of my writing prowess. By 1975, Zeppelin were regarded as a lumbering dinosaur who spent most of their time either in the States or as tax exiles and had just released a self-indulgent double album, "Physical Graffiti". The thought of seeing the band for the first time and the possibility of hearing such epics as "Trampled Under Foot" and "Kashmir" were beyond this kid's wildest dreams. Hell, I was getting paid for doing this shit!

The band played five nights and I saw them on the second, March 24th.

Now anyone who has been to gig at Earl's Court in the 1970s will tell you the experience is similar to what a pigeon experiences when they've been sucked into the fuselage of a Jumbo jet.

Zeppelin managed to obliterate the cold informality of this cavernous "shed" and replaced it with a warm, magical atmosphere that very few bands can create.

It also helped that they shipped over the entire stage set-up from the recent Stateside tour. Apart from the pristine sound, we also had our first taste of video screens. The three-and-a-half-hour set flew by (and this is coming from someone who nearly expired from deep vein thrombosis watching Yes perform "Tales from a Topgraphic Ocean").

Plant's warmth and humanity grounded the performance and were a perfect foil to Jimmy Page's ethereal presence.

He peppered the show with his dry West Country humour, introducing "Kashmir" as a song "about our wasted, wasted, wasted times in Morrocco" and describing John Bonham as "a man with no taste, no manners and no friends".

Bonzo even contributed to the four-part harmonies in "Tangerine" during the acoustic set.

My other abiding memories of the night include seeing the gargantuan frame of Peter Grant coming out of a tiny toilet stall looking rather refreshed. Later that evening at the after-show party, I ended up in a rather more luxurious privvy with a Rolling Stone and a Muscle Shoals studio producer who initiated me into the glamorous world of sleep repellent. I then bounced back to my grim 1970s bedsit – an 18-year-old man-child – possibly having had one of the finest nights of my life.

Peter Makowski, The Snivelling Shits and Sounds journalist

BOB MARLEY, LONDON 1975

I left school in 1974 and started work (after a gap weekend) in a bank called Coutts and Co on the Strand in London. I didn't want to go to university, I wanted to earn my own money as quickly as possible and leave home. I was a clerk in the stock and share department of this old-fashioned bank. In June 1975, a guy that worked with me called Morris said "I've got a spare ticket for this show at the Lyceum – it's a reggae guy called Bob Marley, he's very good. Do you want it? Somebody has let me down." Of course I'd heard of Bob Marley. I had loved the "Catch a Fire" record and had seen him on the "Old Grey Whistle Test" at the time. I said yes, I would love to come. Unfortunately I didn't have time to go home to change out of my work clothes, so Morris and I walked down the Strand to the Lyceum. When we arrived I was amazed that we had tickets in a box that was almost parallel with the stage – you could see everything. Morris and I looked somewhat incongruous in our dark business suits because everybody else in the room was either a West Indian or a hippie – there was a sea of red, green and gold tams and T-shirts on the floor of the house and reaching up to the gods was a miasma of marijuana smoke.

When the band hit the stage, it was like a religious experience; Bob Marley was messianic in his Wrangler dungarees sporting a natural brown Les Paul junior that he only occasionally strummed. The I Threes sported these huge head dresses in Rasta woman style and the nerdy musicians among us were in heaven because we knew the Barrett brothers (Carlton and Family Man) were the best reggae rhythm section in the world. To top this, the organ and guitar player were sublime, and within a few bars the crowd were in a trance. Bob Marley was like no other performer I had seen before – he hopped on the spot, held one hand over one eye and the other aloft in this weird hypnotic dance. Then the message came this was not a pop concert – this was a slave uprising, a religious celebration of rebel music and they were going to burn the fields and bring down Babylon. The message was real. Emancipation is not just a word and slavery is not history – it was real in that room. That night they recorded the version of "No Woman No Cry" that you hear on countless jukeboxes and radio broadcasts – it was live in the Lyceum and they capture the atmosphere and the crowd whooping as soon as they had the opening chords. When Bob sang "Stand Up for Your Rights" and "Burnin' and Lootin'" you knew that this was not throwaway pop music – this was the type of music that I wanted to be involved in. I did not know then that within four years I would be standing on that stage rocking a huge crowd. Bob Marley was my inspiration that night and as I went home on the train in my suit I knew that life would never ever be the same again.

JC Carroll, The Members

BOB MARLEY AND THE WAILERS, MANCHESTER 1975

Back in the last millenium, in 19somethingsomething, I found myself working as a reporter in the newsroom of an Irish national newspaper. There were morning and evening papers and, in truth, the evening one was the more vibrant and thus the more exciting in terms of the immediacy of the stories and the need to get them written as quickly as they were happening given the recurring deadlines for each edition of which, as I recall, there were three and maybe even four every day.

I was of course very far down the reporting totem pole, occupying a position that reflected both my inexperience and my lack of status; my duties frequently consisted of phoning early in the day around all the main Garda stations in the 26 counties with the question "Anything happen overnight, Garda?" which invariably drew the "Divil a bit" response, with the odd car crash or "disturbance" yielding maybe a paragraph or two of a story in the first, or country, edition. Hardly Carl Bernstein/Watergate level but a man had to start somewhere and that was my altogether not unpleasant lot much of the time. It was certainly better that having to knock on the door of some poor distraught mother to ask if she could give me a photograph of her young son who had fatally crashed his motorbike or somesuch the night before. My dreams of an Irish version of the Pulitzer Prize foundered on that particular rock. I just did not have the cold-heartedness to intrude in such a brutal fashion.

One much more rewarding byproduct of my time in the paper was that I ended up, by hook or by crook or by a hard neck, writing a weekly music column every Tuesday evening. I could write whatever I wanted, it being a time when I believed – rightly, I think – that nobody else in the building had a clue what I was on about simply because, in those days, you were into music or you were not and if the latter you may as well have been set adrift in a sea of bewildering names such as Little Feat or Kevin Ayers or even hit acts such as Roxy Music.

One record I reviewed was "Catch a Fire", the first internationally released album by The Wailers. I was familiar with, via pirates like Radio Caroline and Radio London, hit ska tunes such as "The Return of Django" and "Long Shot Kick the Bucket" and I loved the rhythm and the rawness of the sound. The music coming out of Jamaica had changed over that couple of years and this Wailers record was on a whole other level, militant music and righteous lyrics that spoke to the heart and soul, and rhythms that sparked voluntary and indeed involuntary nodding of heads. I was hooked from the minute I heard "Stir It Up".

A short UK winter tour was abandoned when snow fell and Bob, Peter and Bunny, along with their musicians, hightailed it, frozen and teeth-chattering, back to Jamaica.

A couple of years later and, for some reason Peter Tosh and Bunny Wailer were no more and it was now Bob Marley and The Wailers who released the album "Natty Dread" with songs such as "Rebel Music", "Talking Blues", "No Woman No Cry", the titles telling the tale of the record's spirit. It was yet another amazing collection and the minute I heard that shows were lined up in the UK I knew I had to be there. The nearest to Dublin, where I was, turned out to be in the Hard Rock venue (definitely not Cafe) in Manchester on July 20th, 1975. I took the B&I (British and Irish Steampacket Company to give it its full title) ferry overnight to Liverpool on my own and got a train to my promised land.

Having dawdled around the city centre killing a few hours I got directions to the Hard Rock in Stretford and arrived in the late afternoon. My intention was to buy a ticket at the box office but the front doors were locked so I made my way around the back to – lo and behold – find a bunch of dreads hovering around the stage door watching a few more engage in a lively kickabout with some locals. "Yes my brother" was the friendly greeting I got and I bashfully told them I had travelled overnight from Dublin just to see the show. It turned out I was talking to members of Third World, the opening act, and, after a few minutes of chit-chat, I was handed a precious free ticket and encouraged to "enjoy the show". Counting my lucky stars, I bounded away feeling very pleased with myself.

Two hours later and I was inside with a couple of hundred others, an audience I thought surprisingly small. The Hard Rock had previously been a bowling alley; it had a low ceiling and a semi-circular kind of stage with, I think, the bass bins of the PA underneath the front of the stage. It was certainly the loudest, most body-shaking bass sound I had ever heard. Third World had a kind of soul and funk feel to their reggae. They had been signed to Island Records but had yet to release anything internationally but vocally and musically they were powerful and the song "96 Degrees in the Shade" in particular stood out.

After a shortish intermission, the lights dimmed and an MC came out to the front of the stage asking "Ladies and gentlemen, are you ready? I said are you ready?" and, with that, the band, who had assembled surreptitiously in the darkness, struck up the first notes of "Trenchtown Rock" and Bob came bounding out, dressed in denim, seemingly possessed by the rhythm, his vocal clear and compelling. The I Threes, Rita Marley and Judy Mowatt, swayed and swooped to his left, their harmonies sitting perfectly behind Bob. On this night and for the whole tour, the third I Three, Marcia Griffiths (that's right, Marcia of Bob and Marcia who had a hit with Young Gifted and Black), remained at home in Jamaica due to pregnancy.

"Stir It Up", "Burnin' and Lootin'", "No Woman No Cry", "I Shot the Sheriff", followed, each one lifted me higher and higher and my heart pounded in awe and excitement. This was like the church I had never attended, like the firebrand community leader I had never heard, like the most perfect combination of music, lyrics, voices and spirituality I had ever come across. My chest was rattled by the deep bass notes of Aston Family Barrett sitting as one with the cracking snare and the skittering hi-hat and tom-tom fills of his brother, Carlton, on drums. Tyrone Downie's keyboards and clavinet filled out the sound with melody and stabs, Alvin Seeco Patterson's fingers skipped across and around a selection of percussion instruments and lead guitarist Al Anderson, an American, added more rock-flavoured riffs and breaks.

But it was Bob who overwhelmed me; he was Malcolm X, Martin Luther King, anti-Vietnam demonstrations, student uprisings, the Black Panthers, the ANC and the Pan-African Congress, all of those, all rolled into one, a slight but immensely powerful figure, his head back, locks flailing and spiralling around him, high-stepping skanking or staggering backwards almost falling into the rhythm of the band behind him. I had left my faith behind many years before, I was non-religious. Here was this man, proud, defiant, conscious, extolling the greatness of his race, liberating me with his music and his revolutionary fervour in a way that no church and no priest had ever done. His words sounded biblical – "Cold ground was my bed last night and rockstone was my pillow too" – and political at the same time and boy I was converted, hook, line and sinker.

I stood, completely lost and oblivious to everything around me. I felt like I had come home, a ridiculous claim given my knowledge and experience of Bob Marley and of reggae music was relatively limited at that time. But I honestly knew, with every bone in my body, that I could spend the rest of my life happy and fulfilled if only I could remain in those moments with those feelings that I felt for the hour or so that the show lasted.

I have been fortunate enough to have seen some monumentally amazing shows – Jackson 5 in MSG, NWA in Compton, the Bothy Band in Dublin, Nina Simone in Ronnie Scott's in London. The list, luckily for me, goes on and on, all of them lifetime memories – but I have never, ever been so gripped, so possessed by a musical artist the way I was taken over, the way I became one with Bob Marley and his music on that night. He made me proud of who I am, made me want to stand up for my rights and never back down. I was dazed and I honestly do not know where I stayed that night and how I got back to Dublin the next day. Obviously, I got the ferry but sometimes I think that maybe, just maybe, I walked on water all the way across the Irish Sea. For sure, anything was possible after seeing what turned out to be the greatest gig of my life.

Fachtna O'Ceallaigh, manager for The Boomtown Rats, Bananarama and Sinead O'Connor

RORY GALLAGHER, BELFAST 1976

There's a distinct smell that only comes from a wet duffel coat. And a level of discomfort that is difficult to describe. It's heavy, damp and now that you're indoors with 1,800 other people, getting hot. It's my first-ever visit to the Ulster Hall in Belfast and the whole place has a "churchy" vibe to it, aided by the huge organ pipes rising behind the stage, partly obscured by a banner that reads: "It's Crimble Power!" Crimble's was a local music store which I guessed had supplied the PA system for the show. It never occurred to me that this was out of the ordinary and probably should have been a banner with the name of the headliner rather than a wee shop on it. I also remember the seats being hard, wooden, fold-up affairs, but that may be my memory taking the church comparison a little too far. This was my first "real" rock show and I was slightly disappointed at the stage set-up. Everything was so… small. I'd read a lot of music papers and seen stage set-ups from England and America. They were huge. "Thunder walls" of Marshall amps. Drum risers. This looked like a youth club set-up. Tiny guitar amps and what looked like a cabaret piano. Apart from the aforementioned PA system, which I seem to remember looked about right. So, I was undeniably excited for the start of my, as I say, first "real" rock'n'roll experience but slightly worried that it might be a bit of a let-down. The lights go down. There is a roar from the floor. A few shadowy figures move around on the platform. A twanged bass string. A piano run. Kick-drum kicked.

A single spotlight hits the tuxedoed bouncer on stage, and he mumbles: "Ladies and gentlemen, Rory Gallagher."

The stage explodes in coloured light. A very familiar figure in a checked shirt clutching a battered Fender Stratocaster races to the centre of the stage, shouts a quick hello and the band plunges into the first number "Messin' with the Kid". It's deafening. It's blinding. It's terrifying. It's pure excitement. I am lost. Forever. I have found my drug.

Jake Burns, Stiff Little Fingers

DR FEELGOOD, BELFAST 1976

In 1976, I was 15 years old living in Belfast, filling most of my time playing and listening to music with my mates. It's been well-documented that few bands came to play in our city due to the Troubles. I had seen Rory Gallagher playing in the Ulster Hall in 1974 and Focus at a university gig but that was about it. I read Sounds and NME most weeks and became interested in Dr Feelgood and had bought a few of their records. One afternoon I watched a powerful performance on a TV show called "The Geordie Scene". It was with great excitement that I soon learned they were playing Belfast at The Whitla Hall, Queen's University. I rushed out and bought my ticket. This was a band that played three chord R&B songs with attitude, and had even recorded their first album in mono, something that rarely happened in an era where perfected 10-minute guitar solos were played by rock gods who dominated the music scene.

After weeks of waiting, the night of the gig finally arrived and I made my way to the university venue. The band hit the stage and began playing immediately. Lee Brilleaux's aggressive vocal delivery filled the Whitla Hall and Wilko Johnson worked the audience with that psycho stare, playing his red and black Telecaster like a machine gun. Sparko and the Big Figure controlled the rhythm section. They played every song I had wanted them to play including many from "Stupidity", their current album at that time. These no-nonsense guys from Canvey Island had the crowd out of their seats from the word go, their songs stripped down to the primal basics of rock 'n' roll.

They looked different from anything we had seen before in their drainpipe suits and Cuban-heeled boots, not a piece of satin or velvet in sight. For many of us teenagers, this was the start of a whole new thing. The revolution had begun. The band I was making music with immediately started to play Feelgood songs. This gig was important to all of us. Here was a band which was changing the direction of music at that time and delivering it with a different attitude. Many argue that they paved the way for punk, which would revolutionise everything a few months later.

Three years later Protex were playing support to Wilko Johnson and The Solid Senders at the Marquee Club in London. I feel lucky to have been at that Dr Feelgood show in The Whitla Hall, especially with the original line-up. It changed everything for me. What a gig!

Aidan Murtagh, Protex

THE RAMONES, LONDON 1976

I've played hundreds of gigs over the years and equally attended hundreds of shows; but I guess the most important event I've witnessed as a punter rather than appeared at as a player must be seeing The Ramones perform at a small venue called the Greyhound situated above a pub in the London Borough of Croydon, in 1976.

Prior to that experience I was primarily a fan of glam rock, although I had also got into The New York Dolls, Velvet Underground and Iggy Pop and The Stooges through the guidance of a friend who worked in a local record store. He was a great source of information regarding new music and helpfully sold me LPs for a hefty unofficial discount. I had also become aware of a handful of bands that were emerging under the genre banner punk rock in the UK with strange names such as The Sex Pistols, The Clash, Siouxsie and The Banshees and Subway Sect through reading the British music press, as well as their American counterparts – Television, Blondie, Devo, Suicide and, of course, The Ramones.

When I discovered they were playing my home town as part of their first tour of the UK, I was unsure whether to go as I'd been disappointed by The Stranglers the first time I'd caught them some weeks before – for some reason I thought they sounded like The Doors, a band I'd never got into. I really loved them the second occasion I saw them, especially Jean-Jacque's snarling bass sound. But I was still generally unconvinced about this emerging music realignment. But after a friend, Mel Wesson, who had played keyboards in a glam rock bedroom band with me called Marionette phoned to assure me that he was definitely going to attend, I changed my mind. It's strange how these kinds of seemingly insignificant decisions can have such a profound impact on the future direction of your life.

As was my way, I got to the venue far too early and joined Mel for a cup of coffee at a burger restaurant in the High Street. As we drank and chatted, Mel, who was sat facing towards the door, said "Don't look now, but The Ramones have just walked in."

They filed past our table and made for the counter to order their food. I glanced over Mel's shoulder and the first thing that occurred to me was how geeky and tall Joey was. He was wearing a beat-up leather jacket which had its ripped sleeves attached to the main part of the garment by large nappy pins. We both thought this looked really cool. The other feature that immediately came to mind was that there was no doubting that these four individuals were members of the same band. Each was wearing the classic Ramones uniform: leather jackets, Levi jeans, T-shirts and Converse sneakers. There was also something undoubtedly unifying in their bearing and mannerisms which, despite the obvious differences in their physical characteristics, had you believing that they really could be brothers.

We left and walked up the street to order a beer from the ground-floor pub of the Greyhound. The place soon filled up with a multitude of extraordinary-looking people wearing leather jackets, plastic trousers and dayglo-coloured sandals. Most had short bleach-blonde or dyed, jet-black hair, some were flaunting consciously ripped T-shirts over which were worn loose-fitting ties. This crowd was as far removed in their sartorial style from the long-haired and denim-dressed audience that had attended the Thin Lizzy gig of the previous week as could possibly be envisioned. Where did all these weird-looking fuckers come from? I was still wearing my New York Dolls-inspired clothing and started to feel somewhat uncomfortable and self-conscious in this unfamiliar company.

When the doors opened for the upstairs venue, Mel and I stayed put awhile and ordered another beer. I eventually downed my pint and climbed the metal steps to the first-floor bar. I could hear that The Ramones were playing but had one more lager before venturing into the hall itself which was insulated from the drinkers via a set of large and heavy glass- and wood-framed doors.

"Let's go see this band," I shouted to Mel, who was chatting to an acquaintance across the room. We reached these doors together. I yanked them open and a detonation of sound and heat engulfed us. Joey's voice, sharp and sinewy like a wire whip, cut through the beautiful noise of Johnny's guitar while Tommy punished his kit and Dee Dee, deep into his own personal performance, pitched some nice shapes with his white Fender bass... My immediate thought processes concluded: "This is exactly how it should be done!" That moment represented the final destination of what had been the long pursuit to discover a form of music I could unequivocally adopt and make an essential part of my life. It was the catalyst for my conversion to punk rock and of my subsequent professional music career that has spanned over 40 years and continues apace. Seeing The Ramones in 1976 changed everything.

Alvin Gibbs, UK Subs

AC/DC, LONDON 1976

Marquee Club, Wardour Street, June 4th

It wasn't yet "the hottest summer anyone could remember". The heatwave was a couple of weeks away but it was getting there when we got the call advising us to check out an Australian band that were playing that evening at the Marque club. Our band Cock Sparrer – or Cock Sparrow as we were calling ourselves then – were always hanging around clubs trying for gigs or support slots. We had befriended a guy there, the splendidly named Archibald Spears McFarland-Ross who worked at the Marquee on the back door. It was his job to stop the old ploy of one person paying, then creeping around to the exit to let their mates in. He was a great guy and became an occasional roadie for us. He looked and sounded like a smaller Billy Connolly. Archie told us to get down to the club early and that this band were a bit special. We did so and Archie, bless him, let us in. The club held 700 but I wouldn't be surprised if 1,000 people were squeezed in that night.

We took our place at the back – you weren't far from the stage and they placed seats along the back, handy to stand on once the band started. It was gonna be hot! Two huge air-blowing coolers were placed each side of the stage, but they made little difference once the band started.

At this time, a lot of rock music had become very pompous, elaborate, expensive and overblown but this band were nothing like that. Stripped down to the bone, sweaty, beer-soaked rock'n'roll you couldn't help bang your head and stamp your feet to. Singer Bon Scott, stripped to the waist, belting out songs like "It's a Long Way to the Top", "Live Wire" and "TNT" destined to become classics. Lifting a school-uniformed Angus Young onto his shoulders, he walked into the audience playing his guitar, followed by roadies desperately trying to keep his lead plugged in. (No radio controls in those days!) And that drummer! Christ, when you can play that simply but sound that good who needs to do anything else. There was hope for me yet.

I had witnessed an event. Went home and bought the album the next day. This wasn't quite the sound and direction we wanted our band to go in but it was getting there. That was about to happen with the explosion that became punk rock but it still remains one of the defining moments in my humble career and one of if not the best gig I have ever attended.

Steve Bruce, Cock Sparrer

PUNK COMES KNOCKING, LONDON 1976

I was asked if I'd like to write something about a memorable punk night at the Hope and Anchor and I couldn't. So many great punk nights, they blur into one. Between making sure a couple of 14 year olds didn't smuggle themselves in under a mountain of make-up, keeping the pogoing mass from crashing into the innocents while still avoiding the spit and beer, and also running triage for the dance injuries, we got so good at slapping on plasters. There was no time to take in the nuances of the socio-economic politics and teenage angst of the lyrics or watch the guitarists' latest takes on an old Wilco pose. They were as hectic as hell and I loved them so I decided to tell this story.

Like many of the pub rock venues, the Hope was slow to understand and embrace this new musical movement. Our first brush in early 1976 slowed us down quite a bit. It was a quiet midweek evening in the cellar and the band weren't setting the world on fire, but they weren't bad. About 10.30 we closed the charge on the door and opened up so punters from the top bar could wander down for the last half hour. I had gone outside to do my regular stalk round the building to pick up any drunk foolishness before throwing-out time when our doorman came out to tell me there was an arsehole in the cellar. As I hit the bottom of the stairs, I could hear a voice shouting over the band telling them they were a bunch of shit and had no right to play. At first, I couldn't see the culprit – I was looking for a drunken youth showing off to a few mates. But then I realised it was a short, expensively dressed man of about 35 with large tinted glasses standing alone on the far side of the cellar. I moved over and told him to shut the fuck up and politely walked him towards the door with him remonstrating all the way. He even used one of my favourite lines "Do you know who I am?" As we came level with the bar he thrust himself towards Fred who was chatting over the ramp. "You're missing the chance of a fucking lifetime," he screamed and amongst insults, threats and curses we learned he represented an act called Tex Crystal and they were funk. He then got very angry and we realised he was saying Sex Pistol and punk. We just didn't understand why this little guy in a 300-quid cashmere jumper was so angry. We thought it was alcohol – we didn't know it was punk. I walked him up the stairs while he assured me that my "fucking stupid fat hippy" self would be sorry and his band would be "bigger than the fucking Stones". Eventually I got him to the door and he started asking if I could get him a cab. I said no and he stumbled into the night.

We asked that night's band as they packed up if they had ever heard of The Sex Pistol, no one had. We also mused on the fact we had never seen an agent use that approach. We wondered if they were an American band because the punk thing we associated with New York. We decided whatever the Sex Pistol was like they would never play the Hope… We were right they never did.

A few weeks later, after we had learned the guy's name was Bernie Rhodes, a fashion designer, high roller and all-round pain in the arse, the Pistols played the 100 Club and the press told us what punk was all about. We were arrogantly sure we had made the right decision. It would never last. It took meeting and having The Damned play to break the log jam. We realised they were just another bunch of kids trying to set their own agenda, just another bunch of kids kicking over the traces and there might be something in this punk thing. So we let them in.

John Eichler, proprietor, Hope and Anchor

SEX PISTOLS, ENGLAND 1976-1977

The first time I ever saw Punks I was on the back of my first husband's rig on the way home from a club meeting. It was an Outlaw biker club and musical tastes tended towards 70s Rock and for some reason, Donovan at the end of the night when everyone was mashed. As we rode past the strange looking types fagging it outside a pub I had the oddest feeling of recognition. Some months later I had spiky blue hair, a divorce, a job as a bouncer at the new Punk club and was totally in love with the music. Someone said, wanna go see this band from London? I said yeah and we mooched off to see some outfit called The Sex Pistols in a local shithole club. Christ, said my mate 2 songs in, that singer''s a fucking arse. And he was, so we left. Such was my only brush with Punk Royalty. Typical.

Joolz Denby, author, artist, performer

SEX PISTOLS/ALBERT DOCK, LIVERPOOL 1976

Eric's, October 15th

OK, not necessarily my favourite gig, but definite my most memorable, and one that I've dined out on for over 40 years, and even have the poster to prove it! October 1976, I was at Liverpool Art College, starting second year, and we'd formed the typical art college band (influenced by, but not nearly as good as, Deaf School two years ahead of us at the college). The band's name was Albert Dock and The Cod Warriors (to give us our full title): a sprawling, seven-piece, noisy, boisterous gang that could barely play, but were full of attitude and larger than life… We had a frantic three-man front line, consisting of me (vocals/keys/sax), John J Campbell (lead vocals – John would later be in both Yachts and It's Immaterial with me) and Peter Hatton (vocals/dancing – a Northern Soul prototype Bez!).

Before the summer holidays, we'd played parties and the odd Liverpool club (including The Metro, run by future Eric's managers Roger Eagle and Ken Testi) and we'd started to pick up a bit of a local following. We'd heard about this "punk rock" thing, so John and I met up in Leeds and hitched down to London to try and catch this band The Sex Pistols... whom we then found had headed up to do a gig in Leeds that very day! We did, however, witness The Stranglers playing to 17 people at Islington's Hope and Anchor. Little did we know that our chance to see (and, better still, support) The Pistols was only weeks away.

Legendary Eric's Club was about to open and in Paul Skillen's book "Scouse Pop", Ken Testi describes how he and Roger Eagle went about drumming up support for this new club (the first of its kind in the city): Ken: "...So I said to Roger '*Here's the mission. You go into the arcade and turn right and you will see Jayne Casey, we need her and her acolytes... people like Pete Burns, Holly Johnson and so on. I will go to the Art College because I know my way around there'.* So I went to the Art College and immediately walked into Henry Priestman and John Campbell. The people we met that day were the first people to come to Eric's."

John and I went to the first two Eric's gigs (The Stranglers, The Runaways) which were packed, and it definitely felt like this club was the start of something different, a new "scene", raw and exciting. We heard rumours that we were being considered as support act for The Sex Pistols. It was really just a case of Roger and Ken liking us, being in the right place at the right time; days later we were duly offered support slot to the most notorious band in England.

On the night of October 15th, 1976, The Sex Pistols went on first, upstairs. Actually, though I loved the charged atmosphere and the energy, general opinion was that they were good, but not as good as we all thought they'd be. And the gig definitely didn't have the same impact on Liverpool as the legendary Free Trade Hall gig did on Manchester... even Johnny Rotten's audience-baiting wasn't up to what we'd expected: legend has it his best line was "If you don't like it, you know where the door is."

Albert Dock went on later, around 11pm, downstairs, and the majority of the audience stayed. We played our usual ramshackle set, mainly all covers, but mostly so obscure people thought they were ours. I seem to remember we went down OK. Let's be honest, neither performance was *that* amazing, but the gig *was* life-changing... I'd had a taste of what being *in* (and what playing *to*) a sweaty, expectant rock crowd was like, and I wanted more...

Henry Priestman, The Yachts, It's Immaterial, The Christians

ACNE RABBLE AKA SEX PISTOLS, MIDDLESBROUGH 1977

He was an unsure 16 and the troubled fire of punk rock in that summer of 1977 was his very life.

What was on the boy's mind this Thursday afternoon as the train made its way from Newcastle city centre down the County Durham coastline to Middlesbrough station?

He was thinking of the jobs he had been offered upon leaving school, the three main contenders that had been thrust upon him, of coal mine, ship yard and factory, how he had rejected all three, how he didn't know what he wanted to do with himself, just the pure certainty of what he did not want to do, the perpetual sense of otherness of never being able to fit in, of not wanting to fit in, and all this compounded by a lack of confidence and insecurity that nagged away under an adolescent disdain and recently acquired punk bravado.

The boy looked out at the blue skies and the bright blue of the North Sea then both winced and laughed as another thought impinged in on itself, the memory of the rage of his parents when he had popped up on the television's tea time news the day before.

He had been filmed for an expose item, a properly cynical provincial shock horror piece of outrage exploitation. And it had been filmed in a gay club in Whitley Bay, a place called Gatsby's, the only establishment in the area that would host a punk night, whose Monday nights had become a shelter for this new punk movement, where they felt safe enough to flourish and enjoy themselves without getting a bottle over the head and there he was, the boy, in the early hours, slightly drunk, telling the world in all his young dumb foolishness what this punk rock business was all about.

The boy was a novice, but give the novice a beer or two and he could certainly talk.

He hadn't done the cause any actual good if truth be told, so limited was his experience of real life and world view and social perception. Not that his dad cared for such subtlety of nuance – he had swiftly reached across the dinner table to clip him hard. The punk thing was bad enough; but going, *"and being seen in" interjected his mother,* to a bloody gay club. The boy just laughed at this, he laughed again when his dad told him he was "grounded". What kind of word was that? And anyway he was 16 now, he could do what he wanted.

His father retorted with plain common sense that until he was paying some rent and contributing to the household then he was still under his jurisdiction as far as he was concerned, and he wasn't going anywhere until they'd all had a good think about this stupid punk thing. It was not as if the boy had the guts or even the nous to get up and go. Where would he go, where could he? He retreated to his room, playing his singles, The Saints, Buzzcocks, The Adverts waiting for something, waiting for nothing, waiting for anything, waiting to make his move…

There was a phone call for him which his mother allowed him to take. It was a girl and the girl offered up some very interesting information. This "grounded" thing wasn't really going to work. He knew that he could jump from the bedroom window down on to the shed, from the shed he could drop down to the paving stones. He went back to his room and turned The Adverts single over, One Chord Wonders to Quickstep. He'd be quick alright.

That was yesterday though, today was already moving forward at an excitable pace. He also had the girl on his mind, he liked her a lot and he thought she might like him. She was better-educated and better-fed than him, from a very wealthy part of Newcastle. On the other hand though, he was the vocalist in a punk band, and this was punk, they were punks, their homemade dress styles were roughly equal, all normal barriers had been dissolved. They were punks together, they smiled at each other. There were four of them travelling down together. All afflicted by the punk virus. What the fuck would this day bring he wondered.

The train pulled into Middlesbrough station.

If there is beauty in the desolation of the post-industrial northern towns then Middlesbrough is surely an ultimate contender for the beautifully tarnished crown of home-slumming queen.

There was enough industry belching filth into the sky to cast a sickly sheen to the blue-skied summer day and the shabbiness of the buildings surrounding them fair took the breath away. They headed away from the station and walked past rows of boarded-up shops, each block proving more desolate, more depressing, more decayed than the last. This was punk terrain for real, on they walked our four intrepid punks, one a Bowie clone who couldn't quite kick his Ziggy addiction but liked the new pretty vacant vibe and another a fiercely perceptive six-foot African queen of a young woman who was in the process of changing her name from Angie to Ngozi and thinking well beyond this mere punk game, the girl, the boy, our four heroes/non-heroes, on they walked.

A white minibus pulled up in front of them and the back door opened. A corpulent beast of a man with long hair got out and approached them. The boys first instinct was, white van, grebo builder, customary punk beating! For a day did not go by in the northeast when the cry of "Sheena is a Punk Rocker" was not followed by a fist to the face care of a straight beer monster and the boy felt a bit apprehensive as this guy approached. He got up real close and then he leaned forward, he whispered, actually whispered, in a kind of paranoid manner… "Oi mate, which way is the Rock Garden?"

Any apprehension vanished. The boy smiled and pointed down the road, "Down there, we're headed there too." The boy looked beyond the man and into the minibus, where he saw a fiery shock of dirty red hair, and an oily spurge of jet-black spikes bobbing up and down. A little gulp of excitement could not help but surge from his throat as he turned to his three friends. "Fuck, it's The Pistols." The large man now growled and said, "Hey, none of that, keep schtum."

The man threw a pretend fist towards the boy. The boy ducked and everyone laughed at this brief moment of pavement pantomime. The man put his fingers to his lips once more, thanked them for the directions and got back in the minibus. The Rock Garden was just a bit more of a walk down the road, so they followed the van and the band and walked right behind them straight into the venue.

They could not believe their luck. The four of them sat on a bench that was placed on a raised seating area at the back with only the empty dance floor between them and the band as they soundchecked. They were loud, very loud, and played the soundcheck for real, as if they were playing an actual gig.

What was on the boy's mind as the band soundchecked?

He was looking straight at Jones's Fender amplifier with the legend "Sex Pistols, Guitar Hero" scrawled across the front in a totally amateur non-star manner and that started him thinking of his own band and the long winter nights through '75 and 76 rehearsing in Rob Grant's freezing-cold garage under the sickly light of a bare green lightbulb, throats nauseated by aerosol fumes. It had just been the two of them then, going over Bowie songs relentlessly on Woolworths guitars and amps, their only focus seemingly resentment of Rob's posher schoolmates down the road who had better equipment and liked the music of Wings and Status Quo which they could play quite expertly. They really did resentfully hate these fellows. It had given them something to kick against right enough, but they were yet to find a guiding road that would let them kick on.

He knew he loved The Sex Pistols long before he had ever heard them, and when he did hear, and see, them, on a video of "Anarchy in the UK" playing in a record shop in the town one cold November truanting afternoon, it felt like he'd known them all his young life. They felt like they were him. He quite simply fucking loved them to the dirty marrow and he was in on the action from that moment on. Rob and him soon found more members to make up their own band. They called the band Speed. He was designated the vocalist chore. He had been writing lyrics about the life around him for two years anyway so the vocal gig fitted, they had 10 songs already and had played a fair few gigs. Penetration, Raw and themselves. The Newcastle punk scene. Speed.

Sex Pistols. The soundcheck finished and the band trooped off the stage towards the dressing room. Some oversized, tired and bored bouncers had shown up by now and they made themselves busy, their first task being to eject the hangers-on. The small group who had watched the soundcheck dutifully shambled out, not quite sure of what would happen next. The boy was last and, as he was just about ushered out the venue, the door of the dressing room opened wide and he was grabbed by the roadie who had exchanged verbals with him out on the street. The boy was literally thrown in the dressing room and positioned in front of Steve Jones, The Sex Pistols guitarist. A stern request was made of him.

     –   Tell him the time…

The roadie had demanded this of the boy. Jones looked on expectantly.

Erm, half-past three…

What, tell him the time, tell him proper.

Half-past three.

Not good enough, tell him the time.

What was this about? The boy kind of gulped, it was a wind-up obviously, the boy knew enough about the band already to know that Jones was the ruffian in the band, and one who had a background in boxing, but surely they hadn't got him in here to engage in some violent pre-gig sport? Bullying images flashed through his mind, school, the estate, different situations. The boy felt forced into a corner here, the whole room had gone quiet, the large roadie prodded the boy, repeated the request. The boy responded at volume.

Hey man, it's FUCKING HALF-PAST THREE. DIDN'T YOU HEAR ME THE FIRST FUCKING TIME!

He waited for a slap to come, instead he was met with mirthful laughter and the large roadie slapped Jones on the shoulder

I told you Steve, told you they all talk fahking funny up here.

Jones was laughing hard, in a good way though, not at the boy, but with him, a kind of shared respectful appreciation of regional differences.

Yeah, that's some accent mate, where's it from?

North Shields.

North fucking what, where's that?

Newcastle.

Newcastle, that's up near fucking Scotland ain't it?

He turned around to the rest of the room.

This little cunt has come down all the way from Scotland to see us.

Everyone nodded with apparent respect, a can of warm malt Breaker was thrust into the boy's hands. There was no time for thinking now, it was all about the moment. Jones was addressing him again.

So that's like a hundred miles or something, right?

The boy nodded. Give or take 90 miles but he wasn't going to say that. Jones nodded back, he was impressed, and the boy could see, really stoked that this young lad had gone to the effort to come watch his band.

Have you got a ticket?

No, I think it's sold out.

But still, you've come all this way, down here, to see us?

Aye.

Fucking hell, go and get this young geezer sorted someone,
get him on the guest list, whatever.

What was on the boy's mind when all this was going on? He was thinking Jones would give him a pep talk, some words of encouragement. On the passion needed to succeed, the importance of punk, the sheer visceral will, that nothing else matters, that this is your one life and you look like you have that fire in your eyes, you are the one to take it, that this is a matter of life and death, that yes, we mean it maan, bleed for your craft. There was no pep talk though, to talk of passion and intent, of nobility and craft, well that was all just bollocks wasn't it, that would not be punk, they were bored, they were just having a laugh. It was a great laugh though.

Jones thrust another can into his hand, a Colt 45 this time and they were joined by Cook whilst the large roadie left the room. They talked about their band, then his band, about music choices, about football teams, punk girls, teddy boys, violence from other cults, all kind of things, and the boy could not believe their interest in him, beyond this circle of conversation the boy was aware that Sid Vicious was comatose and Johnny Rotten seemed pre-occupied, but Jones and Cook were courtesy itself.

The boy felt himself tapping into another world, the other world, the not-going-to-work-down-the-mines world, an adventurer's world, a scoundrel's world, but also realised he was getting a proper working-class lesson in humbleness and courtesy. Jones wasn't just about good manners though, he could play himself up as demanding musician too.

Where's that cunt Boogie got to?

Boogie was the large roadie. Boogie soon returned with a ticket in his hand which he proffered to the boy. There you go son. A moment later and it was time for the band to go back to the hotel to change before the gig. Hands were shook and Jones exhorted him to enjoy the gig. Vicious snapped out of his coma and Rotten gave the boy a friendly grin as he passed. The boy felt 20-foot tall, he would never admit it though, it was just punk after all and here they were all together, like it should be. He held on to the ticket and followed the band out into the early evening sunlight.

When they had arrived, the streets around the Rock Garden had been deserted: not any more, a huge queue snaked around the block, a thousand people without tickets had turned up hoping to get in and, as the boy went round cries of recognition arose, most people would have seen the news item the night before, this was some fucking gig already. Some mates from Newcastle greeted him. He showed them the ticket. Plans were instantly made; they would get him over the throng at the front door where all the bouncers were dealing with the crush and from there the boy would go straight over to the unguarded fire exit and open up to let the Newcastle mob in.

The boy got into the venue and, giving his mates time to get back round, went over and jammed his palm down on the steel bar of the door and pushed it open. Ten Newcastle mates rushed in and they all dispersed and lost themselves in the chaos of the venue. The place was heaving and the boy felt the electricity inside him. He had seen The Clash and The Damned already, and also The Adverts, Penetration and Warsaw on the one bill and all three gigs were really intense in their own way, but this was another level of expectation and excitement, and partisan too, it wasn't like 20 punks and 800 rugby students in the same room, this was partisan, a tribal gathering of this new wave of feral stylish youth; here you could see punks had travelled all over the North for this, up from Yorkshire, across from Liverpool and Manchester, and great they looked too.

The boy found himself in the company of Nick and Helen, two pals from Newcastle. The boy remarked on how good it was to be in a room full of pure punks, how safe it felt, that this was their moment. Nick, who was older and a lot more considered, said he wasn't so sure that there would be no trouble; he had heard rumours that the Grebos, a biker gang who regarded the Rock Garden as their home, were waiting outside for the gig to finish when they would descend and cause havoc. The boy visualised other tribes, the teddy boys, the beer boys, the soul boys all out there waiting in the industrial shadows, it was grief alright and he himself, the boy, the novice, had said on the television the night before that it wasn't the teddy boys they hated, but the soul boys, opening up factions himself, widening the divide, hate and war, fear and tension, fuck this, fuck that… oh what great piss it is to be young right now.

He hooked up with the girl again and they found themselves pummelled to the front. A lad with a soul boy haircut with a blonde streak in it and a ripped and torn T-shirt smiled at him and introduced himself as Tony, from Whitley Bay, starting a friendship that would last for the rest of their lives. Another pair of older punks from the nascent Newcastle scene, Nick and Helen, were on the other side of him, this felt so good. What was the boy now thinking of as the Pistols took to the stage? Nothing. Nothing at all, for the first time in an age, no preoccupations, no doubts, no mad dreams, and no recent past, no impending long-term future, just the very moment of now as the band seared into "Anarchy in the UK", the sheer explosion of Jones's guitar riff and Cook's rolling drums with a hunched-over Rotten careering over the top with a righteously sneered vocal. He lost himself inside a room of people who were lost inside themselves, not a thing else would he recall or could he tell about the gig, just that one incendiary song, everything after was just noise and fury, style and laughter, pogo and peril, piss and heaven. It was a moment alright.

And later the boy and the girl spent the night in the back of a Morris Minor car that had broke down in the town of Durham. The driver bailed out and left them there. They didn't mind at all. He looked at the girl. Her pale face, the jet-black hair with the pink streak that he loved, and there they were at last, after weeks of unsure hesitation, kissing and cuddling and all that, together, two young punks, wondering if Sid had actually played a note on his bass but agreeing that it didn't really matter, that his style was more than on-point, wondering what that rascal Jones was up to, wondering what kind of performance from any other band could ever beat that, wondering what the boy was going to do and where he would live now that he had left home, and then not wondering about anything at all, just making themselves as closely comfortable as best they could in the back of the cramped old car.

Post script

The boy was such a novice, so fucking naive, but he was learning. He stayed in a squat in the Jesmond area of Newcastle and loved it, but eventually he stunk and needed a bath and went home again and with his point kind of made got a job on a building site and earned and spent some money. The SPOTS tour rolled on to a few more dates and the boy's television appearance sparked a predictable reaction. The presenter had asked him why punks hated teddy boys and without even thinking the boy had replied "Oh no, the teddy boy's aren't our enemies, it's the soul boys we hate." Cue a legion of northern soulers turning up for blood and vengeance for this perceived insult the following Monday. Things evened themselves out, there was crossover on both sides and lots of youth knew each other, but in the toilets that night the boy was approached by the coolest-looking kid he had seen yet. The young man was covered in bandages, bandages as bondage, as fashion statement, the bandages were held together by a badge that said Keep the Faith. The young cat pointed to it questioningly and the boy scratched his mop of spiky black hair… "Weren't they our enemy?"

"You're a fucking idiot Johny," the lad said in a friendly, non-aggressive way. "Soul boys, teddy boys, punk rockers… we're all the same, different clothes, slightly different culture, but same passions, same intent, same working-class background, all of us, and the enemy is not ourselves, the enemy is bigger than that, and we're doing ourselves no favours fighting amongst ourselves, have a think who the enemy is son, my name is Manus by the way."

I shook Manus's hand and stumbled out of the toilets, it is something I've thought about to this day, the first great lesson that I wasn't taught in school. Cheers Manus.

The Boy

Johny Brown, The Band of Holy Joy

BERLIN/SLAUGHTER AND THE DOGS, LIVERPOOL 1976

Eric's, December 10th

The Sex Pistols played in my hometown of Liverpool just eight weeks ago, and I've missed it. Along with The Damned's "New Rose", I've been playing their "Anarchy in the UK" single to death this past fortnight, but information on these intimidating aliens is scarce. The term "punk" hasn't landed in Britain yet, so, this nameless, evolving-by-the-day scene is, for now at least, still plastic in my mind. Tonight, my college friend Roy's band – Berlin – play at Eric's. It's my first visit to the club, and although I don't know it yet, the night the comet hits.

Channelling The Velvet Underground and Ziggy-era Bowie, Berlin and their flame-haired frontman, Roy White, are shoestring glam; and I love it. They are, after all, just playing my record collection live. Their set over, I go to the toilets, where, to my mortification, I am joined by a stranger who stands uncomfortably close to me at the urinal and stares. He hates me and wants me to know it. He hates my too-neat hair, my pleated trousers and my "Bryan Ferry" shoes. Terrified to meet his gaze I stare ahead, pretending to read graffiti. As he leaves, I turn, taking in the zips, safety pins and savagely chopped hair. His openly aggressive disdain has instantly rendered both me and my Bowie/Roxy, art-school sensibilities redundant. For the first time in my teenage life, I feel passé and it hurts. Although Slaughter and The Dogs *are* exciting on stage, they are not quite connecting with me; it's exotic local creatures Pete Burns, Jayne Casey and the music DJ Norman Killon plays either side of the band's set that inform me, not only of what this nascent scene is, but more importantly, what it isn't.

2am, back in the suburbs, I take wallpaper scissors to my hair and a razor blade and a match to a shirt purloined from my dad. Over breakfast he asks me how I "survived the plane crash". Buying "Spiral Scratch" and "White Riot" as they are released, I hide my pre-punk records under the bed. Eric's and its inhabitants are my entire world now. At The Stranglers gig, I meet and bond with trainee teacher Julian Cope. I frown at his "Boredom is for Students" T-shirt and he pulls me up on the decomposing apple core and a razor blade hanging in a tiny plastic bag safety-pinned to the lapel of my jacket. Eighteen months later, we headline this Eric's stage as The Teardrop Explodes.

I've been to better gigs but, for me, the night Berlin opened for Slaughter and The Dogs was the night the comet hit. Thank you for inviting me Roy, and thank you Slaughter and The Dog's front man Wayne Barrett – you fucking bully. You didn't know it, but secreted like a virus, within that Rotten, accusatory stare of yours, was a call to revolt, and the fast-track to my future.

Paul Simpson, The Teardrop Explodes, The Wild Swans

THE STRANGLERS, LONDON 1976-1977

One of my fave gigs was The Stranglers at the Hope and Anchor Islington in either late 76 or early 77.

This was invite-only as it was being recorded. Me and Dave Treganna, later of Sham '69 and three other friends were early fans of the band. We'd see them sometimes when there was only us and five other people watching.

I'd had about 10 pints before I went into the Hope. Jet Black had concocted a really powerful black punch free to anyone who wanted it. Of course, I had loads.

I'd seen the band about 20 times from Oct '76 and couldn't get enough of them.

If you look at the video for Grip, it was filmed that night and I'm in several shots.

I went on to see another 16 Stranglers gigs up to March '77, then I joined the Lurkers on bass and started gigging myself. So watching them waned.

When Grip came out, I'd hitchhiked from Carmarthen to London. I got dropped off at Hammersmith Broadway, ran to Harlequin Records and bought it.

I rushed home and played it on my parent's old radiogram which had a really heavy stylus. I spun it so many times that black dust was coming off the disc. I wore it out and had to buy another and a more modern record deck to boot.

Some of the best days of my life I had at those early Stranglers gigs.

RIP Dave Greenfield, a magician without whom the band wouldn't have had nearly as much success.

Arturo Bassick, The Lurkers and 999

IGGY POP, MANCHESTER 1977

OK, Berlin. Me, James Mealey, John Reynolds, Gerry Garland, Ray Banks (they went on to form Victims of Romance after I left). You can guess from the name we were inspired by Velvet Underground... and Iggy of course. Couldn't get arrested for a gig until Eric's opened really. Apart from a couple of pub gigs expecting chart covers and we were therefore booed off stage. One memorable gig on the Wirral where some guy asked for my autograph while I was onstage, who then set it alight and threw back at me! Yeah Liverpool was fun in those days...

Liverpool 1977 and we are about three shows into our residency at Eric's. The Pistols, The Damned, The Stranglers had attracted capacity crowds and we begin to think that, because we don't have a "The" in our band name, people aren't interested in Berlin as we're lucky to see more than a hundred in the venue (my friend Paul Simpson being one them). However, Iggy is playing Manchester. Forty minutes on the train and we're in our seats ogling Gaye Advert who are the support tonight. They look wrong on such a large stage. We grab a beer. House lights go down and I hear a whiney high-pitched voice announce the "Godfather of Punk". It's the bass player in a cowboy hat talking. He should lower his voice tone I'm thinking. Sounds like a Benny Hill sketch. Strobe lights and flashes of blue darting around the stage. "Sweet Sixteen" at half tempo sounds menacing. Bam, a spotlight picks out Iggy stood at the edge of the stage with a huge smile as in the "Lust For Life" album cover. Electric blue shirt unbuttoned to the waist revealing the famous wounded chest covered in... red paint(????). Black leather trousers with a horse tail sticking out of his arse. That vision alone is worth the trip. Iggy and the band run through an incredibly short adrenalin (coke)-fuelled half-hour set then come back for an hour of encore after encore. Iggy ends the show completely naked, apart from a red sock on his cock! On the train back to Liverpool we bump into a journalist we know from Sounds music rag. His face is bleeding. A bouncer had punched his camera into his face. Camera destroyed along with the photos. We return to our Eric's residency with Sick of You attitude. Then split up!

Roy White, White and Torch

DUBLIN 1976-1977

In 1970, Horslips had hit me with a sledgehammer. I was an early adopter, having first seen them on Fonn, the TV series, when they were still substantially more folk than rock (they've always claimed they used the money they were paid for the first three shows to buy amps etc for the last three!), but where they already had the What The Fuck factor in some measure. The quasi-sacreligious sight of Eamon's long hair draped over his bodhrán as he played is the abiding image I have. I arranged to meet them to interview them for my school magazine and I suppose we've just been mates since. By the time I was 15, I was hanging out at their soundchecks and throwing up in their gardens at the aftershow parties. Horslips never treated me as the awkward adolescent I was, they were the coolest, smartest people I ever met outside my family and later, my own bands, and still are. Though it wasn't quite what they had set out to do, Horslips managed to make a school text like The Táin sexy and relevant, a mythology you wanted to be associated with. And by applying the same logic selectively to Irish music and visual art and so on, that's how Horslips saved indigenous Irish culture from itself.

Dublin, in a musical sense, was pretty hostile to us... We brought The Undertones down to support us at the Baggot Inn and they were astonished at the hostility –

I mean these guys thought parts of Derry were hostile to them, but nothing like on this petty level.

The scene we were actually part of and helped create in 76/77 was more like the early London and New York scenes had been, more art-driven than socially-self-conscious, though there was an element of that. The Radiators from Space, in many ways, echoed the cultural landscape the Horslips came out of 5 or 6 years earlier: art school, literary-minded, fashion-conscious, advertising-savvy, autodidactic. We knew our DC Comics and our Velvet Underground albums and mags like Creem and Punk and our Lillian Gish and Olive Thomas movies. We knew who Riefenstahl and Pabst were. Sufficiently new to the television culture that it remained both compelling and awful. We were deeply suspicious of politics and politicians not so much because they were mendacious and had their noses in the trough but because we knew intuitively they knew nothing about anything that actually mattered, like music and movies and plays and books and The Fugitive. These things were not their daily bread.

But I think what set the Dublin [punk] manifestation apart from New York and London is that almost all the apprentice work that came out of that era, in literature, in film, in theatre, in visual arts, performance art, poetry and music was fuelled by a genuine anger that was about something more fundamental than being bored and on the dole or pissed off cause your drug dealer was late or whatever. We were, after all, the generation who lived through the Christian Brothers and paedo priests knowing how wrong the violence, the abuse, the emotional wreckage was but entirely powerless to stop it. We knew more than our parents because the Church and the State were unable to entirely filter out the messages of change, of progress, that we heard from London or Paris or San Francisco or even Prague which, up till then, had only been the name of a Catholic statue – the Child of "Prayg". The reason why survivors of clerical abuse, when you hear them on radio, even now, deliver the most eloquent and affecting testimony we may ever hear is because for decades, they lived in a spiritual tunnel, an emotional vortex. They had plenty of time to internalise and articulate their experience, if only to themselves. The floodgates opened after the cover-up exploded. When I was a boy, you often heard the men and women of the previous generation refer almost affectionately to having the crap beaten out of them by these adults in loco parentis. Without fail, this recollection would be concluded by "ah, sure, what harm did it do us in the end?" with the implication that somehow all was well, and that used to make me absolutely furious and, of course, it's not something one hears very often anymore.

So, between that and the bullshit nationalism and the fires of hell, we had a great deal to be angry about. Actually, right from the start the Radiators made a couple of attempts at a clerical abuse song but never satisfactorily completed one we wanted to record: "Christian Muggers", aka "Christian Buggers", however sincerely meant, never seemed to rise above punk parody in its execution. I think it's there in the work all the same though. You can smell the fear in the Ghostown songs especially – listen to Jimmy Crashe's "Dead The Beast, Dead The Poison" with that in mind. I suppose, as an artist, you harbour a degree of residual guilt that you were unable to deliver a suitable rallying cry – "Burn all the Priests and Brothers and Nuns, send them to Hell early without Supper", that kinda thing, sung by the masses in Sackville Street. But you can only do what you think you can do.

Philip Chevron RIP, The Radiators from Space, The Pogues
(extracts from a 2012 interview)

THE RADIATORS FROM SPACE, DUBLIN 1977

A message outta the blue from Michael…Write a few words about Your Favourite Gig… It sounded like homework… the hound dog ate my ecker. Christian Brudders.

I agreed as it's such a great cause but Whitney we have a problem… I can't put my arms around a memory… I went, saw, dug and partied… but I took no notes.

Mid/late-70s Dublin was a fairly desolate place… Rory, Lizzy and Horslips. I never got Gallagher. It was black and white… Our world had not yet gone dayglo. Punk arrived… We were saved!!!

Eddie and the Hot Rods and Dr Feelgood were the early outriders… They had energy and didn't rely on wasp in a jam-jar guitar solos. The Clash played back-to-back gigs in Trinity… the first one was the better. That was some gig.

The Ramones played Phibsboro… Rewind… The Ramones played Phibsboro! The State Cinema where as a kid I had seen "Darby O'Gill and the Little People" (a movie not a Boston garage punk band).

Belfield Burnin' was a punk gig where it went wrong… A boy Patrick Coultry got murdered. Punk got blamed… It was a difficult time. Me and Pete were disc spinners that night.

Fast forward to the most important gig of all time... Jimmy... drum roll please...

Moran's Hotel... A new house record. Heat, our fanzine, called it "Punk's first night out since Belfield". It was the debut of the new four-piece Radiators from Space, and the Rads farewell to the Emerald Isle. It included The Fabulous Fabrics who were playing their first gig days after buying guitars in Woolworth. (Whatever happened to them? Woolworth I mean). The Vipers and Revolver completed the support. Billy from Revolver was one of the coolest cats I have ever met.

The Radiators invited Steve back on stage at the end. They belted out "I Feel Alright" by Iggy and the Stooges. Our world was back as it should be, we could all move on.

Later Dublin hosted gigs by The Only Ones, XTC, Elvis and Buzzcocks.

Heat got into a spot of bother with a local band... They had yet to release a record. The High Court agreed we damaged their career. In a roundabout way it led to another classic gig... For one night only The Defenders at the National Ballroom. Paul, Donal and Bill RIP and thanks.

Shortly afterwards I ran away from the circus.

Jude Carr, author, Heat fanzine, Bad Karma Beckons

THE MEMBERS, LONDON 1977

We had a gig. Playing at the Roxy. Not being as plugged-in then, we never realised we were in the fag-end days of this poxy little club. The original thinkers who'd started it had been ousted by the owners in the spirit of "if they can do it, we shouldn't have any problems". Some mistake. We were to be first on the bill, a four-band line up headlined by Ed Banger and the Nosebleeds. We had four or five songs and had learnt Bowie's "Rebel Rebel", which I sang badly. We turned up at the club, impressed by the inner suburban crowd in their second-wave bin liners. The club was already on its way out. Dodgy Management Inc had told us to turn up for a soundcheck – we had no idea what that was about. If I'd known I would have set the precedent of never turning up for them. Arriving to locked doors, we knocked, we knocked harder, we kicked the door, we screamed. Finally, a bored-looking black guy opens the door.

"Yeah?"

"We're the Members."

"We don't have members." Door slams. Repeat the process.

"Whatyoofuckinwant," he says.

"We're the band called The Members. Can we come in please?"

It was a stinky little shithole on Neal Street with a stage the size of a used handkerchief and a dressing room to match. It was heaven, we'd arrived, studied cool an' all. We had a five-minute soundcheck, finally. The idea of a soundcheck is to make sure all the instruments are working and the sound is balanced out front for the audience. We watched, confidently, as the other groups scratched and squawked their way through a song or two. Slouching on stage we did our best. Then I went to the pub and drank until I could hardly stand up. I thought that was what was expected of me. That and the fact I was shit-scared. We were on first.

Stumbling back to the Roxy we took to the stage. I still wake nights sweating at the memory of how truly awful we were that night. Everyone loved it. Whatever audience was there at that early hour obviously had to be home before the last train. In their out-of-date bin liners with carefully coifed hair and dog collars they gave us a marvellously indifferent welcome. A couple of the younger ones who had no idea of the etiquette regarding unknown bands moved around a bit and spat at us. Mmm, nice. We played for about 20 minutes, I forgot the words and realised that I was never going to be Marvin Gaye. The band gurned, the audience turned.

At the time I was calling myself Nicky Ritz in common with every other punk wannabe with a name change. That and the fact that my parents had begged me not to use my real name. After the gig, Jon Moss came backstage. He was playing with London at that time, a real face. "What's that last song called?" "GLC." I almost said sir. "It's good," he said in an off-hand noncommittal way handing down his largesse from above. I liked him. We had no money and I did the unheard-of feat of blagging drinks from the Roxy. It was a Herculean task. Later, on the way somewhere else, convinced that fame and huge fortune was just down the road with its thumb out waiting for us, someone spoke up. "Jesus Nick, you're so cut-price you should be called Tescos, never mind Ritz." My brother called me Tesco until he died.

Nick Tesco, The Members

THE ROXY, LONDON 1976-1977

My name is Rab Fallon. As a musician (well a drummer anyway), I was Rab fae Beith. I was in The Pack, Patrik Fitzgerald, The Wall and UK Subs 1985-1986. After that I was doorman/stage security at the Marquee 1988-1993. I also worked at Virgin Recs HQ 1990-2002, so I've seen a lot of gigs. Too many to pick a favourite.

I discovered punk back in late 1976 while walking along Albert embankment, I came across a gang of punks at a tea stall outside the tube station. I got talking to them and they invited me to the Roxy. I was hooked. I went out and bought a new drumkit on the drip, within three months it was repossessed, I then knew my limits. I got myself a cheap old kit and I was off, got Melody Maker ads, and started going to a week's worth of auditions. One of them was a band, Pack of Lies. Right away I knew this was different, not just some vocalist singing the same chords as the guitar. We did two gigs and had a reshuffle; we changed our name to The Pack. My favourite memories of The Pack were every show really. In those days, we played for any money offered, blagging a van etc. The whole scene was just fun. We even played squat parties for beer (oh the young). It was brilliant in the early days, squatting and having fun. After The Pack, I went to an audition with Patrik Fitzgerald as he decided not to be acoustic anymore. I arrived at the audition and Jack Parnell's son and the drummer for Tubeway Army among others were there. I thought "fuck it, what chance have I got against these professionals". We all got a half-hour spot and just jammed along to what Patrik played. Then bloody hell I was told I got the job. Next thing I knew I was in a studio recording for Polydor (Improve Myself), then out on a UK tour with Teardrop Explodes and The Wall. It was the first time I had a proper roadie and stayed in hotels. With The Pack, we crashed at anyone's house or drove back to London. My unforgettable memory of that tour has to be watching Dave Balfe (Teardrop Explodes) punching our bass player in the gob for getting lippy. Dave went on to be head of CBS/Sony and managed Blur. Country House is about him, so I always laugh when I hear that song.

While touring with Patrik, the support band The Wall asked me if I'd join them at the end of the tour as their drummer. The guy they had was good but he never knew the end of any songs, so he was always playing when the band stopped. I actually thought it was funny. My favourite shows with The Wall were doing The Go For It Tour with Stiff Little Fingers.

That period of punk 1979-1982, I noticed the dark side creeping in. Violence getting worse (skinheads, right wing etc). It seemed that the whole fun bit was just gone. Folk just weren't going to shows as much. The Wall had good record sales but our shows were just getting poorly attended. So in 1982, I just knocked it on the head as I wasn't enjoying it anymore.

FF to early 1985, I was sitting at home and two guys show up at my door, turns out they are Bass and Guitar from UK Subs, they ask me if I want to join for a USA tour. I asked how they knew me, they just said Charlie sent them round. So that was it, I was in a band again. Seeing as this book is about the NHS, it reminded me of this story: Not long after joining The Subs I got a phone call at 3am. It's Charlie, he's having a heart attack. I'm half-asleep and saying "For fuck's sake Charper, call an ambulance." Charlie says "I don't really want to bother anyone" as he was losing strength in his speech. I jumped out of bed just thinking bollocks gotta save him. I raced around to Charper's house, got him out and threw him in the back, then raced over to St James's in Balham where the NHS did their bit. Charlie was rushed into a ward and the rest as they say is history. So all you Subs fans can thank me Charper is around!

Rab Fallon, The Pack, The Wall, Patrik Fitzgerald, UK Subs

DUBLIN 1977-1978

My first ever gigs were in The Stadium about 1972. Slade and then Gary Glitter. I then grew into going to gigs like Dr Feelgood and Thin Lizzy and all the usual 'annuals' who played around Christmas time.

Very few people came here apart from the usual suspects of Rory Gallagher, Thin Lizzy and Horslips in the Stadium. It was an old dilapidated boxing stadium on the South Circular Road with a capacity of about 2,500. All the other venues were licenced, so it was difficult to see anyone until you looked old enough. Horslips and a few bands occasionally played the odd free gig in the hollow in the Phoenix Park or Merrion Square but those were few and far between.

Myself and my brother Dick started going to smaller gigs around late '75. People like the Arthur Phybes band and Jimmy Slevin. Anywhere we could get in really. The Universal Folk Club in Parnell Square was a weekly gig we attended as it was not licenced and entry was guaranteed. Leo O Kelly played there, and he was my introduction to Toners as he had a weekly residency there.

That all changed in 1977 when the Clash played in Trinity College. As my brother Dick said "it was the day Dublin went from black and white to colour". Suddenly out of nowhere there was 1000 bands in Dublin and we were hanging out with people like Jude Carr and the Navan Road contingent, meeting people like Terry O'Neill and George Murray, people who were the engine of the early scene in Dublin and should today be considered as icons because the scene would not have happened without their involvement. They ran gigs and record shops, created fanzines and networks. They were like the glue which held the early scene together. The Fabrics, The Boy Scoutz, The Vipers; these filled the vacuum when the Radiators and the Boomtown Rats left for London

They should all be remembered, every last one of them contributed to the scene. Even the 95% who never played. It was a generation who finally said "Fuck you, If you say I can't see bands I'll create the scene myself". It was liberating, it crossed social and religious divides. We were creating a revolution and we didn't know it.

Revolver in Toners and a Christmas gig by the Radiators in Moran's were particularly memorable as these were my introduction to Dublin punk and the energy just blew me away. Bob Geldof joined the Radiators for a riotous encore of 'My Generation' at Moran's and I decided to accompany him. The jubilant crowd went apeshit and ripped most of Geldof's clothes to shreds while enthusiastically ignoring me. It's at this moment I realised my future was in the background.

I decided to arrange my own gigs.

The Saint Anthony's hall gig in 1978 is probably the best remembered. The thinking behind it was all of the venues bands were using at the time were licenced and it was obvious to me from the numbers of people being turned away at doors and hanging out in record shops that there was a large number of kids not getting to see the bands.

I mooted the idea of holding a "festival" style line up of bands in a larger hall around the top bands in Dublin at the time. The idea was to pre-sell tickets, have a decent sound system and lighting rig and standing room only in the theatre. I got commitments from U2, Virgin Prunes, Berlin, New Versions, Strange Movements, Skank Mooks and The Citizens. Pretty much the coolest dudes around the scene at the time. Bono and Edge later made cameo appearances during Virgin Prunes set.

All 600 tickets were sold out in advance. On the night the attendance was anywhere from 800 to 1000 as there were many gate crashers. The gig itself was a rather shambolic affair but that in itself led to its punk credentials and later legendary status. It was the first gig attended by many people later involved in the Dublin music scene and spawned a second generation of bands and was the precursor to the Dandelion Market gigs and McGonagles Saturday afternoon shows.

Like the Boomtown Rats and Radiators from Space gigs in Moran's Hotel and U2 gigs in the Dandelion, about one million people currently claim to have been in attendance!

George Purdy, promoter, Dublin

JOHN MCLAUGHLIN/SHAKTI, WASHINGTON DC 1977

I don't know if I have an outright "favourite" concert but I have a particularly special memory of seeing John McLaughlin with Shakti in the autumn of 1977. I was 15 and McLaughlin was my guitar god/hero. They were playing two sets in the old-town part of Washington DC called Georgetown at a tiny club called the Cellar Door and I went down with two buddies from high school who were both tripping on LSD. We all had utterly implausible fake IDs but we got in anyway as things were a lot more lax back then.

Anyway, we sit through an amazing set in this tiny club and afterwards I want to hang around to get an autograph. Now, to get from the stage to the dressing rooms at the Cellar Door the artists had to go out through the front door and up an outside stair to the second floor. It was November and dark and rather chilly but there we were out on the sidewalk looking up at the dressing room window where the curtain would open and shut periodically. My two friends on acid decided that the best way to keep warm would be to jump up and down and flap their arms. I just waited.

Finally, John McLaughlin, still in his simple linen stage clothes appears at the bottom of the stairs and asks very humbly, "Er... are you waiting for... me?" My wide-eyed, open-jawed face must have been an obvious answer and he then spent what seemed like a good 15 minutes out in the cold just simply talking to me. What struck me then and stays with me now is that he took care to engage me as a person, not simply as a fan. He must have been freezing, but instead of rushing away he stayed out there on the pavement (while my two friends were still flapping their arms and jumping up and down). And instead of simply looking at his watch while I sputtered familiar hyperbole at him, he turned it into a conversation.

He asked me, "So, do you play guitar too?" The "too: in that question had a profound impact on my psyche. It wasn't simply friendly, it was collegial. We talked about guitars a bit more. I got an autograph and he went back in to thaw out in time for the second set.

That encounter has stayed with me and is on my mind every time I talk to fans or students. A simple act of basic kindness that has benefited me for nearly 40 years. Thanks again John.

Chris Haskett, Rollins Band

XTC, LONDON 1977

Hope & Anchor, Islington, June 30th

Another of those bands first discovered through John Peel's influential and irreverent BBC Radio One programme in the middle of 1977.

I went along with my oldest pal and kindred spirit Robert Mason (illustrator and author). We'd known each other since 1970, having both studied at Canterbury, Maidstone and the Royal College of Art. We had much in common, including our musical tastes.

Notwithstanding the fact that there were no more than about 12 people there including the band, their manager-cum-roadie-cum-van driver and us, XTC were explosive.

Crushed on the tiny stage, and despite Andy Partridge's evident nervousness, they flayed and twitched with jet-fuelled, hard-hitting and visceral energy. Terry Chambers' pile-driving drums left holes for Colin Moulding's elastic bass, while Barry Andrews' frenetic buzzing keyboards swirled within and against Andy Partridge's jagged finger-shredding guitar. They fused the incongruous free-form angularity of Captain Beefheart and his Magic Band with power pop to create music that was noisy, jittery and yet infectiously danceable.

On numerous occasions, Andrews' furious organ-stabbing bulldozed his instrument forward, butting into Partridge's backside, shoving him, tumbling, off stage. Expletives ricocheted as the keyboards were hauled back. Meanwhile Chambers and Moulding were tasked with bravely holding a solid rhythmic ground for as long as the wrangling Andrews and Partridge simmered down enough for them to lock in again.

Even then it seemed obvious that they were slightly out of kilter with their punk counterparts. More inventive and intelligent than most of their peers, their musical craft was too virtuosic and sophisticated to be cool, and their playful melee of complex rhythms, swerving time signatures, tuneful but willfully odd chords and painfully gorgeous melodies stood them apart. Lyrically synaesthetic and poetically sensitive, with English suburbia, surrealism and sci-fi colliding and colluding – Larkin filtered through Viv Stanshall – they were too playfully literate, occasionally too whimsical, and too decidedly apolitical, to be deemed "punk".

While they certainly celebrated the impurity of punk, were they really punk? Or warped power pop? Or a mutant new wave? I didn't know or care. Thankfully it defied categorisation and it was thrilling. It was enough that I was so pumped with adrenaline that on leaving my legs were like jelly.

Russell Mills, artist

THE RAMONES/TALKING HEADS, LONDON 1977

The Roundhouse, Camden Town

I missed the third support band, The Saints, but heard that they'd imploded after two songs and received no sympathy from a hyped-up audience that were there primarily to lurch up and down, slam into each other, and shower a storm of phlegm and lager at The Ramones.

Resembling my favourite childhood comic characters, the Bizarro Superheroes, who were the antithesis of their earthly equivalents, The Ramones were not pretty. Gangly beanstalks, clad in the requisite uniform of the mythologised delinquent: all black leather, skuzzy T-shirts, ripped jeans, shades and fringe-mopped hippy hair. A cartoon band of pretend brothers, they instantly roared into life with a devastating barrage of high-energy, wall-to-wall power chords. What constituted songs, breathlessly barked chants, flashed by at escape velocity, each hook hammering into the next, while any hints of melody or harmony were shredded with the violence of a chainsaw. Apparently, they spewed out 16 songs in 35 minutes. The audience, a raging sea of flailing bodies, was in heaven.

While I appreciated the lure of the pure bliss and energy of frantic, visceral undiluted rock'n'roll, I wasn't convinced. Not a rebellious stance against the moribund music business of the day, nor an attack against the status quo, I felt it wasn't even part of the DIY ethos that fuelled punk. For me they were a one-joke façade; surf rock twisted into a caricature of deviance: all brash fuming, slithery, sleazy and sneering: ersatz hoodlum music. Knowingly stoopid: not dangerous, merely freak show geeks.

I'd come for Talking Heads, an American quartet of white, lean, nervous and wide-eyed nerds, who had very little in common with the headliners. They entered the stage awkwardly as if somewhat dazed and confused and immediately burst into life.

There was magic in their minimalistic yet intricate instrumental interplay. Chris Frantz's solid, unflashy, occasionally staccato, drumming locked with low-end anchor Tina Weymouth's pliant rubbery bass to create the funkiest rhythm unit I'd heard, a structurally meticulous grounding that enabled Jerry Harrison and David Byrne to intertwine chiming, jangling guitar riffs with swirling organ melodies. Alternately ominous and uplifting, with adrenaline-rush eliding into the trippy, their music created a sense of disorientation that appealed to me.

Byrne, wire-thin and all trembling nerve endings, was the band's mesmeric focal point; jerky and crackling like a wired insect, his flailing limbs threatened to disconnect from his body. Switching from reticent mutterings to extended crooning or yelped whines and geeky falsettos, with idiosyncratic vocal phrasings, inexplicable pauses, he sounded lost, brain-addled, urgent and in total panic, like a crazed preacher warning against impending catastrophes. His lyrics were quotidian observations delivered as a delightfully unhinged stream of consciousness; simultaneously disquieting and heartening, like a fractured commentary of consternation and alienated wonderment at the world's strangeness.

Like me, they'd been to art school; they understood the importance and potential of Dada, collage, fragmentation, appropriation, quotation and juxtaposition. Here was music that, without sounding smug or descending into pastiche, engaged with the mind, the soul and the hips, meshing art-rock with dance music. For me it was the most exciting sound I'd heard since Captain Beefheart chopped up the Magic Band's component parts and threw them up into the air, or early Roxy Music's pop art magpie plundering of contemporary music, or Eno's restless innovatory explorations of sonic landscapes within a pop framework. They were sharp and smart and irresistibly danceable; they seemed like the future.

Russell Mills, artist

PENETRATION, SIOUXSIE AND THE BANSHEES, X-RAY SPEX AND MANY OTHERS, LONDON 1977

In mid-June in the summer of 1977, I board the ferry at Dun Laoghaire port in Dublin, to make the three-hour crossing to Holyhead, and began my pilgrimage to London.

My parents have reluctantly driven me from Wexford, an 80-odd-mile trip. I have no recollection of the journey but remember our farewells in a hotel bar near the harbour, my mother fussing because I have a serious strep-throat infection and a burgeoning high temperature but I refuse to cancel or defer this trip.

A recruitment drive for seasonal workers by a UK hotel chain had offered me the chance I was looking for – to finally get to London and the epicentre (or one of them) of the first wave of punk. I would go to gigs, hang out with bands, and acquire some "proper" punk attire. My formerly flared Levis had been carefully taken in to "straights" by my mother painstakingly hand-sewing the tough denim, but for me, they were still a poor substitute for proper bondage trousers. I would buy the few punk records available and most importantly, I would finally find my tribe. I was 18. I had been listening avidly to John Peel and reading the gig reviews in Sounds and the NME since the previous summer and now I would get to see these bands myself.

The boat and train journey passed in a fever dream of anticipation, excitement and vague anxiety. Power plants, lit up like giant fairgrounds, loomed out of the darkness as the train sped past. I couldn't sleep, pressing my face against the window and willing the lights of London to appear out of the gloom as dawn started to brighten the horizon.

Negotiating the tube from Euston station, I make it to Kensington and the hostel accommodation. I figure out how to get to the King's Road and walk its length hopefully, peering into the closed shops, pressing my nose against the window of Boy and gawping at Seditionaries' display. But the street is virtually empty, with not a punk in sight.

On my first day of work as a chamber-maid in a hotel near Marble Arch, I spot a guy in the staff canteen and know he would be my in. Richard was a 25-year-old former art student and his work boilersuit was emblazoned with badges and safety pins, his hair bleached and spiked, he had more earrings than I had ever seen on anyone, man or woman, before. I played "Roadrunner" by Jonathan Richman and the Modern Lovers on the canteen jukebox and mustered the courage to ask him where I could go to see punk bands playing. He was going to a gig that evening and offered to bring me along. The Roxy was over he told me, now the bands were playing The Vortex in Soho instead.

I don't remember who played at that first gig with any certainty, just the dub reggae music played between sets, and the cans of revolting-tasting but strong fortified beer. But over the course of the next four months, I would see Penetration, Siouxsie and the Banshees, X-Ray Spex and many others on that stage. I saw The Boys and Generation X at The Marquee in Wardour Street. Although I wasn't as impressed by either of these bands as Richard (a gay man) was for some reason. Of the bands I knew beforehand and had heard back home on the radio, I would not see The Clash that summer, nor The Sex Pistols, who were allegedly "banned" by the GLC from playing anywhere in the city.

I was inspired by the strong female performers I was seeing; Pauline in Penetration, Sioux of course and the most impressive of all, the one-off talent that was Poly Styrene. The most exciting and eagerly anticipated gig I attended was The Cognoscenti Orchestra – a band name nobody was familiar with – at Camden's Electric Ballroom. There were rumours that it was actually The Sex Pistols playing a secret gig. It wasn't. But on the bill that night were The Slits and they left me exhilarated. I loved the way they occupied the stage, especially and the confrontational, provoking, feisty yet playful way they faced-off the audience. This, I thought, is what I want to do. I want to create, to perform, not just consume passively and be entertained.

I toyed with staying in London, of giving up or postponing my university course, but in the end, I regretfully headed back to Ireland on the ferry in early October. I was dreading college now and what I foresaw as a place devoid of other like-minded punks. But I didn't have long to wait before I found them. A few weeks later I finally got to see The Clash play, but in Dublin, in Trinity

College's exam hall, looked down on by 18th-century portraits. Although I didn't meet them all that night, the majority of my soon-to-be friends and future band mates were at that gig too. It was the crucible for our little 1980s post-punk scene to come.

Bernie Furlong, The Golden Horde

THE SLITS/THE RAINCOATS, LONDON 1977

The Tabernacle, Powis Square, Notting Hill Gate, November 9th, 1977

I'd first heard the Slits on John Peel's BBC Radio One programme a few months earlier and was intrigued by what I assumed was their extremely youthful innocence, which came through as a vibrant energy and chaotic joie de vivre. My pal Rob Mason had heard the programme too and was as keen as I was to go. The Raincoats were a mystery to us.

This was a benefit concert in aid of the Community Arts Centre housed in the Tabernacle, a vast Victorian, grade-II, listed church built in 1888. With its curved Romanesque façade of red brick and terracotta and twin towers, it was an incongruous venue for the first all-female punk gig that ignited the Riot Grrl movement in the 1990s.

The audience, which was perhaps predictably predominantly female, all black string vests, rainbow knits, leather, slashed T-shirts, Doctor Martens boots and military surplus, seemed far less threatening than that of the testosterone-driven, gob-shooting, male punk gig. A bobbing sea of voluminous multi-coloured knotty dreadlocks and dyed buzz cuts obscured my view for most of the night, but what I did espy was a wonderfully shambolic display of all the primary characteristics of punk: the DIY enthusiasm, the pulsating energy, the attitude.

This was The Raincoats' first gig: they were nervous, tentative and delightfully tattered. They were also genuinely inept musicians, learning on the job – with no rulebooks – flirting with imminent catastrophe. Plundering their imaginations and accepting their limitations, their honest, unashamedly amateurish sound was tinged with a naturally anarchic edge. Fidgety drumming tumbled and sprawled beneath a scratchy violin and restless skewed guitars, while the songs, alternately lilting or jarring, delved into the way they lived, and the scrappy contingencies of life at the margins.

The group's playful meanderings and wayward delivery melded a bristling folk with elements of the avant-garde, reminding me the likes of Kevin Ayers, Soft Machine, Caravan, Hatfield and the North, and other bands of late-1960s art-rock of the Canterbury scene, much of which I'd experienced while on foundation at Canterbury School of Art in 1969-1970. This was the kind of serious play always on the verge of ecstatic collapse that I liked.

The Slits were also a lot of fun. With their murky hair snarled up into hornets' nests, they leapt and bounced and raged, all scratchy guitars, with bass and drums slip-sliding in and out of grooves, while voices whooped, trilled, yowled and cooed a gleefully shambolic tirade against the stifling stereotypes of femininity, or the constants of disappointing boyfriends. Like a gaggle of sassy schoolgirls teasing boys or casually reducing teachers to microbes, they turned their aggression and wit into a giddy game.

While the gig itself was an exhilarating experience, it also marked a hugely pivotal moment in what was, until then, the overwhelmingly male-orientated world of music. With their audacious, defiant sense of autonomy, here were some very young women making music for women, rather than the male gaze. And they were having a lot of fun at the same time.

Low point: I would've enjoyed the evening far more had I not spent most of it too scared to move, as my feet were pinned to the floor under the huge and heavy heels of a brawny, army-camouflaged, crop-haired Amazonian stood in front on me flanked by a gang of equally formidable females.

Russell Mills, artist

HAMMERHEADS, HAMILTON, ONTARIO 1976–1978

We were all hopeless to begin with. Born to lose, blue-collar devils, completely out of fashion. We were just kids really, surrounded by a whole town that looked like Peter Fonda's dim-witted cousin with an STP oil treatment.

Kinda handsome and kinda really fucked up. The great male character combo that filled the bars and bowling alleys, the Running Pump, the Elamar and the Jockey Club… bruised knuckles and crooked noses, perfect hair.

Our youth was aimed but misdirected, erected and we were spilling out of broken homes and onto the streets of Hamilton, Ont.

Religion and school and politics had driven us further into the ground. We believed that we'd never pull ourselves out of the holes we were drilled into, so our spirits thrived on chaos and the perfect storm was coming our way around 1976/77.

There was nothing before that for us to cling onto. We weren't hippies and we didn't have the proper clothes to go to a disco. The radio was slowly killing us dead like frogs in slow-burn saucepans.

Passing cars and DJ booths in clubs playing four-on-the-floor kick drums and then middle-of-the-road acoustic guitars ringing out some white-boy sadness.

We were being fed a steady diet of music that was impossible for us to imagine being a part of.

Songs that we could never figure out how to play on our shitty guitars.

We needed the door of possibility to open a crack so that we could barge through and proclaim ourselves. We found it on the wings of one, two or maybe three chords hammered out and blasted off with sweat and blood and piss that blew past our gaping mouths and stung the backs of our throats.

Punk rock was simply the rock'n'roll that came at us from Detroit.

The Stooges, MC5 and Alice Cooper along with bands like The New York Dolls and The Flaming Groovies made sense to us.

These bands opened the door, asking us to walk though.

My hometown, "the Hammer' as it's known across Canada, is and always has been a cultural island that sits amongst a rusting steel industry.

The art that's made there is often shadowed by a broken-nosed attitude that walks the streets looking for a fight. The town is known to have an overall bad attitude.

We stand far apart from the shiny-shoed giant they call Toronto, but we can look across Lake Ontario on a clear day and see its golden towers shining in the bright sun.

It's annoying. We hate it there. We as in the collective psyche of Hamiltonians that is. I don't really care either way to be honest with you.

Hamilton is also a great town for original music.

Conway Twitty wrote "It's Only Make Believe" here.

King Biscuit Boy ruled all who attempted to sing and play the blues and was in fact anointed the greatest white blues singer by Muddy Waters. I could go on. I won't.

So when Hamiltonians tapped into rock'n'roll we avoided looking to England like the rest of Canada and instead took our cues and aimed our needles towards Detroit, Michigan which was so close we could smell it.

We played music to stay out of the steel mills.

We didn't want to lose what we had to shift work... We weren't better than those jobs. We just wanted to rebel, and the punk movement was our way out.

Now, the actual punk bands that came out of Hamilton weren't actually just punks who got guitars.

They were gangs.

Groups of young men who sold drugs, robbed convenience stores and broke into houses to make money to buy instruments. They vomited on stage and got into fights with whoever showed up to see them. Not many people ever showed up to see them btw.

My friend Ray played in one of those bands and got arrested on stage while opening for Stiff Little Fingers one night. They took him away for playing a drum kit he stole from a home earlier that day. The kid whose parents house got broken into was at the show and fingered Ray. He ran to a phone booth and hit 911.

Ray became the king of the punks after that even though he looked nothing like the fashionable punks. Ray was skinny as a starved dog with long black curly hair. He walked the downtown core selling LSD and looking like Gilbert Sheldon's character "freewheeling Franklin".

The bottom line is that in my hometown punk got put into a midway mirror and from the most part didn't look much like the punk movement going on everywhere else in the world.

It was more like our roots. Detroit rock'n'roll

It was Eddie Cochran and Gene Vincent riding a wave aboard a Les Paul jr and destroying every bar room through Marshall amps.

Hamilton punk was Teenage Head who got some hits and caused some shit, caused a few riots that got reported in Rolling Stone and almost got really famous but for a terrible car accident, some addiction issues and overall Steeltown bad luck. It got old and fell to the sidelines and now we are all old and looking back at glory days that look more like a three-alarm fire in a warehouse.

Rave on y'all.

Tom Wilson, artist, author, songwriter, Junkhouse, Blackie and the Rodeo Kings

FOLK FESTIVAL, TRIER 1977

The charm, if there is any, of the unreliable narrator, is that he believes he remembers the truth. So this is how I recall events one night in the summer of 1977.

My band, Bluebell's Anus, a bizarre punk-edged traditional Irish unit, played in the square at the heart of the Trier castle ruins, early in the afternoon – though the level of our set was perhaps best measured by the fact that the songs which went down best were a couple of English acapella Copper Family songs. In contrast, a band of young lads based in Liverpool came on in the evening called The Green Groves of Erin – at their core, two brothers who played pipes and fiddle, and a huge bodhran player called Finbarr, notorious for taking on phalanxes of German police when he was pissed. They played jigs and reels with real power and authority. I thought their set was mesmerising.

But it was neither formal part of the gig that I remember best. Late in the evening, we gathered in a stone arch, near the bar and burger stand, for a session that lasted hour after hour. I recall, I was taking care of our bouzouki player, who'd struggled to the bogs and vomited into a basin – one hand splashing him with cold water, the other unblocking the sink of its new contents – when a crew of Borussia Monchengladbach fans arrived, fresh from their defeat to Liverpool in the European Cup Final. Much as an earlier generation of German youth had been wooed by traditional culture to support the kind of values enshrined in Nazism, for which the current one was mortally ashamed, these weren't ethnic music enthusiasts.

It wasn't long, inevitably, before Finbarr and the rest of us were involved in a heavy argument over the football, which would any minute turn sour and bloody. The first glint of dawn was rising. I don't know why the idea came into my head but, before fists could fly, I suggested we settle the score by playing a game in the meadow down by the river, and whoever won, won. No arguments. So it was we lined up in the grey air and kicked off: Irish musicians against German skinheads. It was close and dirty. But a few minutes before time was blown on a tin whistle, the Groves' fiddler scuttled down the left wing and put over a cross, almost too high to get my head to. But, with the benefit of alcoholic leverage, I threw myself through the air, dived full length, and headed into what would have been the roof of the net. That settled it.

Unfortunately, I landed heavily on my right hand and bent back the fingers so badly that the rest of the gigs on that tour were a nightmare. But then I was a shit mandolin player anyway, so I don't suppose it made much difference.

Ah yes, Trier Folk Festival. Never to be forgotten. Gig, session, football match at dawn. At least that's how I remember it.

Nick Burbridge, songwriter, The Crack

THE RAMONES, LONDON 1977

It is said that the music of your youth is the one that you never tire of. I was 20 years old in September 1978, living in Swansea and working at Virgin Records there. A few of us Swansea punks piled into my mate John's red van and headed to the Locarno Bristol (now an 02) for The Ramones... I'd seen them at the Roundhouse in London before this, and was at the legendary Rainbow gig NYE 1977 (still have the ticket stub thankfully) but this felt really special. This felt local.

The venue was smaller than it seems nowadays, with a low stage. I always had to get right down the front to feel part of the atmosphere at gigs, but remembering that Johnny Ramone had coshed someone from the stage for spitting at the Roundhouse, I took my spot in centre front of Joey's mic stand. I can't remember a set list, I don't have that kind of memory, I do though recall the wild, sweaty, loud, pogoing crowd going mental. I was probably one of a small number of females in that crowd, in my narrowed-hem jeans and homemade black leather jacket (skins from a Welsh abattoir). I was being pressed up against the stage until my face was almost level with Joey's and I had indentations on my shins for the journey home from that stage. It was that low and my hearing has never recovered!

The spirit of punk has lived on in me and that energy was what inspired those rowdy Boothill Foot Tapper gigs for sure!

Wendy May, Boothill Foot Tappers, DJ

THE RAMONES, ANN ARBOR 1977

In early 1977, The Ramones played the Second Chance in Ann Arbor, Michigan. We, my brothers and almost all my friends at the time, had just heard their first album and knew we had to be there. It was not a choice, it was a necessity. The minute they hit the stage, I and all my allies were on the dance floor. It was a tribal dance. It was the dance of finding a community we did not know was there or that we needed. But it was, and we did.

It was so loud that there was a discussion thread that they had actually planned for certain decibel levels at certain frequencies to alter your brain. This is unlikely to be true, but it sure felt like it.

As the set went on, song after song, back to back with no breaks, the tribal vibe intensified. It was pure released human joy, mixed with tragedy of course, like any good play in 440BC in Athens, Greece. When Joey grabbed the Gabba Gabba Hey sign and carried it proudly aloft, we all knew why. Was this high art? Was this going back to the reptilian portion of the brain? Likely it was both.

Later that year I was talking with a friend from high school who loved that "Classic 70s rock stuff". I put on the first Ramones album and, as three songs sped by in the time that one of his favourite bands were still struggling to get to a chorus, I nudged him and asked "Hear any guitar solos yet?" He was baffled, but I knew what was going on. The ground had shifted and I was just biding my time until I found my new footing.

In 1979 Mission of Burma formed in Boston, MA. It took a while. But it was The Ramones that cleared everything off the table. Time to cook up some new victuals motherfuckers...

And when Mission of Burma played with Gang of Four in NYC, in early 1980, Andy asked me to be his guitar tech and change strings if he broke any. I was honoured.

Roger Miller, Mission of Burma

BLONDIE, NEW YORK 1977

When you work in songwriting like I did, nothing is more important than the song. It is always a thrill to first hear a song, a fresh raw recording by a writer, you might even be one of the first people to ever hear it, and you think "that could be a hit!" People forget how many exceptional songwriters punk and new wave and post-punk produced.

I was one the few women executives in the music industry at the time. I hit the glass ceiling when I was eventually promoted to senior vice president and general manager of the Chrysalis Music Group USA. Sadly, there were few women in this position, but I was determined to help female label workers, managers and artists.

I was really lucky to work with Blondie, one of the world's best punk rock bands, with the beautiful Debbie Harry.

I first saw them perform at the then famous CBGBs. The music was raw and very loud. Ear-splitting.

Their debut album was produced by a friend of mine, Richard Gottehrer (also a songwriter "My Boyfriend's Back"): "Blondie" (first released on Private Stock) and subsequently on Chrysalis. I remember visiting the band in rehearsal with Mike Chapman and inviting them for lunch. Debbie was hesitant and I carefully replied that she didn't have to join us. She did.

A few years later I remember going to visit Debbie with Jack Craigo. I asked if there was anything I could do to help (she was looking after Chris, who was seriously ill) and she replied – "Help me clean, please?" I responded "Absolutely I would love to help you." Sadly, Debbie never took me up on the offer.

It would be hard to pick a favourite Blondie gig. On one occasion, they arrived at the Beverly Hills opening of Fiorrici in an army tank!

Perhaps the Hollywood Bowl gig was my favourite. I never knew this at the time – it was designed by Lloyd Wright, Frank Gehry and Myron Hunt – seems fitting for the modern-pop-with-attitude of Blondie. I took Frankie Miller and Doctor John as my guests. They are also very talented songwriters, but they were quite funny afterwards. They definitely did not understand punk.

Another outstanding gig was seeing the very talented Jack Lee and his band, The Nerves, for the first time. Again, ear-shattering. Madam Wongs, I believe. Jack is an amazing songwriter. Blondie covered two of his songs – "Hangin' on the Telephone" and "Will Anything Happen?" He became and remains a good friend of mine. Later Paul Young covered three of his songs, including "Come Back and Stay".

Billy Idol, with the curled sneer and managed by Bill Aucoin and Brendan Bourke, was another talented punk singer/songwriter. "White Wedding" is my favourite. Billy's shows were loud and exciting with the very talented guitarist Steve Stevens.

With Billy and Bill Aucoin in a hotel on Sunset Boulevard, I was more than amused to be invited by Billy to try on the frilly underwear he had bought his girlfriend.

Another fond memory I have is of meeting Henry Rollins for the first time after watching his show. I told him I had loved his show and had he ever thought of producing a get-fit video. Everyone around gasped. However, Henry said only one word: "Yes."

Ann Munday, senior vice president, general manager, Chrysalis Music America

DEAF SCHOOL, NEW YORK 1977

CBGB's, June 18th

We had formed in the autumn of 1973 at the Art College in Liverpool. From day one we had consciously aimed to be an antidote to the plethora of hairy prog bands that seemed to be noodling everywhere at the time. By the spring of 1977, we'd made two albums for Warner Bros and were about to benefit from their bloated "Hotel California" profits as we stepped off a Jumbo Jet in San Francisco to start a seven-week tour of the USA.

As punk emerged, we recognised so much of our core ethic: making an impact took precedence over musicianship. We even gave ourselves daft stage names. Long before Johnny Rotten, we had Eric Shark, Max Ripple and Cliff Hanger in our ranks.

After six weeks of constant gigging across America (two shows a night being the norm) and despite our credo, we were as tight a musical unit as we would ever be. As anyone who listened to John Peel's radio shows at the time knew, CBGB's was already a legendary club and we were booked to play three consecutive nights – six shows!

Manhattan at this time was on the brink of bankruptcy. Apart from the really posh areas, everywhere was dirty and smelly and The Bowery, where the club was situated, certainly played its part in contributing to the general June ambience.

Nevertheless, we readily embraced it as our second home – our first home being Eric's club in equally distressed Liverpool.

Of the six gigs we did at CBGB's, the second set on the second night is the most memorable for me. We took the stage at around 1am and were delighted to recognise many faces in the crowd from the previous night. By this time, we had got the measure of the quirky acoustics in the narrow room and the quaint electrics – we were buzzing. We launched into our first song and almost immediately I had what can only be described as an "out of body" experience. (I should explain that we didn't drink much* or partake of other substances… to speak of). I guess we were so well-drilled at this point that my fingers knew automatically what to play. After 44 days of only needing to focus on playing the bass to my best ability I was able to stand back, metaphorically speaking, and appreciate the joy of it all. In that moment, I objectively knew we were at the epicentre of a particular universe and there at a special time.

Earlier that day I'd been introduced to Joey Ramone and, as we shook hands, it felt like we were peers. And now, here I was on the stage of CBGB's, bathing in its historical context when, suddenly, our keyboard player burst the bubble. The panic in his voice was blood curdling as he bellowed to one of our roadies for a screwdriver. In a flash, the tool was delivered to him only to be immediately cast aside. "No!!! Vodka and orange juice!!!!"* Well, it was bloody hot and our tastes in alcoholic beverages had come a long way from Whitbread bitter and Skol lager.

The significance of CBGB's has grown over the years. The significance of our six gigs there has dwindled. Joey and The Ramones went on to bigger and better things. Deaf School split up within a year of our tour of the USA. I've experienced more euphoric gigs, from both sides of the stage, but nothing as enjoyably weird as that night.

Steve Lindsey, Deaf School

THE HEARTBREAKERS, STAFFORD 1977

18th June

Set out from west London with a couple of mates to see The Heartbreakers at Portsmouth Polytechnic. After an uneventful journey apart from driving at speed through a very large puddle and soaking some locals, we parked and went to find the venue. Strolled up and found the door blocked by a jobsworth who then refused to let us in as we had to be "signed in by a student". How could we, we were from London and didn't know anyone? The argument continued and we spotted Jerry Nolan on the phone, called him over and, after hearing our plight, Jerry went to get their manager, Leee Black Childers, who was livid! Long story short: the jobsworth would only let us in if Leee took full responsibility for our actions. "I'll look after these boys," he grinned and in we went to see a memorable show with the band on fire.

A few days later we're walking down Oxford Street and bump into Jerry and Leee again who recognise us and invite us to that night's gig. Where is it I ask? "In Stratford I think," said Leee. We were skint but that didn't matter. Track were providing a coach and free beer and we wouldn't have to pay – just meet at Track Records office on Carnaby Steet later that afternoon!

We arrive and survey the scene, more than a bit shy and terribly excited – there's a lot of familiar faces and everyone seemed to be in a band we'd seen before. We are herded onto a coach and spot the piles of beer that some people grab greedily and find a free seat. The coach fills and then Gail Higgins (Breakers co-manager), an imposing vision in yellow hair, looks at the pillaged beer and yells "If this fucking beer doesn't get returned right now, the coach ain–––'t fucking moving." Silence then a steady procession of embarrassed punks sheepishly return the cans and we finally move off.

We then find out by chatting to some gobby Irish kid throwing badges at us telling us they were going to be big one day, that the gig is actually in Stafford, Stoke on Trent not Stratford, east London. The badges say "The Boomtown Rats" and the gobby kid is Bob Geldof. The journey is a hoot, beer being passed around, frequent piss stops when assorted household-names-to-be line up along side the hard shoulder and frighten the motorway traffic with the occasional arse flash, V-signs and general abuse.

Arrive at venue, stagger in and queue up alongside Johnny Thunders, some Rats, Models and the odd Banshee for burger and chips. Johnny takes a bite and promptly throws up on my shoe and complains about "shitty English food" before slipping off to "prepare" for the gig. We watch Siouxsie photographing her tits in the photo booth, and talk to an Italian camera crew who are filming a punk special. And before we know it, The Heartbreakers are on stage and play a blinding set which is still one of the best gigs I've ever seen in my life. I don't remember much about the journey home but to see my heroes, knock about with them, share coaches, beers and food all for no pounds sterling, well it don't get better than that.

I was fortunate enough to recount this tale with Leee on his last visit to London before his premature death at a launch of his "Drag Queens, Rent Boys, Pick Pockets, Junkies, Rockstars and Punks" and we were both in tears as he repeated, "I can't believe you were on that bus!"

Tom Crossley, The Phobics

THE HEARTBREAKERS/JOBY AND THE HOOLIGANS, BRIGHTON 1977

I remember a gig by Joby and the Hooligans who I played bass for, the first band that I was ever in. We formed accidentally in Brighton in 1977 and found ourselves in the position of being quite popular, mainly because our lead singer Joby was completely unpredictable, offensive and hilariously funny.

We found out that Johnny Thunders and the Heartbreakers were due to play at Sussex University and, being massive fans, we decided to go there with our equipment and beg their manager to let us go on to play before their official support band.

After we blagged our way into the dressing room and practically begged him on our knees to let us play, he flatly refused so we decided to get completely drunk to drown our sorrows.

He changed his mind!

Rather unwisely we took to the stage, absolutely off our faces. I thought it was only me: I was too out of it see the guitarist on the other side of the stage, and definitely couldn't fit in with what he was playing. I could only just see the neck of my bass but wasn't quite sure how to play it. Joby seemed to be singing another song entirely, and in another key and at another speed, kind of howling. God only knows what the drummer was doing.

We had the plugs pulled on us.

I'm kind of proud of that.

(In memory of Joby Visigoth)

Helen McCookery Book, The Chefs

THE STRANGLERS, BANGOR 1977

It's hard to pick out one punk gig memory to write about. I wondered about some of the fabulous live shows when I played with Peter Perrett or even a brief time when I did a couple of tours on bass for Eddie and the Hot Rods, but for me punk really happened when I was at school and was as far removed from everyday life in north Wales as the Beach Boys or Kraftwerk were. Our connection with music was the radio and obviously John Peel, so a small group of us added The Pistols, Stranglers and Buzzcocks to our Deep Purple and Thin Lizzy albums. This got more real when in 1977 The Stranglers played at Bangor University, which was in our nearest decent town. We all asked our parents if we could go and inevitably mine said no. So I lied and said I was going round to a mate's house that night. I phoned home at 7pm to say I was gonna stay over with my mate and my dad asked "Where are you now?" "I'm at Joe's house...". "That's strange," my dad said "because Joe is here with me." The sinking feeling of being caught out big time!!! "I'll deal with you later, lad" and down went the phone. So I watched The Stranglers with a sick feeling of fear in my stomach and a spinning head, wondering what I was gonna face later that day. The band were great, but I remember being overwhelmed when they got going because it was so "real". They were loud, raucous and threatening and combined with the fear of what was coming when I got home, it was really unsettling. The only security I had was the familiar songs. I had bought a bass by that time and had learned all Jean Jacque's basslines – I was pretty much glued to his hands all night and the band sounded fantastic. I remember it passed so much faster than it should have because I didn't want it to end, partly because they were brilliant and partly because I was in for a huge bollocking. I remember the gig like it was yesterday and also the bus trip home which was as close to dead man walking as I'd had up to that point. The gig was great and the parental telling off was biblical.

Rich Vernon, Peter Perrett band, Eddie and the Hot Rods, The Mission

CURED BY PUNK, LONDON 1977–1978

Ramones/Talking Heads, Roundhouse

I open a cubicle door in the gents and find a kid struggling into a black bin liner, arm holes and collar scissored out. The clobber he wore on the train from Croydon or Romford lies on the floor, with half-a-dozen safety pins and some eye-liner, yet to be applied. It's probably his mum's. He's about 15; I'm 10 years older, an old fart. But he's busted. He sneers and blushes, simultaneously.

Buzzcocks, Lyceum

I'd bought "Spiral Scratch"; best UK 45 since "Virginia Plain". My wife hated it; I knew we'd split up; we did. A year later, on my tod, I'm watching the post-Devoto band, a monolith of perfect punk-pop noise. Four black sweatshirts with a single scarlet square on each, a Mayakovskian echo of The Shadows.

Only Ones, Hope & Anchor

Not punk, they say; Lou Reed rip-off, they say. But Peter Perrett seems very English to me, an androgynous music hall crooner in thrift-shop drag, a welfare state Bowie. And the band, unfashionable old pros though they may be, gel beautifully but casually, like Free did a decade before (though a lot faster). There's this ramshackle grace.

XTC, Hope & Anchor.

Sweatiest gigs ever. The tiny stage hardly contains their energy. Andy Partridge the charismatic gaffer, nonchalantly reeling out brittle angularities and peering down at the bouncing faithful. Balding Barry Andrews, wearing a Paracetamol Kid T-shirt and stabbing his keyboard with screwdrivers (I fear for him: *Kids! Don't try this at home!*). Chambers and Moulding a duck's arse rhythm section, though Moulding always seems too aware of his good looks and gets on my tits. Maybe I just envy his cheekbones.

Slits, some venue in West London.

The bulky woman in front of me lurches back, and her biker-boot heel pierces the upper of my favourite DMs. I shove her away; she inspects the damage and laughs in my face. The shoes were my Dad's work shoes for years before I "borrowed" them, and I'm pissed off. So, I shove her again. Her friends, all women, all scarier than me, round on me, while Ari warbles and shrieks.

Various, Hope & Anchor.

I'm working on a Radio Times illustration and my lung collapses. "Spontaneous Partial Pneumothorax," the medics tell me. I'm lucky: a week in hospital and it heals itself. "Bed rest," they say. "Boredom," I think. I call my Dutch girlfriend and she nips over from Paris: Merci, Marida. We blitz a bunch of gigs at the H&A. Maybe we see good stuff. Doesn't matter. I'm cured by punk.

Robert Mason, illustrator and writer

THE CLASH, DUBLIN 1977

It's a wet, cold October morning, meeting a few friends for a walk around the Dando. That was the normal Saturday for the punks in Dublin. Wander around the market looking for T-shirts, badges and other punk-related stuff. Walking up Grafton Street, I noticed a lot of punks hanging around in groups, not saying hello or even recognising any of us, very odd. Anyway, got to the Dando. Mods and rockers all over the place. I'm thinking, "We are gonna get a kicking here."

Myself, Jem and Git backed away. There were a few lads in there looking very shady. Someone said "I suppose you're going to see The Clash?" We said "What???" "Don't say you didn't know they were playing?" a voice from behind the counter said. "No, where is it on?" "Trinity, it's sold out." He said if you go down and hang around you might get lucky, so we quickly dashed down to Trinity.

In through the big gates and out into the big square looking for a sign or someone to ask. Then boom. A gang of punks standing in line outside a building, we quickly walked to the end of the queue. We stood there for about two hours. The queue started moving. Great, here we go. We got close and a voice cried out, "Tickets, tickets." We started letting on we were looking for our tickets. The ticket man asked why all three of us couldn't find our tickets. "Can we go in?" "Come back tonight, there's another show tonight."

We backed away slowly, went around the side of the building and waited. A little while later the screams from inside told us the band were coming on stage. We danced and sang every song. People walking through the college were looking at us – three mad-looking young punk rockers trying to dance or whatever you might call it. We asked some of the guys coming out for their ticket and got three. Got into the Buttery Bar for a coke. We sat in the cold watching everything, it soon got dark and cold. People started coming in for the late show, and an exciting atmosphere was beginning to happen. I had butterflies in my belly, I was 14 years old, 6ft 3 tall, I felt invincible. "Hi lads, Did you find your tickets? GO AHEAD LADS."

I was bursting with excitement, ran to the front of stage. The heat was overwhelming. THE CLASH, BOOM Guitar, drums bass and fucking Joe Strummer standing three feet away. Have I died and gone to heaven. "Garageland", "White Riot", "Clash City Rockers", "Complete Control", "White Man". I sang every song as if I wrote every one of them. My first-ever gig and it's

The Clash. My mam and dad are going to kill me. It was worth it. Joe shouts to move closer. Fuck I was standing with my foot on the stage, The Clash's stage. Mick Jones kicking me every so often, Joe too. At one stage, Simo looked at me and said "alri". I was made up.

Last song and the place went mental. I couldn't breathe. Joe asked me "Oi are you alright?" I grabbed my inhaler, had a squirt and said "Yea thanks Joe." He replied "Good." Fuck, Paul and Joe spoke to me. Mick Jones kicked me. I was the happiest kid in Ireland that night. it was like all my Christmases all at once. Gig was over and The Clash left the stage, people were grabbing set lists, posters etc. I saw a black plectrum beside Joe's mike stand. I dived on it. Next, I hear a roar and look up. Joe is standing over me. "Here kiddo" and handed me two plectrums. Said goodnight and walked away. I went home and sang every song again on my way. My dad battered me for being out all day, but fuck it, I had just seen The Clash. Go easy, step lightly, stay free. Viva la Clash!

Andy Keating, The Cathedral, Purdah, Complete Control

THE CLASH, DUBLIN 1977

I'm not the first and I won't be the last to write about The Clash's debut Irish gig in Dublin in Trinity College. In terms of shear impact and velocity it was intense. The sort of gig that was catalyst for many, that motivated them to action either in their own musical endeavours or in other forms of creative activity. The music, from memory, was not particularly laced with sonic clarity but rather was a wall of noise laced with political ideas and self-motivational encouragement. The set was largely based on their debut album and was delivered with an unmistakable zeal and commitment.

No one who was there would have been unaffected by what they heard, either in a positive or negative way. I did hear comments from certain quarters that it was an incomprehensible, badly played racket that they would rather not hear again. But that wasn't really the point, rather it was the visible (and audible) assault of the status quo – and, perhaps, on Status Quo.

For many, things would not be the same again. For some it set a template for the future, one that would barely change from that point onwards, while for The Clash themselves it was a starting point from which they would retain a "punk" sensibility but would explore many different musical forms and indeed explore other sartorial looks that were often based in imagery of earlier musical times.

The next time The Clash played Dublin, at the Top Hat in Dun Laoghaire, they were a very different band. Better sound, better musical ability and a more broad-based audience but somehow the ferocity of that earlier gig had been lost to be replaced by something different, equally compelling but less the "shock-of-the-new".

As a footnote, the band who brought some of that same kind of confrontation to the night were the support band The Virgin Prunes who after only three or four songs were removed from the stage in the face of a negative reaction from the audience. I witnessed this first-hand as I was a guest with the band that night playing some analog synth. Will we see such things again? We can only hope so.

Steve Averill, The Radiators from Space, SM Corporation, Trouble Pilgrims

THE CLASH AND THE JAM, DUBLIN 1978

Although The Clash at TCD in 1977 was a seminal event, and is rightly cited as having a major impact on the fledgling punk/new wave scene, the sound was awful and I don't really remember any particular songs. The Clash at the Top Hat was a different band, a year further along, tighter, more in control but still energetic and vital. Although a year away from releasing "London Calling", they had matured and had developed their sound, which was crisp and clear on the night, I specifically remember "Complete Control", "White Man in Hammersmith Palais" and "Tommy Gun" as being standouts on the night. By the way, I'm pretty sure I heard Dave Fanning say it was the best gig he ever saw, and I would guess he's seen a few!

Regarding The Jam, I was a big fan, I went to Reading to see them headline in August 1978. "All Mod Cons" was released in November and "Down in the Tube Station at Midnight" was out as a single. We knew all the words, so for me, the gig was just fantastic – every song sounded so good. I remember at the end Weller rushed off stage and reappeared up leaning over the balcony to the right of the stage; he was grabbing one of those large dayglow orange Jam posters! We missed The Vipers that night but I had seen them loads of times – they were a great new wave band.

I got my Jam ticket signed by the Modfather himself; we ran into him at the coffee dock after the gig.

Jake Reilly, The Blades

THE JAM/THE VIPERS, DUBLIN 1978

In October 1978, I was playing bass with The Vipers when we were offered the support slot with The Jam on their two gigs in Ireland; in Dublin (Top Hat) and in Galway (Leisureland). The Jam were promoting their make-or-break third album "All Mod Cons" and The Vipers had a ringside seat watching them introduce brand new songs like "'A' Bomb in Wardour Street', "Down in the Tube Station at Midnight" and "Mr Clean". They sounded great and looked sharp in their mohair suits. The Jam were managed by Paul's dad, John, a big, stocky individual with a boxer's physique, who was ever-present and always looking out for his boys.

One thing I remember from those dates was when Paul, Bruce and Rick used to finish their last number, they would run off the stage and a roadie would have a lighted cigarette ready for each of them as they came running past. To us lowly Vipers, this was the big time.

Paul Weller was quite shy. His girlfriend Jill was over with him and he spent most of the time with her. He was only 20 years old so you couldn't blame him for wanting to be with the love of his life. Though, I do remember George Sweeney, our lead guitarist, sitting down with Weller at some stage after the soundcheck and they started trading guitar riffs. They were both massive Who fans.

Bruce and Rick were very sociable. I remember being surprised when Bruce and Rick started complaining to me about the price of a bottle of coke in the bar of the hotel they were staying in. They were drinking whiskey and coke at the time. Though looking back I suppose they were only on a small wage, as The Jam still hadn't broken big yet.

Bruce was very generous to me all the same. He had just got a sponsorship deal with Rotosound and he had a flight case full of their bass guitar strings. He very kindly gave me a few packets.

It's hard to believe but we nearly got kicked off our little mini-tour with The Jam after the first gig in the Top Hat in Dun Laoghaire. It just so happened that Paul,

Bruce and Rick had nice electric fans mounted in front of them while they were on stage. I suppose they needed them as they wore heavy suits and shirts and ties when they performed.

I remember we were near the end of our set and going down really well when George launched into one of his blistering guitar solos. His fingers were squeezing the life out his strings and he was throwing all sorts of shapes. He ended his solo on some impossibly high note and kicked out his foot at the same time. Unfortunately, his foot connected with Paul Weller's precious electric fan, which went flying across the stage.

Well, all hell broke loose and the road crew were lining up at the side of the stage giving us menacing looks. The fan was in a crumpled heap, damaged beyond repair. When we finally came off the stage there was a lot of bowing and scraping and apologies. John Weller suddenly appeared, eyes bulging, veins throbbing in his neck. Explanations were sought. More profuse apologies. Some restitution was offered. Finally, it was accepted that there was no malice intended and with that we were back on the tour.

Mind you, Paul Weller didn't half sweat that night.

Brian Foley, The Vipers

THE STRANGLERS, CORK 1977

I've been lucky to catch so many great gigs over the years that it's difficult to pick just one, whether it was my first experience of a big open-air concert with The Who, complete with all the original members, at the Oval in September 1971, supported by Rod Stewart and The Faces, America, Mott The Hoople and more, or Pink Floyd in Earl's Court launching "Dark Side of the Moon" in 1973; that gig was very different from any I'd been at before, a surreal, all-embracing experience with surround sound and all sorts of technical wizardry, so that wherever you were in that large space you were very much part of the experience. And, in those pre-laser days, the magic continued with a light show outside the venue after the show, provided by the army using searchlights with coloured gels, to ease the transition back to reality as we made our way to the tube station and home.

Dr Feelgood at the Hammersmith Odeon in 1975 was a revelation too in a very different way – a pub rock blues band with a punk attitude, and brilliant live performance with the anarchic chemistry between Wilco Johnson and Lee Brilleaux. While I had both Wilko and the Feelgoods play my Cork venue, the Downtown Kampus, in their separate line-ups, a couple of years later, the magic wasn't quite the same – interplay between the two was special and had created something way more than the sum of the parts.

My first big gig was Led Zeppelin in the Stadium in Dublin early 1971, and I had a seat just over the stage and a great view. The Stadium, normally used for boxing events, had limitations as a venue but, crammed with enthusiastic fans and a powerful performance by the band, there was an energy and magic I hadn't experienced before. A standout moment was Robert Plant sitting front of stage as he sang "Stairway to Heaven", which they were performing live for just the second time, having debuted it in Belfast the previous night. The atmosphere was brilliant, and the crowd just didn't want to let the band go – and they were happy to oblige, playing several encores.

And then there are the other elements that make a gig extra memorable, such as being responsible for the production and seeing the gig goes safely. The Stranglers in Cork's City Hall stands out as one of very heightened tension; it was 1977 and the band were at the height of their popularity. It was only my second big show as a promoter, and The Stranglers' self-appointed mates and minders, the Finchley Boys, accompanied them and insisted on making their presence felt from the start. They set out to intimidate, insisting that the band were not going to play a seated venue, but that was the only way it came at the time – rock'n'roll, and certainly punk, were new to the civic premises, and there was no way it would be available any way other than seated. Band and minders exuded an air of menace, and the tension cranked up as the gig progressed with a frenetic performance by the band and the audience getting ever more frantic with excitement to the point where things could tip over into complete anarchy at any moment… but ultimately held together. I managed to catch the second half of the set from the balcony and could see some of the audience had managed to climb up onto window ledges and the balcony edge for a better view. There were several nail-biting moments as they precariously swayed to the sound but somehow gravity was defied and no injuries occurred. Those lived-on-the edge moments that ultimately work out well are pretty special, giving an extra edge to experience. Speaking to Hugh Cornwell in recent years, he remembered the gig well, and was surprised at how well their music was known in Cork as they had thought of it as some strange outpost on the fringes of Europe – this was prior to the Downtown Kampus gig, and Cork becoming a regular part of the music circuit in Ireland. And three years later, on August 30th, 1980, a night of local bands featuring Nun Attax, Microdisney, Mean Features and Urban Blitz, all of whom had developed from watching the visiting bands play the Kampus week after week and were inspired to have a go themselves, was special too, and happily recorded for posterity on "Kaught at the Kampus"; three of the four bands went on to sign with English labels and all continue to be involved in music to this day.

So what makes a gig memorable or special? I've seen artists perform that I had revered for years and loved with every album recorded, but who so disappointed with a lacklustre live performance that it took years before I could recapture the magic of those albums. And others who had not necessarily been listened to much on record who created such a riveting unforgettable live show that they lived long in my memory.

Elvera Butler, promoter, Reekus Records label owner

CIMARONS, IRELAND 1977-1978

Back in 1978 not many English bands wanted to play in Ireland as there was a war in the North with the IRA and loyalists making their presence felt and bombs going off, but when our Irish agent asked us to do a college tour we saw it as a challenge and a new territory for reggae. Our first stop was Belfast with bombs exploding and soldiers patrolling the streets; to be honest we were a bit nervous, but it wasn't too bad. Our first gig was at Queen's University where the crowd gave a very warm welcome – the hall was full. When we got on stage, Winston said to the audience all Catholics put your hands up – there was a lot. Then he said all Protestants put your hands up, it was like half and half. And he said tonight reggae music is going to unite everyone. And there was a loud roar from the crowd.

Starting off with "Ship Ahoy", it was the first time the people there experienced reggae and they were going frantic. It was wild, and the crowd couldn't get enough and were shouting for more and more. There was a queue a mile long for autographs and everyone was saying how much they loved it and how it brought everyone together. We didn't want to hang about Belfast too long and made our way to Dublin the next day for a gig in Trinity. We really enjoyed travelling through the countryside which was beautiful. Again the gig was packed – people were really keen to hear live reggae but again we were surprised as we didn't know what to expect. We had them singing "Ship Ahoy" from the start – it was like a football crowd with the roar from the crowd.

Our next gig was in Cork. It was a massive dance hall and roller-skating place. We didn't know what to expect. Would anyone turn up? But to our surprise, it was a sellout. The reaction we got from the crowd was like we were superstars. The people were going crazy and were singing along to "Ship Ahoy", "Freedom Street" and "Civilisation". They took a real liking to "Civilisation" and it became an anthem. I've never seen an audience reacting in such a way – some of the people got on stage and we had to stop so the bouncers could clear it, and the encore was like an hour. We got an instant rebook from the manager and played there several more times over the next few years.

Our next gig was in Sligo. The scenery along the way was beautiful. We stopped in a little village to get some food, and the people were so surprised to see us. They hadn't seen black people or dreadlocks before and they all wanted to touch us – they said it would bring them good luck. The tour was a success. We made our mark and made a lot of new fans, but Cork was the greatest.

The first outdoor festival in Ireland was set to take place in Macroom, a little town in Co Cork. They wanted The Cimarons to play, but the date clashed with a gig we had in Scotland. We didn't want to let the fans down in Ireland, and we couldn't cancel the Scotland gig, so we had a problem, but the promoter said he would work something out, and he sure did. There was an eight-seater plane waiting for us at Heathrow; when we got there, the pilot shook hands – there was seven of us including Chili our road manager. When I got on the plane the first thing that came to mind was how small the space was, like sitting in a car – this was our first time we ever flew in such a small plane, and the take-off was scary. I thought the plane was going to fall apart. These small planes fly very low and you could feel every bump from the wind and turbulence, and I wasn't really enjoying it. The pilot said it was okay to smoke – we all needed a spliff to calm us down, but it got so smoky at one point he asked us to cool it a bit.

When we landed, a car was waiting for us at the airport and when we got to the festival it was in full swing. It was on a farm and you could feel the vibes – rock'n'roll and pop bands were doing their thing in the countryside in Cork. Some fans spotted us and were more than happy to share their Merrygold and we smoked with them for a while. They told us they had a surprise for us after the show and as we were making our way to the backstage, I noticed this guy following us with a red bucket over his head. I thought he was a hippy, the way he was behaving but then he got hold of Maurice's hand and said what's that you're smoking. Maurice said someone just gave me this as we were walking – it's tobacco. He then told us he was police and said smoking weed is illegal in Ireland. We told him who we were and he said okay but if you're smoking, do it backstage. I don't think the fans would have let him arrest us though.

When we got on stage the place erupted – by now the fans knew every song word for word and we had them singing away to "Freedom Street" and "Ship Ahoy". But "Civilisation" was the anthem – we couldn't stop playing that one. The energy from the audience was electrifying and, as we left the stage after a long encore, there were a few fans waiting to present us with a trophy engraved out of stone. It's priceless when you get something like this from your fans. Our fans in Cork have got to be the best in the world.

We couldn't hang around too long after the show as we had a plane to catch for the show in Scotland. I wasn't looking forward to flying back on that eight-seater in the dark but to my relief it was a larger plane and we were all smiling. The only downside was we couldn't smoke our Merrygold on board.

Locksley Gichie, Cimarons

DC NIEN, DUBLIN 1977

A personal account.

DC Nien in 1977 comprised Brian Seales (bass), Paul McGuinness (guitar), Ken Mahon (drums), Brendan Gannon (synths) and Damian Gunn as lead singer in its final line-up. Another guitarist and friend, Paul Duffy, was a founding member but left to pursue more guitar-orientated music at an early stage. I continue to write music with Paul Duffy to this day and a strong bond between the original band members still exists.

Formed during the booming punk era, DC Nien came together as a bunch of friends who saw few if any prospects of getting a job or going on to third-level education. Ireland was in the grips of a long recession and job opportunities were at a minimum so in the true tradition of punk we made our own jobs. A little-known fact: most of us had worked in one well-known north Dublin garden centre. Damian started work there first and eventually most of the band worked there at some time or other. Come on, you need money to buy instruments! This story has been repeated over the years with the focus of it being on me alone. Well now the truth is out. We all worked with plants but I was the only one to make a living from it after leaving the music business. I am proud to say I have managed to make a living out of both of my hobbies: music and plants.

DC Nien came together in Santry, north Dublin, in 1977, after some months of us learning, or trying to learn, to play our respective instruments. Remember, this was at a time when prog rock was the rule and bands like Yes, Genesis and Emerson, Lake and Palmer set a very high target when it came to musical competency. The arrival of punk opened doors for many of us ordinary and not very gifted musicians to have go and that was the key point about that era. I have never regarded DC Nien as being a pure punk band in the sense of The Sex Pistols, The Clash etc, but their success was a major factor in inspiring us to go out and do our own thing. Quite simply, the punk scene opened doors for many aspiring musicians and still does.

The name came from the district of Dublin we lived in, Dublin City 9 and a popular commercial plane, the DC9 which we had watched landing at nearby Dublin Airport as young kids. We then gave it a Germanic ring in a nod towards the brilliant Kraftwerk, who were one band we all liked. We used to meet for our first rehearsals in a small cottage right beside the airport which conveniently had a pub next door. In fact, the cottage was the best place to rehearse as the noise we made could not disturb anyone because the planes were way louder, particularly that DC9. So rehearsal involved a few pints, some time rehearsing, more pints followed by more rehearsing and a rush to catch the last bus home. Who played what in the band was solved by asking questions such as "Who wants to play drums?" or "Who wants to sing?" Few of us had any experience on our respective instruments but constant practice gave us confidence, if not expertise.

Our manager was another friend, Philip Kavanagh. Philip was the only one of us at the time who could drive and he owned a van, so to keep up with the pattern of using friends only, we asked Phil to become our manager. Another friend, Martin Gallagher, was asked to do the stage lighting for us. Martin worked in the offices of the Electricity Supply Board (ESB) at the time and knew nothing about stage lighting or even electricity for that matter. That never stopped him, and he soon developed a striking light show based around UV lights and strobes. At least when venue owners asked us if the light show was safe, we could answer with a straight face that Martin worked in the ESB. This of course was long before computers and computer-controlled light shows. It all had to be done by hand with Martin feverishly switching light switches on and off as he battled to create some space for himself in the crowd to prevent people spilling their beers on his electrical gear. Some of those early gigs would never be allowed these days with all the health and safety rules in place. However, it all added to the somewhat aggressive and edgy feeling which surrounded DC Nien's gigs. Tony O'Meara became our sound engineer and worked with the band throughout its lifetime. Top all that off with another couple of friends in Peader Gaffney and later Billy Louth who became our roadies. Our first gig, run by Smiley Bolger was in Moran's Hotel in Dublin in July 1977 and all it did was make us go back to the rehearsal room for more practice. We were not happy with our performance and most of the crowd just stood with their mouths open wondering what we were all about.

DC Nien were a hard-working band who constantly gigged through 1977-1981. Our main venues in Dublin were the Magnet Bar, Toners, McGonagles and the Baggot Inn. All of these were small venues by today's standards but perfectly suited to DC Nien's aggressive stage presence and light show. People smoked indoors back in those days. Almost every town had a ballroom which mainly booked country and western-type bands or showbands as they were called back then. This Irish version of American culture was very prominent back in those days and few villages didn't have a local hall used as a music venue. Schools in Ireland were mainly all same-sex back then and run by religious orders. The dance halls often were the only way young Irish people could meet the opposite sex. Picture this then. All the guys sit on one side of the hall and all the girls sit on the opposite side. That was standard practice back then and looked very odd to us coming from cosmopolitan Dublin. I remember one incident in a dance hall in Sligo when I asked an attractive local girl for a dance only for her to shyly refuse. A local guy I knew at the time showed me how it was done. He sauntered over to the same girl and said loudly "Are you vacant?" whereby she giggled and got up and danced with him. He later went on to become a priest! So it wasn't just music we had to learn about back then as playing outside Dublin and the other main cities was quite an experience, like travelling back in time to the 1950s. One venue which we all remember fondly (and which most definitely was not like travelling back in time) was the Downtown Kampus in Cork. It was massive and a real test of your pulling power as a band. Kudos to Elvera Butler for running this great venue.

The few local fans in those days who were into punk would stand in front of the stage dressed in the way that only punks can dress. These were the local rebels, those who thought differently to the rest of the town and in many ways their dress sense was a visual intimidation to the rest of the kids around them. These local punks were the ones we played for because they were listening for starters and they remain a loyal fan base to this day. DC Nien and other contemporary bands such as The Atrix, The Virgin Prunes and The Blades had a go at bringing a different and new music to these venues with surprising results. As we returned to certain venues for a second and third time, we noticed that the local punks were being joined on the dance floor by other locals. The combined efforts of many Cork, Dublin and Belfast bands both to do something new with music and bring that to a new audience of Irish youth appeared to be working. In hindsight, I can see now that we were doing what Kraftwerk, Roxy Music and others had done to us.

DC Nien were heavily influenced by many bands of that era. Roxy Music, The Stranglers, The Clash, Ultravox, Devo, David Bowie, Talking Heads and even the famous German electronic bands Kraftwerk and Tangerine Dream all had an enormous influence on what we played and how we sounded. DC Nien even did some covers of their favourite songs by those bands. DC Nien did support gigs with the likes of XTC, The Specials, Squeeze, Dr. Feelgood, Psychedelic Furs, Rory Gallagher at the Sense of Ireland Festival in London and… AC/DC in the Olympia Ballroom. That last one was one of the best gigs the band were ever involved in. AC/DC were one of the true super bands and we learned a lot from them, watching how they worked the audience. What a live band AC/DC were and what a great bunch also being so supportive of upcoming bands. Despite us being completely different to them music-wise, they made us feel welcome as their support band. I will always remember the late and great Bon Scott walking into the dressing room before we went on stage and wishing us luck. He asked where was our food and beers and we told him we were only the support band and didn't get any. He left and came back with two of his road crew with their arms full of beers and food for us, AC/DC's own food and beer which he gladly shared. It's amazing how these little gestures meant so much to me over the years. However, there was one incident that night which remains with me forever. Towards the end of the gig, Angus Young started a guitar solo and was then lifted by a large roadie up on his shoulders (he had just popped some still mysterious pills), carried down off the stage and then the roadie forced a way through the crowd on the dance floor with Angus still playing away. A stunning example of getting the audience involved.

Only one DC Nien single was ever released, on our own record label known as NineteenEightease Records (no one else would have us and it was all about record labels back in those days) and that was a song called "Nightclub", which was a moderate success in the charts and got favourable reviews in the music press. Prior to that we had released a cassette tape, The Red Tapes, in a limited run of 500 copies. We financed this ourselves and even distributed copies around record shops in Dublin and sold them at gigs. Now, wind forward 40 years and see what happened.

The Red Tapes has a cult following to this day and has been restored to a more modern audience in the last few years by remastering it into a digital format. It now also has a home on the web which didn't exist back in 1980 in the format we know today. The source cassette tapes which were used to restore the songs were supplied by long-time fans of the band who had worn them out listening to them over the years. "Nightclub" was only recently used in the soundtrack for an Irish film written and produced by Ferdia MacAnna of Rocky De Valera and the Gravediggers fame. So after all these years, my dream of having a song I was associated with used in a movie was fulfilled. The film was called DannyBoy and if you want to know what we all went through back in those days, then it is as good a place to start as any.

Brian Seales, DC Nien

THE STRANGLERS/UNDERTONES, PORTRUSH 1978

Punk Comes Rolling down from 55 Degrees North.

On Friday 8th Sept 1978 two of the world's best punk bands, The Stranglers and The Undertones, took to the stage in Portrush, the sleepy seaside town, on the North West coast of the island of Ireland. The venue for this great celebration of the new wave of music was Chester's. When I say Chester's, I should point out that I'm not talking about Marshall Dillon's shadow, but the club name used for non-showband nights in the New Arcadia. The (old) Arcadia was a ballroom built (quite literally) on the seafront in 1953. It was a favoured stop-off on the Irish showband circuit.

By September 1978, I'd just signed The Undertones to act as their agent. I'd also booked The Stranglers for a few of their Irish tours. Portrush was as close as you could get to an actual hometown gig for The Undertones, so it was obvious to suggest them to The Stranglers for the opening-act spot. Thanks to John Peel everyone in the UK loved "Teenage Kicks", which had just been re-released on the Sire record label, and The Stranglers happily approved them.

The Undertones sauntered on stage looking like they'd just come from their local youth club. They dressed like punks might have dressed on their way to church. Their moves were initially a little self-conscious but when they started to play, they were so tight, so together, so unpunk in fact, they won over each and every member of the audience. They were a complete revelation. And to top all of the above they had a set of perfectly crafted short pop songs, proving to all in attendance they wouldn't become a one-trick pony. Working on the theory that a prophet is without honour in his own home, in his own time, they received a phenomenal reaction from the 600-strong audience who had paid £2.50 a head. Fergal Sharkey wasn't best-pleased though. He was wearing his brand-new, parka-jacket and, as the lead singer, in the centre of the stage and further forward than his bandmates, he was the perfect target for the gobbers. Within a couple of minutes, he looked like a dozen full spittoons, from the nearby Harbour Bar, had been thrown over him.

The Stranglers were fresh from their current album, "Black and White", nearly topping the UK charts. It peaked at No 2. Most artists would give their eyeteeth in advance for a No 2 album, but when you get so close and then don't make the pinnacle, well then the massive disappointment is the predominant memory you take away from the experience rather than truly enjoying your major achievement. The Stranglers had two No 2 chart positions out of their run of seven top-10 albums. They also enjoyed seven top-10 singles, one of which was their exciting cover of the original punk band, The Kinks' "All Day and All of the Night".

The Stranglers *looked* like a band, they looked like they belonged together. Lots of dark clothes and leather jackets. Jean-Jacques Burnel looked like his bass guitar was playing him and dragging him around the stage. They were loud but more importantly they produced a BIG sound. They were a gigging band, they lived on the road, they lived for the road. The Stranglers were still buzzing from their amazing show the previous night at the Ulster Hall in Belfast. They were an extremely musical band, part of the current punk movement but not *from* the punks. They took no prisoners. JJ proved he had a much more effective way of dealing with the gobbers than Fergal's earlier attempt at a Clint Eastwood lethal Dirty Harry glare. No, mid-song, JJ merely took off his guitar, jumped down into the audience, chinned the leading offender, and was back on the stage playing his bass before his band mates even knew he'd left the stage. Just to amplify his point he announced that any further gobbing would result in the entire band leaving the stage and not coming back. From behind the scenes, The Stranglers were a great band to work with, especially for their support acts. If their support act hadn't had time for a soundcheck, as was usually the case, then The Stranglers would hold the opening of the doors to ensure they set up properly. Talking about The Doors, I always thought Dave Greenfield was as vital to The Stranglers' sound as Ray Manzarek was to Morrison and co.

It was a brilliant gig, an exciting gig and a genuine double- header. And as to who took the honours on the night, well that would be debatable and, in fact was still being debated quite recently. The super-duper reformed and revitalised versions of The Undertones and The Stranglers were appearing together on a European festival a year or so ago, and Jean-Jacques made it his business to track down Michael Bradley and Damien O'Neill from the Undertones. JJ told them he had heard someone in The Undertones' camp had claimed to have blown his band off the stage all those years ago in Portrush. "Oh," Damien, who was very aware that JJ was a black belt karate master, offered very quickly, "that would have been Sharkey."

Paul Charles, author, booking agent. Paul Charles © 2020

TOM ROBINSON BAND, DUBLIN 1978

When my friend Paul came home with the first Clash album, we were immediate converts to this strange new visceral rock music. Naturally we went to see them when they played Trinity College in October 1977. And it's fair to say that gig alone was responsible for many a garage band forming in Dublin over the next few years.

On weekend nights we found ourselves in McGonagles nightclub. Quickly enough, we got to know many others from our newfound punk tribe. Paul had suggested to some new friends in McGonagles that, given the chance, he would love to be a drummer if he was ever in a band. The following week he was introduced to Maurice Foley who was starting a band called The Threat. Maurice was a few years older than us but had a striking appearance, spiky green hair, and an enthusiastic demeanour. He dropped a snare kit round to Paul a few days later and within a month the band were practising regularly. I took on the duties as manager of the band. Sadly, this first incarnation of The Threat met its demise when a gig ended violently in Dundalk.

Overseas bands came to McGonagles. The Lurkers visited from the UK and played a high-powered punk style not unlike The Ramones. It was not unusual to have access to bands like this in the local hostelries before a gig. To meet your new musical heroes, face to face before a gig, was a refreshing new experience shared as part of the punk ethos. Unfortunately, a legacy of violence tainted many early punk events in Dublin at that time, and many a good gig was spoiled by the few troublemakers. For the most part there was a camaraderie and healthy tension between most of the local bands we encountered. We caught most of them, The Vipers, The Vultures, The Radiators etc, and loved the way most bands supported each other.

The Tom Robinson Band played Belfield also around this time and I can remember well the whole crowd singing along to "Sing if you're glad to be gay", an amazing feeling. Especially for myself at that time being a young closeted gay man. If Bowie had broken the mould by suggesting he was gay or bisexual and Lou Reed had invited us to walk on the wild side, then Tom Robinson most certainly had nailed it on the head for me. Rock Against Racism and oppression of minorities were subjects that were cleverly addressed in the sleeve notes to the band's music, especially on their first album, "Power in the Darkness". Up to that point, most storylines and mentions of gay identity had been tainted with pejorative terminology and certainly did not end well. To be actually happy or glad to be gay certainly challenged the status quo. When Pete Shelley of Buzzcocks sang "Ever fallen in love/With someone you shouldn't have fallen in love with?" I could certainly relate to those lyrics.

Eoin Freeney, Chant! Chant! Chant!

BIRMINGHAM 1978–1979

In 1978, myself and my friend Shane O'Neill left Ireland and went to live in Birmingham. Coming from Ireland where gigs were scarce on the ground the music scene there was for us a real adventure. It was so diverse it's hard to narrow it down to one gig so I thought I'd give you a flavour of what was going on around that time. There was a club called Barbarella's that we went to a lot, one floor was electronica and played Kraftwerk and a lot of the German bands and Bowie's album "Low". The other floor was a reggae club and another section for live bands.

There was a pub called the Crown where we used to go to see a band called Coventry Automatics, which then became the Specials. We also saw The Clash in a club outside Birmingham, I can't remember where. It was my second time to see them as they'd played Trinity College in Dublin the year before.

Going back to Barbarella's, we saw Devo, George Thorogood and the Destroyers, Graham Parker and the Rumour, and The Tourists that later became the Eurythmics. But one band that really stuck out was Pure Hell, an all-black punk band from Philadelphia. The band were really powerful and what was interesting for us was that the guitar player played with the guitar over his head, reminiscent of Hendrix. After the gig we ended up in the company of the band and their manager who turned out to be Chas Chandler, Jimi Hendrix's manager. We talked for the night and heard great stories about Hendrix from Chas. After the Pure Hell gig we were on our way home, we were trying to stay out as late as possible because Shane's flatmate Keith, a Rastafarian, had asked if it was okay to have a blue party in the flat, It was called a blue party because they put a blue bulb in the light fitting. He had a huge home-made sound system.

As we were heading up the Bristol Road towards the flat, we could hear the music in the distance, so we waited outside for a while and then Keith spotted us and brought us in. We were the only two punks among all the Rastas. The place was filled with smoke, you couldn't see yourself. To come from listening to a black punk band to dub reggae played at ear-splitting volume in that small space was amazing. I think that time spent in Birmingham gave me a real love for reggae music. Which brings us back to Pure Hell – the crossover between punk and reggae was there from the very start.

This diverse range of music had a huge impact on me and definitely influenced the eclectic nature of my own work.

STANO, artist, musician

BUZZCOCKS/REVOLVER, DUBLIN 1978

Summer of 1976 July to be precise. I was with Dave and Yat hitchhiking around Europe and busking in Lyon in France playing probably something by The Eagles and getting quite a lot of nice French francs.

My wonderful older brother somehow got hold of me through a local hostel where we were staying and told me he was paying for me to get back to Dublin asap as my Dad was nearly at the end. See I had in May/June run away from his lung cancer and buried my head in so much sand.

I got back to Dublin and was so shocked by his condition. He had gone from being a giant to a frail, extremely thin man who I had to help up the stairs. Unreal.

My memories are of him being a brilliant singer – his voice was rich and so full of life so to see him like this was unbelievable. He used to belt out "Boolavouge" at the house parties we all went to in Crumlin and The Liberties.

He flew away at the end of July and I went back home again to Dublin as Mum could not cope. His voice is the reason I got into music.

I was very aware of punk then but mainly from the USA vibe. Television, Heartbreakers, Velvet Underground and The NY Dolls fascinated me.

Now I was a fully paid-up lifelong member of The Faces fan club and Thin Lizzy were on my radar as well but when Billy Morley invited me to audition for Revolver and played me "Trash" I was 100 per cent in.

I got the gig as lead singer.

The Clash came to Dublin. We all went – it was a must-do. I had to beg the money from Mum but she gave it to me as I promised I was not going to put a pin in my face.

Then somehow Revolver got the support slot for Buzzcocks at Trinity in the Exam Hall. Wow this amazing room! The chessboard floor and the minds that had passed through there. It was about to be totally immersed in several hundred crazy Irish punks from all walks of life.

I think I got the gig as I was always hustling for the band. Once I was in it, that was it. I was a million per cent.

I remember the soundcheck and Buzzcocks checking us out. We were so excited, and they were so great to us. Beers backstage, the dressing room was through a secret wall at the side of the stage and they let us use a corner of it. Fab.

Revolver absolutely nailed that show.

We were – I've been told – brilliant although my memory is a bit light on it. I remember looking across at Billy and him winking at me mid-song and then

Kevin Helly and I collided mid-stage and I almost pushed over Johnny Sullivan's drum kit. It was fantastic!

I also recall one chap spitting at me constantly.

It was like every time I came across to his side of the stage, he had saved up a large gobfull of awfulness especially for me. Kev and Billy had noticed it as well so at one point I ran across the stage mid-chorus and they joined me. We dived on him and kicked him! I smashed the mic stand into him as well. Horrific looking back.

We were never violent, but this guy had pushed us over the edge. Security jumped in and the maddest thing is as he was being thrown out, he was shouting at us that he loved us. And thanking us for the new tunes!

Buzzcocks were fantastic and after the show I think we all went to the Berni Inn. We couldn't get into the Bailey as it was full. Full of the usual posers of course but we were the real deal and the Berni was just grand.

What a night. And Revolver had only just started.

Phil Byrne, Revolver/Teen Commandments/The Reasons

CARNIVAL AGAINST THE NAZIS: PATRIK FITZGERALD/X-RAY SPEX/THE CLASH/ TOM ROBINSON BAND/STEEL PULSE, LONDON 1978

The thing I remember most vividly about this Victoria Park concert was the size of the crowd. Never seen so many people all in one place in my life. Plus the diversity of the crowd – it was really incredible to witness (specially in those times) but nurtured over two years of reggae and punk bands sharing gigs, doing joint media interviews, forging friendships and spreading that bond to the fans. I remember seeing people up in trees, dancing while clinging to branches! Plus there was a massive anti-Nazi march before the actual festival, from Trafalgar Square to Victoria Park which had a carnival vibe.

I recall the energy, it was electric all day. Every band fed off the collective energy of the crowd. Felt like a celebration of the power of collective desire for racial unity mixed with a fierce determination to defy and openly challenge the institutionally racist establishment. Was also a celebration of the fearlessness and passion of youth.

Selwyn Brown, Steel Pulse

STIFF LITTLE FINGERS, DUBLIN 1978

It all started in a pub called Longs, which funnily also had long seats in it, like those in the back of an old bus. Me and the boys, yes we were under age, had a few scoops and then headed off in the cold damp night to the Belfield university campus.

The lads knew of a punk band playing. When we got there, it was one big dark cavernous, uninsulated, cold hall, the type that used to rain on you on packed nights with the condensated sweat dripping onto you. This was going to be a dry night. The band were late, the PA and lights never arrived and there was less than a hundred cold souls in a hall fit for a thousand.

Guitars amps and drums quickly set up, strong Northern Irish accents apologised for the mess. They then announced that here were Stiff Little Fingers.

What happened next was so profound that it became life-changing. It defined my angle on life, as the band sang some of the most insightful, intelligent songs. And coming from a war zone, they managed to say so much without antagonising either side but were more a unifying force.

It's not easy to play in a hall that should be dripping wet when it isn't and is devoid of the critical mass of humanity. Well, they played like when they were in Wembley at Live Aid and were so powerful in their message that you would want them pleading for you to the executioner before your impending death. While the walls didn't drip that night, we got cold going home in our sweaty clothes.

I was young, so I don't have more detailed memories of the night but they played their part. Crass were another band with the message and so were The Clash. The Clash, who I love, somehow never inspired me seeing them live. A close second to the best live band would be The Ramones, while not so ideologically punk in the European sense, they do simply blow you away. PIL, another favourite, really surprised me by how loveable and humorous John Lydon is. I had never before noticed listening to an LP just how musically talented they are. Then, of course, I'll sign off with Steve Ignorant and "Do They Owe Us a Living?"

Barry Cooke, Dead Fridge in the Road

PATTI SMITH, NEWCASTLE 1978

patti smith

newcastle city hall

august 1978

i am 17

growing up in the bilious backwater of billingham

a noxious nauseous new town

full of dread and foreboding

malevolence and violence

punk explodes and we delight in the fallout

blinking and squinting into the future

we embrace it all

we are on our own voyages of discovery

into a new world

where even newcastle seems exotic and faraway

I hitch there

alone

up the a19 and onwards

i don't have a ticket and couldn't care less

there would be a way

there always was

and there is

my mind is blown into tiny pieces by the pop group

they are supporting

like a headliner though

their what the fuckery stuns me

they are an incredible inedible sonic assault and battery

i take a breath

i wait and i wait and i wait

until

she strides on, kicks in and

we're straight down the piss factory
no ceremony, no quarter
no music and it's loud as fuck
smith incants
it's straight in your face
it's up your nose
we can smell it
it's breathtakingly-away beautiful
drink it in
soak it up
she is five foot six going on seven foot tall
she is joey ramone
she is punching above her weight effortlessly
she is shamanic street preacher
she is bitch, whore, mother, lover
she's calling the shots
i am completely smitten
and that's when i fell in love
with this giant
her fragile frame fills the room
she's at home
but there's no turning down the lights
it's an aural atmosphere we're wrapped up in here
she's on a roll
we are rocked
if she called in her debts she'd be filthy rich
so many IOUs
but now she wanna tells us how it's gonna be
a wild horses finale segueing into gloria
hosanna! we cried

tears of joy
for the boy
who looked at patti and here i go
and i don't know why
i spin so ceaselessly
could it be she's taking over me?
some strange music draws me in
makes me come on like some heroin

oh god I fell for you…

I grew up in the bilious northern backwater of Billingham, a town famous for, in fact infamous for, the overwhelming presence of the ICI chemical works which relentlessly spewed out its effluent and noxious gases into the atmosphere, giving the sky a toxic orange hue which we largely, laughingly just took for granted.

Punk hit me hard in the solar plexus in 1976 when this weird and wonderful music started to gradually wend its way up north. While still arguing vehemently about the various merits and downfalls of Jimmy Page versus Richie Blackmore with my mate Mick Wicks, a towering menacing presence of a man, we meanwhile submerged ourselves in this burgeoning new music scene.

It didn't take long before a small gang of us gravitated towards each other and became a tight group of piss-taking, rabble-rousing, attention-seeking ne'er-do-wells. Billingham then was a staunchly working-class town with few if any airs and graces. We eagerly consumed everything we found. We religiously listened to Peel, we regularly walked home from Middlesbrough Rock Garden in a huge entourage, the braver and drunker ones climbing the Transporter Bridge on the way home while we all swapped records, clothes and partners on a regular basis.

I first discovered Patti Smith on vinyl when I found her 12" single of "Gloria" in a brown paper bag in Fearnley's in Middlesbrough. She'd previously blown my mind on The Old Grey Whistle Test late one night doing a version of "Horses" that was so what-the-fuckingly amazing for a 15-year-old boy that nothing would ever be the same again. She seemed as though she was from another planet, quoting Burroughs, referencing Rimbaud; it was so alien, so other and she was so androgynous, so strong, so damn sexy and sexual. My already raging hormones went into overdrive.

I didn't even have a ticket for her show at Newcastle City Hall but it was the summer holidays and I thought fuck it! I'll hitch up to Newcastle and see if I can blag my way in somehow. I did. Well, I bought a ticket outside for the balcony; it's all there was (in those days it was essential to be in the throng downstairs, swaying and sweating and bouncing about) but once in I found myself in the front row upstairs with a bird's eye view of the stage. I'd never even heard of the support group, The Pop Group, but fuck me! I was completely mesmerised by their full-on agitpunkfunkstorm headed by the gangly shouty, enigmatic front man Mark Stewart. Their sonic assault completely hooked me in. What was I witnessing?

Punk suddenly seemed so lame and safe and traditional; this was taking things to another level. I loved it with a passion. And still do. I loved how I was witnessing something so different and new. So challenging, so defiantly un-punk. It marked the beginning of the end for me. Another adventure was about to begin. But then Patti came on. She made me cry that night. She still does. Every fucking time. Despite her inconsistencies and her foibles – all the best characters are flawed anyway. That's what I love and accept now.

Dunstan Bruce, Chumbawamba, Interrobang

ELVIS COSTELLO, DUBLIN 1978

The Stella Cinema, Rathmines, March 16th

Elvis Costello was in the midst of a mad, crazy streak when he landed at the Stella Cinema on the eve of St Patrick's Day in 1978. He'd made two albums and a handful of 45s on the hop (mostly with pick-up musicians), was wrapped in a thick blanket of hype and had just finished an acrimonious US tour.

This was Costello's first gig in Dublin, and the coalescence of the Attractions as his new band.

Dublin was a grey place then, but it was being lit up by the explosion of punk and new wave both within and without. It was certainly ready for Costello's appearance at that wreck of a small, suburban movie theatre. (Dublin had many such cinemas. Once packed with movie-goers, most are gone now or turned into bingo halls.) The Stella was not just declining then, it was almost fully declined. Its brown wood was scarred and bubbled, its red velvet shiny and gum-stained. The only mystery about attending a rare movie showing at the Stella in the late 1970s was which species of parasitical insect you'd return with.

That night in March presented different dangers. I am sure the fire marshals would have had conniptions had they seen the crowd jammed into the Stella that night. Never mind fire safety though, the city engineers would have had coronaries. I was convinced that the building was going to fall down on top of us, because it was heaving and pouring with sweat from the moment the Attractions hit the stage.

My memory is that Costello spat into the microphone that they were just home from an American tour, and it was "nice to be back among humans". Then he tore into the opening number, "Mystery Dance". (I was right about the first song, but John Little, in a contemporary review for In Dublin magazine, placed that comment as the intro to the encore.)

Then it was a demented rollercoaster to the finish a massive wave of energy that the band blasted at the audience, and which they blasted right back again. This was rock'n'roll at its most visceral – the niceties of Elvis's melodies and the complexities of his lyrics subservient to the energy of a band at its peak.

Thanks to my friend, John Foyle, an avid Elvis fan, I can tell you that the band played several songs from their then new album "This Year's Model", a few from "My Aim is True", a couple of the singles, one as-yet unreleased song, and a cover of Kilburn and the High Roads' "Roadette Song".

I remember none of those specifics.

I just know that it remains one of the greatest gigs I have ever seen – certainly top five if not top three. It was not life-changing – that honour belongs to The MC5's free concert in Ann Arbor, Michigan's Gallop Park in 1968, and The Ramones in the Club in Cambridge, Massachusetts eight years later. Nor was it the most memorable, which was The Damned at the Rat in Boston on the opening night of their first American tour, when they ate pizza onstage (and the audience threw them bottles of beer). But Elvis at the Stella was sure as hell life-affirming. This was full-tilt rock'n'roll the way it was meant to be. Energy and emotion in one huge rush. I wonder if the band ever played a better gig again.

I may not remember much of the specifics of the night, but, like an old dog lying on a porch, if I tilt my head just the right way, I can still smell the decrepit room and the sweating crowd. Most of all, I can feel the energy rushing into my body. And, for that moment, I am lost in the moment.

(After lying empty for several decades, the Stella recently got a makeover as an upmarket bar/restaurant/cinema. Now you get posh nibbles and cocktails where you once got stale popcorn and scabies. It would be a perfect venue for Elvis to return to with his current jazz stylings.)

Karl Tsigdinos, designer, DJ

DEAD RINGER AND THE CLONES, BANGOR 1978

All our gigs were bonkers, but the weekend we were supposed to support The Boomtown Rats at Bangor University stands out.

The convoy set out for Wales on a frosty Saturday. A Ford Transit belonging to Pig Style, the moustachioed, mulletted DJ who'd opened for Sabbath, Zep and Budgie, led the way with his roadies, Marvin and Tog, with him in the cab and most of our gear, bassist Big Malc and me in the back. Our roadies, Lee and JD limped along in a grey Morris Minor van. Phil the Ted and Suzy followed on Triumph and sidecar. Behind spluttered a collection of band members, girlfriends, siblings and fans in a train of smoke-belching wrecks.

The three hours from Kidderminster took five, thanks to Pig's insistence on stopping at the last pub in England. He wasn't sure which pub, so he played safe. There were lots on the A5 in 1978 and at every one, he gave our manager, Nigel, a pint of mild and a Jack Daniels. By the time we reached Bangor, Nigel was incoherent. Tog had matched him drink for drink, just to be sociable. In Bangor, Tog fell out of the Transit, vomited, crawled into the back of the Morris and slept till Sunday.

We piled into the student's union excited to meet Geldof and the Rats.

"They've cancelled. You're it."

"We're headlining?"

"Yeah, but not the hall. You're in the bar. That's the stage. Change in the toilets."

"It's not big enough for the drum kit."

"Take it or leave it."

A negotiation ensued. There were eight of us, four roadies and some pretty mean-looking girlfriends, so they agreed to build something bigger. Jonny B Rigid, guitarist, drifted off to the pool room to avoid the aggro. He thrashed the best player in the uni, not a student, he just played pool there. It was a mistake.

The rest of us went to see Bangor, which was closed. We passed Pig and Marvin pushing a catatonic Nigel in a shopping trolley. We heard later they were pushing him down a hill when the police pulled up.

"Oi! What are you lot doing?"

"Don't worry, officer," letting go of Nigel and walking in the opposite direction. "We're English!"

The police shrugged and drove off. Nigel crashed into some railings but was so drunk he bounced and was unhurt.

The crowd that night was a respectable size but an awkward match. On one side of the room were faux hippies in Millets Afghan coats and cheesecloth smocks. On the other were wannabe Travoltas and their molls in cheap white suits and ra-ra skirts. In the middle was a 10-foot space filled with the looming presence of Cool Hand Luke from the pool room, leather-clad, stone-faced.

We played energetically, a mix of our own stuff, Petty, Dury, Feelgood, Thunders. Three songs in, Liquid Lil entered stage-centre like a B-list Vanian, white fumes belching from the smoke bombs in his hands. "Fuck off!" he said. The audience cheered.

We stepped up the pace, ragged R&B and R&R. The hippies and the disco kids started dancing together, all but one. And then Lil did his party trick and swan dived into the throng. His head struck Cool Hand Luke in the sternum.

All hell kicked off. Lil curled into the foetal position as the boots pounded him. We couldn't see him for bodies and smoke. And then the girlfriends and Phil the Ted advanced, dragging Lil from the ruck and beating off all comers. It was very impressive, but the gig was over.

The bar was cleared, the roadies grabbed their gear. We went looking for chips and found girls from the gig who wanted autographs. I signed a stage-prop wad of photocopied fivers in my pocket. We played rock stars for a moment, then drove through the snow to my dad's miner's cottage in Blaenau Ffestiniog, 17 of us, £125 richer. Gods all! Roadie Lee slept in the dog basket. He'd be the only one of us to make a million in this game. Phil the Ted was officially employed as Lil's bodyguard for all future gigs.

Neville Farmer, author

THE CLASH, DUBLIN 1978

I was 18 with longish hair and a combat jacket – very far from a punk. I remember being absolutely terrified of the real punks in the audience. Berlin were one of the support bands and got gobbed on unmercifully. The lead singer was wearing a pale suit which gradually changed colour as he was the main target in spite of his regular pleas for them to stop. The Virgin Prunes were the most bizarre thing I had ever seen but seemed completely fearless in the face of the terrifying audience.

The Clash were very late on and incredibly loud and moving constantly around the stage. I know it's a cliche, but it was genuinely an assault on the senses and to this day no other gig has ever made quite the same impression on me.

I had never seen a band as loud or who played as fast as they did but it wasn't just noise, they were amazing. The last thing I remember was sprinting to get the last 46A home, terrified of being stuck in Dún Laoghaire with the rest of the audience! We just made the bus and I don't think my ears stopped ringing for a week.

I feel so lucky to have been there and haven't hesitated to dine out on having been there many times!

Brian Walker, bookseller

MAGAZINE, COVENTRY 1978

The first I knew of the band Magazine was when they appeared on Top of the Pops in early 1978 with their single "Shot By Both Sides". I didn't begin listening to John Peel's late-night radio show – or even know about it – until later that year, so the only way I could get to hear any of the new bands was via limited daytime radio airplay and TOTP appearances. I only got to hear The Sex Pistols once "Pretty Vacant" had gone top 20 and was played by Paul Burnett on his afternoon show on Radio One in July 1977. I remember this because it was my birthday and I was camping out in a tent with my friend Tony Power in his back garden. We were eager to hear what the band sounded like, having read all the lurid tabloid headlines, so when the DJ announced that he was about to play them, the volume on the little transistor radio was turned right up, and we gave our full attention. We thought the record was brilliant and hilarious, and with our limited knowledge of the musical reference points of rock 'n' pop, concluded that it sounded like a harder-edged Status Quo with an Albert

Steptoe impersonator on vocals. Tony was more of a record buyer than I was, due to him being better off financially, ie pocket money doled out in notes rather than coins. He bought the single and was delighted to report that the song on the B side had the word "fuck' in it.

I was quite intrigued by this band Magazine, watching them on telly that Thursday night in February 1978. I liked the song and thought that the singer looked like a horror film psycho killer – one that lived with his mum and whose victims were dispatched by some elaborate method that probably involved dolls. Tony didn't like them at all – too weird.

His opinion of Magazine changed in the school summer holidays of that year. Having gone on a trip to Manchester while staying with his aunt in Halifax for the week, he spotted the singer from Magazine in a record shop and decided to follow him. Howard Devoto soon became aware he was being pursued by some kid in green flares and a sleeveless denim jacket, with a chain and padlock around his neck (I'm assuming this was Tony's attire on the day, because that's what he wore for most of that school holiday). He stopped to ask if he was indeed following him, at which point Tony began to blurt out a barrage of inane questions, "Weren't you on Top of the Pops?", "What's it like?" etc. Surprisingly, Devoto didn't tell him to piss off, but instead took some tobacco from his army shoulder bag, rolled himself a cig, and leaned back against a wall, fully obliging and happy to hang around for a few minutes for a chat. This agreeable encounter lead to Tony purchasing Magazine's recently released debut album "Real Life", and the record became a big part of the soundtrack of the rest of the school holiday and beyond.

A few months later, we got wind that Magazine would be playing Tiffany's in our hometown, Coventry, on December 7th, and decided we had to go. We'd been to see Buzzcocks with Subway Sect at Coventry Theatre in October, which was the first gig either of us had attended, and we were ready and eager for a second. The only problem was that Tiffany's was a nightclub and we weren't sure if we'd be allowed in. Maybe they let kids in for concerts, we hoped. Only one way to find out – see if we could buy tickets. We nipped into Virgin Records and Tapes in Coventry city centre one day after school and handed a over a couple of quid each to the future drummer for The Specials, who manned the counter at the time. The tickets were issued without question, despite the fact we were wearing school uniforms. So this had to mean that there'd be no age restriction, same as Coventry Theatre, right?

Fast forward to December 7th. The first ominous sign came on the bus into town. When we went to see Buzzcocks, the bus had filled up with kids from all over the estate, punked and primed for the occasion. There was hardly anyone on this bus, let alone anyone our age who looked like they were going to a gig. Okay, so Magazine weren't as popular – it was probably that. We got into town and headed for Tiffany's lift and stair tower that stood in the middle of part of Coventry's shopping precinct and took you up to a glazed walkthrough that lead to where the action was. I'd been inside the place once before, earlier that year, to attend a disco for schoolkids, where I'd spent an hour standing around aimlessly, ketchup sticky fingers from a recently scoffed hot dog nestled in Harrington jacket pocket, as Cov teens shuffled about half-heartedly to Althea and Donna and The Bee Gees, and a queue formed to snog an accommodating young lady from another school. It was a dismal and crummy experience, and one that I'd missed Star Trek for.

So myself and Tony are now standing in the glazed walkway, where a few concert goers are beginning to gather, waiting for the doors to open, and it isn't looking promising. They are all blokes and look to be in their 20s. I'm feeling very out of place in my towelling hoody, cheap jeans and plastic Co-op trainers. At least I'd put a bit of an effort into my appearance for the Buzzcocks concert: school blazer, straight-leg black cords, Millets baseball boots but here tonight I'm 14 with the dress sense of a 10 year old. It dawns on me that we're not getting in – this ain't for kids! A bouncer arrives, "You two, eff off!" he snaps in a menacing-sounding Scottish accent, giving a dismissive backwards thumb gesture towards the lift as he passes us. Okay, that's it, we're going home. Tony, who has a lot more front than me, heads over to the bouncer in an attempt to rectify the situation. Somehow he manages to persuade him to let us in, with the proviso that we keep well away from the bar. Well, we only have our bus fare home, and alcohol doesn't figure much in our lives at this point anyway – we're just here to see the band.

So in the end, we did get to watch post-punk, art-rock band Magazine do their thing live on stage. It was a very different experience to the supercharged affair we'd witnessed six weeks earlier, when Devoto's former band had played Coventry Theatre, but it did now seem that our initiation into a new night-time world of youth culture and blaring decibels had well and truly begun.

Paul Court, The Primitives

IAN DURY AND THE BLOCKHEADS, DUBLIN 1978

Dublin was great in the late 1970s. The music, the venues and the people.

Having spent my early days listening to Pink Floyd and Led Zeppelin and coming from Dun Laoghaire, it was time to shed my hippy skin!

Something new was happening in music and it was exciting.

The Olympic ballroom had the faded glory of old dance halls (just like the TV Club around the corner in Harcourt Street) but it was now hosting punk and new wave acts from the UK. So, my pal Gary and I went to see Ian Dury and the Blockheads who had released the album "New Boots and Panties" the previous year.

What a gig! What an incredible band! Amazing brass section, infectious funk punk grooves, and the man himself. A great performer, with an incredible stage presence the likes of which I'd never seen before. We were mesmerized by this new shift in music and the promise it brought.

"Wake up & make love with me", "Billericay Dickie" and "Hit me with your rhythm stick", all songs to remember.

There have been many gigs since and hopefully many more to come, but this one just stayed with me. Such energy, hope and spirit. Just what you want from a great gig.

Pat O'Donnell, The Fountainhead

THE STRANGLERS, LANCASTER LATE 1970s

Stranglers. Lancaster University. Their psychedelic take on punk blew us away. We saw them play in Lancaster in the punk years and everyone went home and formed a band. The way they were surly outsiders with this incredibly aggressive attitude – their music really hit a raw nerve. They were imaginative. I liked the way they did their own thing and didn't give a fuck. I loved their music and I still do! The less fashionable they are, the more I love them. The night was tense and full of violence but the band cut through all of this. They were at the top of their game.

John Robb, Membranes, Goldblade, Sensurround. Writer, Punk an Oral History, Louder Than War magazine/website

TOM ROBINSON BAND, BELFAST 1979

At 56, I've been an avid gig goer since February 1979 when I saw AC/DC and got the bug for gigs. Anytime there was a gig on, we would hang around the back entrance to the Ulster Hall. We got to know the caretaker, Jackie, not sure he liked us as we were always trying to sneak in. Anyway March 24th, 1979, was TRB at said venue. I didn't know much about them, possibly only "2-4-6-8 Motorway". I was standing outside the back door when we were allowed in. They were soundchecking – it was great. Some bloke came over and asked if any of us could use a pin spot. I put my hand up and ended up controlling the pin spot up on the balcony. The only instruction I got was "shine it where Tom points".

The first *free in* gig! They are always the best and I've been blagging ever since. Uppa Punx!

Buck, The Defects

PUBLIC IMAGE LTD, MANCHESTER 1979

Nearly 41 years ago, on the afternoon of June 18th,1979, Public Image Ltd were filmed for Granada Reports. Understandably, given Lydon's track record with early evening magazine programmes, the interview was pre-recorded. This left the group with a free evening, so John Lydon asked Tony Wilson if "he still had that club of his" and a gig was arranged for that night. Fall producer Grant Showbiz was drafted in to do the sound and let the various members of The Fall know that the gig was on. I was allowed to tag along, though I was clearly under age (I wouldn't be 16 for another eight months) – a point not lost on the doorman. I was only allowed in after personal intervention by Tony Wilson himself.

I'd seen PIL before, at The King's Hall in Belle Vue in February of the same year, but that had been a fairly underwhelming affair. Though they were seriously under-rehearsed on both occasions, the first time had been properly advertised and promoted and was hard on the heels of the release their brilliant first album, so audience expectations were running high. The group were obviously unwilling, not to say incapable, of living up to such lofty preconceptions, and their short performance, like the whole evening, was tense and tetchy.

This evening's appearance came with no such baggage. The group were in the middle of recording "Metal Box" and, as became clear when the album was released, were at the absolute peak of their creativity. They'd just engaged the services of Richard Dudanski on drums after a series of stand-ins, and were sufficiently impressed to let him play on a fair bit of the album. Though they were old hands at projecting an air of detached boredom, you could sense their collective excitement as soon as they took to the stage. They started with a scintillating run through "Chant" (which unlike subsequent live renditions featured a full complement of "Mob/War/Kill/Hate" courtesy of Richard), followed by both sides of the new single and a tentative go at second single "Memories". In some ways it wasn't really like a gig at all – it felt like you were being allowed a glimpse into their creative process.

Wobble then took "Public Image" at such a gallop that Lydon had to stop the song. "Give him a break he's only been in the band two days," Wobble explained to the audience, motioning to the man behind the kit. "What a c**t, blaming the drummer," Keith reminded everyone, smiling. It was that kind of an evening – as well as being among the few punters to ever see Keith Levene in a good mood, we were also treated to the first recorded sighting of Jah Wobble standing and playing at the same time. Despite the brevity – they only played five songs – it remains one of my favourite gigs to this day. Not all memories are useless.

Paul Hanley, The Fall

FUTURAMA, LEEDS 1979

Queen's Hall, September 8/9th

I moved to Leeds two years ago to take up a job and one of the first shows I went to was a Jon Langford solo gig in Northern Guitars. Before the last song, Jon offered his thanks to the rather large and jovial man who had taken my eight pounds at the door, one John Keenan…

…The first time I came to Leeds was close to 40 years before then, to a show promoted by the same John Keenan and for the same price, if I recall correctly, but at a much larger venue that stood then, as it doesn't now, maybe five minutes from Call Lane: Futurama 1 at the Queen's Hall, a venue so unsuitable few can mention being there without an involuntary shudder. Leeds has generally been overshadowed by other northern English cities musically: in 1979, Manchester was already way ahead of the pack, Liverpool was coming up on the outside with the whole Zoo package, and Sheffield was Dusseldorf on the Don. The bands that did emerge from Leeds around then were notable in comprising students at the university and poly rather than natives – Gang of Four, Mekons, Delta 5 (none of whom played that first Futurama, oddly). If Leeds was a bit behind the curve, without an identifiable "sound" or a record label of its own, with Futurama, it helped clarify the way out of the identikit punk/skinny tie new wave impasse. What we didn't then call post-punk became an identifiable culture at shows like this.

Looking at the poster to check my memories, there are bands that seem to have played of whom I have no recall: apparently Cabaret Voltaire were there, as were Adam and the Ants. The other band I don't remember is PIL, since I managed to sleep through them completely, exhausted from the Dublin-Liverpool crossing the night before, even though my so-called friends claim they tried to wake me.

The bands I do remember well are Echo and the Bunnymen (still with the drum machine), Teardrop Explodes, OMD, with the Revox on stage, Scritti Politti (in their squatter Gramsci-quoting phase), The Fall and Joy Division.

Joy Division were a revelation, obviously, but the abiding memory is of seeing The Fall for the first of many times. I'd bought the first two singles, but didn't yet know "Live at the Witch Trials"; but already they'd passed that point and the motoric/glitterbeat stomp allied to the sight of a man who looked like the quiet, weird guy at school possessed by something or other was both more ordinary and more unearthly than anything I'd seen on a stage up to then.

The gig was a mere three mins from the station, so we probably saw less of Leeds than I can currently see from my window. Two memories: being kicked awake by a policeman at 6am on the station concourse on the Monday morning, and seeing posters warning women about the still-at-large Yorkshire Ripper.

I brought home copies of "Rowche Rumble", "Pictures on My Wall" and "Sleeping Gas" purchased at the stall in the Queen's Hall and a copy of "Unknown Pleasures" from Probe in Liverpool on the way back.

 Stan Erraught, Stars of Heaven

WIRE, LONDON 1979

Dome Cupol (Performative event conceived by Bruce Gilbert (Wire), Graham Lewis (Wire) and Russell Mills), Notre Dame Hall, Leicester Square, London, July 19th

I'd become good friends with the members of Wire in 1977, having met them at a few of their London gigs. We'd all been to various art schools so we had a lot in common and understood the likes of Duchamp, Dada, Schwitters, Joseph Beuys and the Fluxus group. We'd been talking about our frustrations with how most concerts/gigs were so formulaic, and had discussed ways of making them more interesting and diverse, more open and inclusive. Out of these usually alcohol-fueled discussions came the idea for a one-off multimedia evening involving a mixed programme of performers and events.

Our marvelous little-known venue was at the very heart of London: the Notre Dame Hall in Leicester Square, part of the Notre Dame de France Church, which contains three wall murals by Jean Cocteau painted in 1959-1960. The hall, despite its near-secrecy, had an illustrious history having hosted groups such as The Small Faces, John Mayall, The Who, The Rolling Stones, The Sex Pistols, The Clash and Boy George.

The evening opened with Costa del Song, a performance by Wire's manager, Mike Collins. Sat on a high stool under a pin spot light, he was dressed as an Italianate 1960s Eurovision song contestant; red frilly blouson shirt open to the waist, huge, gaudy gangster/pimp chained medallion hanging from his neck, fingers clustered with flashy rocks-for-rings bling, and wrists wreathed with tawdry shiny bracelets and trashy ornate bangles. Accompanied by mock-flamenco guitar, played by Bid (Monochrome Set), he sang an emotionally charged, but completely cracked nonsensical cod-operatic ballad. As the song became more climactic and his gestures became more flamboyant, his garish jewellery flashed off like stars. The audience, having initially thought it was all deadly serious, were completely befuddled by the time Mike stormed off the stage in mock exasperation.

Blurt's ambush immediately followed with a blistering set by erstwhile poet and puppeteer Ted Milton. Out blasted berserk babbles of saxophone and existential lyrics rasped over his band's ferocious, stripped back avant-garde funk.

The debut screening of the Quay Brothers' stop-frame animation film Nocturna Artificialia (Those Who Desire Without End), followed. Graham, Bruce, the Quays and I stationed ourselves by an exit door as we feared the audience, most of whom were pissed-off because, contrary to their wishes, Wire would not be appearing, might erupt and trash the place. Instead, and much to our relief, they quickly sat down cross-legged on the floor like dreamy hippies, totally engrossed in the film's extraordinary, disturbing, dream-like qualities.

Next up was us, under the name Dome Cupol, performing a 20-minute piece called Kluba Cupol. Graham, Bruce and I played behind a hanging screen of construction weld mesh sprayed black. Graham and Bruce switched their instruments and Graham sang a screed of lyrics about the ongoing conflict in Afghanistan, that he'd scrawled on a toilet roll, which unfolded wildly during his recital. Meanwhile I attempted to play a Moog synthesiser (which I didn't really know how to play), and operate a cassette player loaded with a tape of pre-recorded DIY and found sounds, which, governed by my nerves, I punched on and off at random.

I also designed the "set" and the lighting, and the "choreography" of the performer, a Japanese artist friend of mine, Shinro Ohtake, who had been tricked into thinking he was being asked to play bass with his favourite band, Wire. Appearing to be blind, he hesitantly entered the stage wearing dark glasses and tapping a white stick. He had been directed to a large black box at the front of the stage, within which were lengths of luminous security ropes, and about eight A4 sheets of my handwritten stage directions. These instructed him to weave the ropes into approximate shapes in the weld mesh in response to the music/noise we were making. Simultaneously we tried to interpret his movements through the sound we were producing. The low light levels caused Graham to struggle reading his lyrics, causing him to miss his timing. At the end of 20 minutes, the sound went dead and the stage lighting was abruptly killed, leaving Shinro alone to finish his crazed weaving. With just a UV light illuminating the darkness all that could be seen in the pitch black was a weird calligraphy of glowing floating lines.

The evening ended with the UK debut of the German extreme electro-punk band DAF. (Deutsche Amerikanische Freundschaft), who stormed through a pulverising set of jagged, stripped-down, brutal electro-noise. Later John Peel would hail them as "the godfathers of techno".

Russell Mills, artist

BUZZCOCKS/GANG OF FOUR, SAN FRANCISCO 1979

I always struggle with these. Which one do I choose? I've been so lucky with great shows that I've been at – my first-ever being Creedence Clearwater Revival at the Royal Albert Hall; seeing The Who with Moon a bunch of times, the first at the Rainbow doing "Quadrophenia"; seeing Free at the RAH, standing right down front at the lip of the stage; Genesis played at my grammar school down in Kent – right after "Nursery Cryme" had been released, and everybody craning upwards to look at the ceiling, from which Peter Gabriel promised us a giant pair of knickers would descend during "Harold The Barrel"; Bowie at the Rainbow in early 1972, with the Lindsay Kemp Troupe flitting around the stage and David coming out after the encores in a short kimono to apologise that they'd played every song they knew; Bowie again when he was Aladdin Sane at Earl's Court, standing up on the back of a chair… but not falling because the crush of the crowd of reaching, crying Ziggy Kids was so tight; the mind-blowing Roxy Music at an old cinema in Medway, Kent – we'd skived off school and driven up there… to see the band arrive in a space ship, getting out and going in IN FULL SLAP, ALL DRESSED UP, AT 5 O'CLOCK IN THE AFTERNOON (OKAY – it was a Ford Transit); The Anarchy Tour in 1977 at Leeds Poly, when Matlock was still in the Pistols, and with the pre-Topper Clash… and on and on. And, of course, a few unbelievably intense and fantastic shows of my/our own – the most unbelievably amazing show opening for Buzzcocks at Geary Temple in San Francisco in 1979 – the hottest day of that summer, over sold by probably 1,000 people, hanging out with old BBC DJ Johnny Walker before it all began (I know – what the hell, right?!), one of those shows that you float above yourself when you're playing… Watching yourself play so perfectly, trying and succeeding at anything your mind drives you to, in Complete Control and utterly 'NSync with those three other Great Men, and blowing Greil Marcus's mind. And then… 25 years later, in a pub in south London (my old manor) – getting back onstage with those same three Great Old Men (all on the cusp of 50). Probably the first time with them I'd actually been truly nervous. But halfway through the first song, I caught Dave's eye – and we just grinned at each other. It felt like we were 23 again (it smelled like it, too in that weird old pub on a small stage with crappy monitors and a crazed crowd.) It was a time warp… until I looked over all the steaming heads to the back of the room – where my 23-year-old nephew was giving me the hairy eyeball. Oh, well. And then… the show that truly broke me up. Watching my 12-year-old daughter rip it up as Ursula in The Little Mermaid – singing like Chrissie, Dusty, Adele and Elkie all rolled into one.

So there you have it. I can't choose just one. Sorry.

Hugo Burnham, Gang of Four

BUZZCOCKS/GANG OF FOUR, SAN FRANCISCO 1979

It was Gang of Four's first tour of the US in the summer of 1979. We didn't have a record deal over there, and people only knew us from the "Damaged Goods" EP and live reviews. The whole tour was brilliant, between shows opening for Buzzcocks – who were great supporters of Gang of Four – and our own headlining club dates. We often played two sets a night, on at 9 or 10pm and then back again at midnight or 1am; meaning we played maybe 40 times in 30 days. Intense, a rock "n" roll boot camp. We were six on the road, the four of us plus manager and one crew; so every day we all loaded up the shit Econovan, drove a few hundred miles, unloaded at venue, soundchecked, hung about, gigged, loaded up the van, drove to motel, unloaded van and (unless there was a party) went to bed. We could only afford two rooms with two doubles, so every other night we had to share a bed.

We were tight, the buzz was growing, the shows just got better and better. It was like a downhill juggernaut. A very loud one.

My favourite show has become legendary. We played with Buzzcocks in San Francisco at Temple Beautiful (aka The Geary Temple) on 9.11. It was at 1839 Geary, formerly the cursed Jim Jones People's Temple and on the same block as the storied Filmore West.

The show was totally sold, way over-sold, on the hottest night of a hot summer. We were on top of our game. Outside the venue, it was still in the 80s early evening, and onstage over 100 degrees, hot as fuck, with sweat condensing on the ceiling to fall like a gloopy monsoon. We hit the stage at 100mph and barely paused between songs; we were totally on it. The set went by in a trance and when we were off, I could hardly recall what we'd done. Soaked in sweat, I lay down with my head in a deep tray of ice, steam rising.

Reviews were sensational. We'd stolen the show. America had opened her arms – we went in for a big hug.

Jon King, Gang of Four

THE RUTS, BRADFORD 1979

I'd heard The Ruts' signature song "In A Rut" on John Peel and I knew we had to be there – Sunday night at the Royal Standard on Manningham Lane was when the punk bands played. Perhaps just 200 of us crammed into the little concert room at the back of the pub and me and Joolz standing on the bench seats along the side overlooking the tiny stage, trying to keep our balance as the room seethed and boiled. The three-piece band were brilliant: aggressive, tight, tuneful – all seasoned players and at the centre was the fourth man, Malcolm Owen, singing, snarling, wheeling through great song after song. He seemed to care so much and not give a damn all at the same time, spitting love and rage in equal measure, effortless, unstoppable. It was the best gig I've seen. Ever. Not much more than an hour of power, fury and joy. Afterwards I felt completely burned, cleansed, exhilarated and truly happy and still remember how we slipped and giggled through the freezing night, singing in the subway "You're in a rut/You've gotta get out of it/Out of it"… and there we were, completely out of it. There was no hurry to get home. Our whole lives stretched before us, suddenly filled with limitless possibility.

Within a few months The Ruts' "Babylon's Burning" became the soundtrack to Mrs Thatcher's riot-torn Britain, followed by a string of other hits. And then suddenly Malcolm was dead of a heroin overdose. And that's it. That was all.

The precious things in life are just moments. And the way that The Ruts made me feel that night has been my template for everything New Model Army has done and tried to do all the years since.

Justin Sullivan, New Model Army, Red Sky Coven

ANGELIC UPSTARTS, LONDON 1979

In April 1979, I watched the Angelic Upstarts play a gig inside Acklington Prison. It sounds unlikely, but it happened. Naturally it was a cock-up. The prison chaplain, a pleasant mild-mannered fellow, had booked the notorious South Shields punk combo on the strength of their name alone. The *angelic* part sounded heavenly; but the *upstarts* element became apparent as soon as their roadie hung up their banner, a Union Jack embellished with the words "Upstarts Army" and an angry socialist clenched fist along with various unprintable thoughts on the local Northumbrian police.

It was the ultimate irony – the band the local cops loved to hate were guests of HM government for an exercise in subversion. Naturally the convict audience cheered faster than the colour drained from the poor chaplain's face.

Singer Thomas "Mensi" Mensforth had been nervous beforehand. "They always said I'd end up inside," he said. "I never thought it'd be like this." He shouldn't have worried. The 150-strong crowd were on the Upstarts' side as soon as they exploded into the opening number, "Police Oppression".

The younger cons jerked with the ferocious beat; the older ones looked bemused, but they all clapped in thunderous approval at the end of each song. The more they responded, the more Mensi loosened up, dropping in the odd "My name is Sue, how do you do?" throwbacks to Johnny Cash's pioneering 1969 San Quentin gig, swearing at the mixing desk, spitting at the ceiling (they loved that) and bellowing along like a wounded bison to the raw rock'n'roll that made the Upstarts one of the handful of street punk bands left back then.

"There's crooks everywhere but it's always the wrong ones get nicked," he said to much applause.

Then came a specially amended version of Sham's "Borstal Breakout" called "There's Gonna Be An Acklington Breakout", followed by the delicate lightness of "F*** Off and Leave Me Alone", "for all the screws".

The wardens weren't happy; the chaplain looked like he was praying to be struck down by celestial lightning; but even the cons who weren't into the band's primal din were loving the spirit. Never more so than on the emotive set-closing "The Murder of Liddle Towers". Mensi reinforced his opinion that the Northumbria police had unlawfully killed the electrician from County Durham by subtly unveiling the fresh head of a pig which he left gurning from atop the amps. The hall exploded with cheers and whistles as cons leapt up and punched the air.

An encore was inevitable and the Upstarts slammed through "Acklington Breakout" one more time. The band were happy, the convicts were ecstatic, the prison officers… let us leave. I just felt sorry for the chaplain.

Garry Bushell, journalist

THE CLASH/NEGATIVE TREND/THE ZEROS, SAN FRANCISCO 1979

The Temple Beautiful (An Old synagogue next to Jim Jones' People's Temple and The Fillmore), February 8th. Benefit concert for New Youth Productions.

$3.50 entry fee! All ages

I was 19 years old, bass player and founder of punk band The Zeros from Chula

Vista, California, a city in San Diego County, 101 miles south of Los Angeles,10 minutes north of the Mexican border and Tijuana.

In September 1978, The Zeros moved to San Francisco to live and play as many gigs as possible in the city. We had been living there for only seven months when The Clash concert took place.

Peter Urban, our manager, wanted to open an all-ages punk rock venue in SF so he created New Youth Productions in order to realise this goal.

NY Productions started having meetings and in one of those meetings a member of NYP suggested The Clash could possibly get involved.

Apparently this NYP member knew Joe Strummer and Mick Jones and said he would contact them via telephone and ask them.

We all knew The Clash would be touring the USA for the first time and would be playing at the Berkeley Civic Auditorium with Bo Diddley as the opening act. And San Francisco was just across the Bay Bridge and perhaps it would be possible for them to play after all.

So they were asked and they agreed to play! Unbelievable!

I went to The Clash/Bo Diddley concert in Berkeley. It was amazing. The next night I would be in the opening band for The Clash. Wait, WHAT????

The day of the gig, The Zeros roadie, Tony "Flattop" Bentley picked me up in his early 1960s Volkswagen Bug with no back seat and no passenger seat so we could have more room for the amplifiers, drums and guitars.

We loaded the music equipment into the VW and drove to The Temple Beautiful located next door to Jim "Drink the Kool Aid" Jones' People's Temple and The Fillmore West on Geary Street.

We arrived around 3pm, walked into the venue and The Clash were on the main floor kicking and passing a soccer ball around to each other while they waited to do a soundcheck.

A surreal moment for sure.

Tony Flattop immediately joined The Clash in the soccer ball kickaround and The Clash were totally cool and inviting to Tony's intrusion.

Soon after, The Clash left the main floor and disappeared up into the balcony section of the venue. After unloading the music equipment out of the VW, I made my way up to the dressing room. I open the door and The Clash are in there. I walk in, say hello to the band and they say hello back.

I was wearing my fake leather jacket and I had a lapel pin attached to it. It was the Sandinista emblem – a black triangle next to a red triangle.

Joe Strummer noticed it and he said, "I like your pin there" while pointing at it.

"Thanks," I said, and we had a quick, brief chat about the Sandinistas and their cause. Yes, Joe Strummer and me. It still seems like a dream to me.

After our chat, I took the pin off my jacket and offered it to him as a friendly gesture.

Joe said: "Oh I can't take that from you." And I said "Come on, please take it. I insist." And he did and said "Thank you."

Then he exited the dressing room to do the soundcheck.

Show time: 3,000-plus people filled the Temple Beautiful. The concert line-up was firtst The Zeros, second Negative Trend and third The Clash.

So we hit the stage: 6,000-plus eyes and ears looking at us and listening too.

Was I nervous? Hell yes. When we finished playing our set, I was relieved.

Next up was Negative Trend, but at the last minute The Clash decided to go on next. They played second after The Zeros because they were under contract with Bill Graham Presents to only play his concert in Berkeley the night before and nowhere else within a 100-mile radius. That is why the actual name of the band was not used in the promotional flyers. Only their slogan at the time, "The Only Band That Matters" and/or an image of the band.

The Clash were true punk rebels for defying Bill Graham Presents and helping New Youth Productions. That concert and that day is one of the highlights of my Zeros/punk days.

Hector Penalosa, The Zeros

RUEFREX, WEST BELFAST 1979

Cross the Line. Turf Lodge Community Centre, November 1979

If a band can be said to have an ideology that underpinned their purpose, then Ruefrex's mission –through the politics of our songs – was to contest social injustice and challenge the evils of sectarianism. It might sound pretty grandiose now but in 1970s Belfast, it required "walking the walk".

Martin Lynch is an internationally respected playwright but it was his brother, Seamus, who I had most looked up to.

From north Belfast, Seamus became a republican activist around the start of the Troubles, and sided with the official wing of Sinn Féin in the split of 1970. He was a strong supporter of the Official IRA's ceasefire in 1972 and official Sinn Féin's vocal socialism.

Somehow Seamus and Martin (already active in Community Arts) had heard of the work and the message that Ruefrex had been promoting and contacted me with an interesting, if daunting proposition. "Come to play for the kids of the fiercely nationalist Turf Lodge housing estate in west Belfast and your pint glasses will never run dry!"

Turf Lodge lies in the shadow of Belfast's Black Mountain, which for most of its history has been the scene of poverty and social unrest. Originally, the estate was built to house people from the overcrowded terraced housing of the Lower Falls Road. With no shops, schools, public transport or roads infrastructure, life for the population of largely young families with children, was challenging to say the least. Poorly constructed flats exacerbated the problems. To further aggravate an already dire set of circumstances, the impact of the Troubles on the area was immediate and calamitous.

It is something of a minor miracle then – and to the enduring credit of the Lynches and other activists like them – that an unbreakable sense of community identity and spirit maintained throughout.

When I discussed the proposition of the gig with the other band members, it is fair to say that there was a considerable amount of trepidation. Sectarian murders were happening daily. By young working-class men, of young working-class men. For a band from the loyalist Shankill Road to venture into the area to perform would have been unheard of at the time. The risks were just too great.

But Martin had given us a guarantee of safe passage (and that offer of unlimited free drink). After some discussion, we agreed that this was effectively the central raison d'etre of the band and agreed to play.

A rusty, brown Nissan car with some heavy-looking older men in it met our hire van on the fringes of the estate. We would normally move our gear by any means possible – sometimes by black cab – but that was out of the question here.[1]

When the community centre came into view, we were at once reassured and unnerved. It looked like all the community facilities located on our side of the wall. A concrete block of a building, pebble-dashed and set on a sea of black tarmac, sprinkled with broken glass, bottle tops and crushed cigarette cartoons. The kind of place we thought from which bad men ventured abroad to spread carnage and waste lives.

Martin met us at the door and his effusive welcome and generosity helped steady our nerves somewhat. The interior again bore a striking resemblance to loyalist clubs I had been in. The only key difference being the photographs and flags on the walls; not the queen or King Billy but images of The Starry Plough, James Connolly, Che Guevara.

Soon, the locals began to arrive and file in. They were predominantly men our own age or younger. They dressed and carried themselves much like we did. They danced wildly to the upbeat, frenetic songs and bled into the shadows on the slower numbers. Just as the kids in the loyalist estates had done when we played there. They faced the same problems daily and sought refuge and escape in the same ways. If ever there was an affirmation of a shared cross-communal affinity, it was here.

The gig culminated with much backslapping and hand-shaking. Pints were quaffed and jokes told. It was as if an epiphany had been visited upon all there. Most of these kids would never venture out to the Pound Club or the Harp Bar. It wasn't their scene. They were "Spiderman"[2] just like us. The message, if it was to be heard, had to be taken to them. And for a brief window in time, there was no difference to be made among Prods and Taigs or Spides and punks.

It was to be the first of many cross-community ventures that saw Ruefrex play around the province. But it was Turf Lodge that put the steel into our resolve, both in terms of performance and in a determination not to compromise our mission; through the songs or in our stance to challenge the scourge of sectarianism.

Paul Burgess, Ruefrex

---

1 Throughout the Troubles, black taxi cabs – often overseen by paramilitaries from both sides – provided a community transport service in north and west Belfast
2 "Spidermen" or "Spides" is a derogatory term used to describe Belfast working-class youth.

ATV, LONDON 1979

Greenwich Theatre

London in 1979 was a seething mass of every type of humanity; an overflowing magician's cauldron fuelled by fun, fear, hope, violence, new ideas, good times, bad times, drugs and music, music, music. We were living on the fringes of the fringes and were pushing the boundaries of communal living, human relationships, gender conformity and a whole bunch of other stuff we didn't even have names for yet. We knew ATV and decided to travel south of the river and see their last gig before they transitioned into the more experimental Good Missionaries.

Mark Perry has more claims than most to inventing UK punk rock, but by 1979 he had become frustrated and bored by a punk reductionism that was rapidly sucking the life and joy out of a slowly dying scene. The Pop Group had burst out of Bristol with an altogether new take on punk and stuff and Perry seemed to fall under their influence. He decided to lead his ATV compadres out of the narrowing punk wasteland and into the sunny uplands of weird noise, confrontational sounds and improvisational anti-music.

We arrived at the plush and inappropriate Greenwich Theatre after a breakneck drive across London in a clapped-out, overcrowded Post Office van. Racist Special Patrol Group stormtroopers stopped us outside Buckingham Palace, but they let us go when they saw we were white and tore off looking for black people to beat up. We got back on the road, nearly colliding with a double decker London bus sporting the legend 666 on its number plate. It seemed like a good omen.

We piled into the Greenwich Theatre and a band called Fashion played first. All I remember about them was they went on interminably meaning ATV would have to cut their set short. The group at this point consisted of Perry, vocalist Anno Wombat from Here and Now, and regulars Dennis Burns and Mick Linehan. They were joined on drums by Dave George, who warned the band he couldn't actually play drums, a fact that became apparent to everyone as the "show" progressed. There was a rumour that Genesis P Orridge was on stage that night, but I couldn't confirm that.

The first number was a version of "Nasty Little Lonely" and was almost normal, except for the addition of a saxophone being tortured rather than played. It seemed to go down quite well. But then the music became stranger, no discernible rhythm was evident and no melodies were played. Nothing that resembled a chord sequence, or any sort of sequence, occurred that night. It was an unholy racket and the sort of noise most people would never recognise as music. It was random, in every sense of the word. I thought it was thrilling.

The crowd started to show their impatience and it looked like they might turn ugly. The band reacted by pushing the performance further out on a limb. Then one of the band started to push the grand piano towards the edge of the stage. It looked like some serious damage might be on the agenda. The theatre management must have freaked out. The house lights came on and the PA went off. Some people booed, most looked confused and started to head towards the exit. The band also seemed bewildered and drifted off stage.

Then out of nowhere a swarm of about 50 riot cops marched through the theatre looking mean and ready for action. No one was up for getting beaten up so we wandered out into the night and off on another adventure. London in 1979 was a great place to be, and every night there was a great gig or some weird shit happening.

Steve Lake, Zounds

XTC, DUBLIN 1979

From Dublin, at 18 I became Thin Lizzy's first manager. I managed and/or was agent and/or publicist for many other acts and events including Granny's Intentions, Moving Hearts, Hothouse Flowers, The Real Wild West, The Pogues, Shane MacGowan and The Popes, Bob Marley Dalymount 1980, Bob Dylan at Fleadh Mor Tramore 1993, the Lisdoonvarna Festival and the Galway Arts Festival; and in the UK, the Reading Festival, Phoenix, The Fleadh and the Mean Fiddler Organisation's 17 live music venues in London.

In 1978, I ran McGonagles as a seven-night-a-week live music venue and booked all the Irish punk acts including a very young U2 who played there regularly. Other acts included John Otway with Wild Willie Barrett, The Damned (The Doomed) and XTC. I also booked the Electric Ballroom in London and Bang On! in New York… acts there included Rick Danko from The Band, Robert Gordon, Jeff Buckley and Elvis Presley's band, The Sun Rhythm Section. Benefit shows included The Verve at Brixton Academy for The Big Issue.

XTC played a few times for me when I ran McGonagles in Dublin in 1978. Their first was a one-off and brilliant. About six weeks later, they came back and did three nights in a row which were amazing. They were really cool nice guys who loved what they were doing and just wanted to play. They had a great tour manager called Paul Cummins, a nicer guy you couldn't meet. There were positive vibes all around this band.

About a year later, Hot Press magazine got XTC to do a benefit show for them to help support the magazine. They got a venue in Ranelagh called The Chariot Inn. It was usually used for cabaret.

Hot Press asked me to put the show together. So I did. It sold out and was totally stuffed on the night.

All was good until it was time for XTC to go on. I assumed someone from Hot Press would announce them on stage. I honestly hadn't given it any thought. Close to showtime I couldn't find any Hot Pressers. The crowd were going apeshit. They wanted XTC. Even though I'd been in the biz for years I'd never announced anyone on. The crowd wanted the band. The band wanted to play. It was beginning to feel like it could go off at any minute.

Thinking back, I suppose I was filled with what must have been a shyness that most people wouldn't associate with me, combined with loads of self-consciousness and lots of self-doubt.

Every minute that went by sent the crowd wilder and the band were becoming more frustrated. They just wanted to play.

There was only one thing for it. XTC were ready. The crowd was ready. I ran from the back of the stage to the front and grabbed a microphone. Before I said a word, something happened that I should have expected but came as a complete surprise. I was gobbed. Seriously gobbed. I was instantly covered with the biggest gulliers and greenest and slimiest snot I'd ever seen… or felt. Honestly, it was horrific. Somehow, I said, "XTC" and they came on and played a blinder. What a great band – in the times before social distancing.

Terry O'Neill, promoter

INSPIRED BY PIL, DUBLIN 1979

The Sex Pistols disintegrated a few days after their gig at the Winterland, San Francisco. Johnny Rotten returned to London to his house in Gunter Grove, Chelsea, which he had just bought before his American tour with The Sex Pistols.

Here, he formed a new band, Public Image Limited, with Keith Levene on guitar and Jah Wobble on bass. He went back to his original name, John Lydon.

The three spent a lot of time in Gunter Grove listening to dub reggae through Lydon's huge speakers while planning what music they were going to write and record themselves.

I first saw and heard them on the video for their debut single "Public Image". It starts with a speeded up dub bassline, followed by a chiming glacial guitar with Lydon's vocals drifting beautifully over it. It's a brilliant first single.

Around October/November 1979 while flicking through the NME, I came across a full-page advert for "Metal Box" by PIL. The advert was the handwritten lyrics for the album's songs printed on the whole page. After reading those lyrics I was hooked. And then when I found out it was going to be three 12-inch records in a metal film canister box, well I had to have it.

"Metal Box" was released just before Christmas 1979 and I bought it on the first day it became available in Ireland.

I took it back to my friend's house to play it as his dad had a brilliant stereo to listen to his classical albums.

We opened it up, took out the first record and put it on, and the first song "Albatross" started.

After a few minutes (the song was over 10 minutes long) listening in silence, we stopped the record. We asked each other were we playing the record at the right speed. We had it at 45rpm. So we put it on at 33rpm. No, we were right the first time, 45rpm was the right speed.

We just had never heard any music like it ever before, and it was wonderful.

To this day, it's still one of my all-time favourite albums. There isn't a bad song on it.

It's their masterpiece.

Then in February 1980 I saw PIL playing live on The Old Grey Whistle Test and it was a magical performance. Lydon was wearing a long red coat down to his ankles and singing his lyrics from a music stand, Wobble's trousers were blowing from the sheer volume of his bass amp and Levene was playing his choppy, chiming guitar and his homemade synth noises at the same time.

As John Lydon sang "Hindsight does me no good/Standing naked in this back of the woods/The cassette played poptones".

Then around 1980/1981, I started going to gigs in the Magnet Bar on Pearse Street.

I remember going to see a Mean Features/Nun Attax/Micro Disney gig.

Finbarr Donelly from Nun Attax in an army jumper with his skinhead haircut dyed green, white and orange, Giordai O'Laoghaire from Micro Disney wearing a cool hat with a feather in it playing brilliant spacey guitar riffs and Cathal Coughlan from Micro Disney singing "Let's go down, down to Mitchelstown".

I loved the energy and madness of those two bands.

I also played in the Magnet Bar in a band called Amuse.

The only thing I remember about that night was Finbarr Donnelly sitting at a table in front of the stage moving his head up and down to the music.

Years later, Finbarr Donnelly's band Beethoven and my band Into Paradise were the first two releases on Setanta Records.

Dave Long, Into Paradise

JOCK'S PUNK FOOTBALL TEAM, LONDON 1979

With the football season hopefully returning, my story is how I managed with punk rock and footie to put together a combination of famous punk and rock heads combining in a Christmas Day concert at my club in London. Here we go… Over a few beers at my Studio 21 London club I discovered that Phil Lynott, Steve Jones, Paul Cook, Billy Idol, Steve Severin, Paul Young, Richard Jobson and many more wanted me to form a football side for charity. So I did. We played at Spurs ground, Chelsea, Middlesbrough, Capitol Radio and I discovered just how good these guys were. Philo was made captain, wow what a player. Some of the guys like Billy Idol played in make-up as they came direct from TV studios. Wow what a player, we WON everything. We played in the green of Ireland, raised lots for good causes like this book is doing for the NHS. We played matches against the Met Police, various pub sides, and in the big grounds against BBC etc

The climax to all this was when I did the impossible. On Christmas Day, the club was opened, and I put together The Sex Pistols with Billy Idol on vocals, Youth (then in the Bollock Brothers, now Killing Joke) on bass, with back-up from the Bollock Brothers and the very first performance of Bananarama in public. Their second gig was with us at Futurama with Joy Divison!

Back to the gig, only brave souls made this historic concert as with the early lockdown of everything on Christmas Day, there was no transport of any kind. They had to walk to come. Numbers played were "Roadrunner", "Did U No Wrong", "God Save the Queen", "One of the Lads", "No Fun", "Waiting for the Man" – I have it on film, alas quality not great, but working on it.

Football and punk rock and one very historic concert.

Jock McDonald, The Bollock Brothers

THE CURE, AUSTRALIA AND NEW ZEALAND 1980

Our first tour in Australia was a mammoth affair if just in concerts. Twenty-three shows over pretty much the whole continent with the exception of Darwin and Alice Springs, I suppose.

We played in Sydney at the Bondi Lifesaver, a revelation to us nice proper English boys. There was so much beer drunk they had to use a mini backhoe to clear the empty, crushed cans off the floor afterwards. A brief trip to some hippies in the middle of nowhere (hello Bangalow), and then south to Melbourne. Playing the Crystal ballroom, in amongst the Old Victorian buildings. Next to Adelaide, most notable to me for a day off to relax, which we did. We were the only patrons in the cinema on a wet Thursday afternoon watching Can't Stop the Music – yes that Village People movie.

But my most vivid memory for several reasons was Perth at the end of our Antipodean sojourn.We played a nightclub and had our first stage invasion for quite a while by some skins. We should have guessed what was coming when the lady owner asked us before we went on if we "Could try and keep them [the audience] off the tables". After the predictable skirmish on the stage, we apologised to her for not being able to do so. "No worries," she said, "they don't think they've had a good time unless they get a guitar round the chops!"

However, the real memory I still carry from that tour was the last week we were in Perth waiting for a flight to go back to England. We stayed in a small hotel on the coast. Every day for that long wait to go home, we walked and ran along the seashore, jumping with glee into the pure white soft sand on the edge of the Indian ocean. Nobody was visible for miles in either direction on the shore. The water lapping warm on our pale-skinned feet, we strolled along, sockless, talking and laughing about the previous three weeks' adventures. But mostly, we just stood on that soft white sand, staring at the sea and marvelling at our incredible good luck at being 21 and here on the other side of the planet doing just what we had always dreamed about.

Laurence Tolhurst, The Cure

THE SCIENTISTS, PERTH 1980

I recently took an astrology reading and the astrologer asked if anything hugely significant had happened in my life around the age of 16. I thought for a moment – nobody died or was born, we didn't move house, I didn't play the saxophone yet … just sweet 16 at high school with the boyfriend I thought I'd be with forever (we're still friends, so in a sense I was right). Just high school, my boyfriend, and PUNK ROCK. Punk rock, I told him, and we both laughed.

After the reading, my mind kept going back to that and I came to feel that my initiation into the world of punk rock at 16 was in fact no joke and has played out enormously in my life for the ensuing decades, even though I'm more on the easy-listening tip nowadays. I'm talking about the most crucial, essential sensibility at the heart of punk rock, an invisible significator I pocketed early on which gave me confidence walking down the street in Perth and confidence walking into the Governor Broome or Hernando's Hideaway, the strictly-for-initiates punk rock venues which were home to a thriving and innovative live music scene. It later transported me to the stage of CBGB's.

I don't really remember where I first saw The Scientists, but I think it was at the Governor Broome Hotel, a seedy affair under the Horseshoe Bridge in Perth. Roe Street was dangerous, known for streetwalkers and drug traffic. Getting out of a car and walking through that neighbourhood in pointy shoes and some kind of outfit which looked completely obnoxious to almost everyone felt like walking on air. Entering the club, paying the $3 cover to the groovy guy at the door in a white leather jacket and going into the back room where the show was felt as exclusive as it must have felt to be allowed into Studio 54, not that I was thinking about Studio 54 whatsoever at the time.

The Scientists were, and have been on and off for 40 years, a great band. Kim Salmon is a true rock star – a great guitarist who prolifically writes great songs and sings them passionately and charismatically. Seeing The Scientists at the Governor Broome is a rite of passage I'm really glad came my way. I was obsessed and at some point I'd see them every Friday and Saturday night.

The line-up I loved was a later one, the trio of Kim Salmon, Ian Sharples and James Baker. I knew I wanted to have a band, but couldn't really picture what it was like until so much later – I wasn't even a musician yet when I used to see The Scientists, but they certainly inspired me. When I finally started my band Moisturizer in NYC, I'd say our attitude was directly influenced by The Scientists, even though the music was instrumental and there was no guitar.

The atmosphere at the Governor was electric – punks, mods, rockers and skinheads pogoing and doing the swim. Girls with dyed black hair and mini skirts, lads in leather jackets or suits. The band created the perfect sonic installation to contain all that teen angst and energy – even the people in their 20s were teenage dreamers.

By the beginning of 1980, The Scientists left Perth, moved to Sydney and became swampy. They were still great and I saw them on New Year's Eve when they returned.

I moved to Melbourne and became a saxophone player. People often ask me who my influences are; I'd be remiss not to mention Kim Salmon. Later he moved to Melbourne and made Kim Salmon & The Surrealists, and I finally got to play with him before leaving in the early 1990s.

I saw the Swampland version of The Scientists in 2007 at ATP in England and in 2018 at Union Pool in Brooklyn, a club where I've had a weekly gig for over 10 years with Reverend Vince Anderson. It was so amazing to see Kim playing the best versions yet of the songs I loved in my early 20s on the stage where I've stood every Monday night since 2009. Kim Salmon really has made my life more surrealistic.

Moist Paula Henderson, Moisturizer, James Chance and the Contortions, Lubricated Goat, Nick Waterhouse, Burnt Sugar Arkestra

THE RAMONES, DUBLIN 1980

Cabra Grand

Growing up in Dublin in the late 1970s, we were surprising close to the punk rock scene developing in the UK and the States. This is down to some outliers in bands, venues, radio DJs and promoters.

I found it an enabler…. let me do the things I wanted to do, not worry about what others thought or wait for the right moment whenever that might be. Just do it… You can!

The Sex Pistols' "Anarchy in the UK", that stopped me in my tracks … that industrial chug chug of the guitar intro, the sneer… then it all kicked off. It galvanised me to do the things I wanted to.

But it was The Ramones that I fell in love with… their music, the look, the attitude. The songs were stripped down to a primitive driving beat and chord progression that instantaneously made you want to jump around … and smile! Yes, there is something magic about the Ramones and their songs that lifts you. "Gimme Shock Treatment", "Blitzkrieg Bop", "Teenage Lobotomy" etc. Lyrically they're tough, but magical.

When our band started out, the only covers we did were three Ramones songs. Not that they were easy to play (they weren't if you wanted to do it right). We did them because they made us feel great on that stage. And yes, you can get lost in a two-minute song. We tried to get some reflected glory by having our band badges "The Strougers – Faster Than The Ramones". But we weren't really.

We also recorded "Blitzkrieg Bop" coupled with "Teenager In Love" on our first demo tape. It sounded great. A prelude to "Baby I Love You".

So when The Ramones were playing right beside us in the Cabra Grand cinema in 1980, myself and other members of The Strougers – Bitzy Fitzgerald, Peter McCluskey, Denis Rusk – got our tickets.

On the night, after a few pints before the gig, I said to the lads, as you do, let's go and meet The Ramones before the gig, show our badges and tell them about our version of "Blitzkrieg Bop"/"Teenager in Love".

Being a punk, anything is possible, so off we went and I blagged my way into the Grand. They were just finishing the soundcheck. We watched and as they were going back to the dressing room, we just went back with them.

It was surreal in the dressing room. Fairly packed but a small room. There beside us were our heroes (even punks have heroes) warming up for the gig. I distinctly remember the courtesy (a strange word when talking about a punk rock iconic band) of the band to us. But they were! Tommy was warming up by drumming on a normal office desk. Surreal. Dee Dee and Johnny were listening to us… and Joey well Joey was actually listening to me, Bitzy and Pete rabbit on, looking at our badges and pretending to listen to our demo tape! Was he really listening, well he asked about why we coupled "Teenager In Love" with "Blitzkrieg Bop" and liked it.

Then, the gig was to start and we ran to the front of the stage. The Ramones came on to a great reception, Joey strides up to the mic… and says "Hi Dublin, we the Ramones. This is for The Strougers. Take it away, Dee Dee."

He was listening!

I would like to be able to talk about what songs they sang, how good they were etc but from first chord to last we were lost in Ramones magic! We jumped, pogoed, sang cheered and laughed. Then, it was over. Still drunk on that magic and "This is for The Strougers". What a band, what great people and what a night. Later that night, Joey was on the Dave Fanning radio show (it started at midnight then) and Dave mentioned us, and played a Strouger song. Although not "Blitzkrieg Bop"/"Teenager In Love".

If Carlsberg did pre-gigs…

Shay Hiney, The Strougers

THE RAMONES, DUBLIN 1980

It was a Wednesday evening… October 8th, 1980… Ticket price four Irish pounds. Steep enough at the time seeing as it was only one pound 50 pence to see The Clash in TCD three years earlier and The Ramones for three pounds in 1978 in the State cinema. As I approached the gig, the tension was palpable. There had been lots of trouble at punk gigs between rival factions just for the hell of it. Dublin punk gigs were violent affairs in general back then anyway.

As I approached I had to run a gauntlet (like everyone else) of mods and skins who were trying to punch, kick and stab anyone in their midst who didn't look like them. I made it through relatively unscathed. Before the gig started,

I managed to blag my way onto The Ramones tour bus with other members of the band I was in at the time (The Strougers). We gave Joey a demo tape that included some Ramones songs and one of our badges which read "The Strougers – Faster Than The Ramones". They were chuffed that anyone would cover their tunes.

Later as The Ramones took to the stage, Joey grabbed the mic and said "Hey, we're The Ramones and this one's for The Strougers. Take it, Dee Dee, one two three four…"

Cue my jaw dropping to the floor where it stayed for the next 20 songs.

It was a night to remember plus the four stabbings and unnecessary aggro after.

Bitzy, The Strougers, The Lee Harveys

THE PASSIONS, NEWPOP FESTIVAL, ROTTERDAM 1980

September 7th

One of my favourite gigs The Passions played was right after a big upheaval, Claire had left, we'd been dumped by Fiction, and then we found David or he found us. Polydor signed us to a singles deal. And we got invited to play at the NewPop festival in Holland. I think we were first on in the afternoon. But on the same stage as The Ramones were going to be on later, massively exciting, especially as we had all access passes and so were going to be able to watch from the sectioned-off area right in front of the stage. (I remember feeling the ground move during their set.) But back to our own, the awesome sight of 80,000-plus people. We were really on form that day, then suddenly I broke a string on the only guitar I had. Gary "the Healing Gleam" our roadie and I looked at each other in horror. Then this kind man from Q-Tips, who were waiting by the stage to go on next, handed up his white – a Gretsch or a Gibson or a Guild – hollow-body guitar for me to play. And we finished up to great applause.

Barbara Gogan, The Passions

THE DB'S, STOCKHOLM 1980

Possibly the single greatest experience I had was when my band The dB's were sent to Stockholm where our debut album "Stands for Decibels" had made a momentary foray into the national top 10 in 1980. We were just four transplanted southern boys who'd made our way to New York in the late 1970s, just a little late for the first wave of bands like Television and The Talking Heads. We got to be part of the next batch of bands as we improved our sound and learned dozens of new songs we'd been writing. We wangled a recording contract with an English record company called Albion, and they, in turn, got the record released in Scandinavia.

It was our first trip to Stockholm, and we were very excited for our reception to the record. We were booked at the Göta Lejon, a beautiful theatre built in the 1920s; it was the biggest place we'd played by far, unless you count the Rainbow Theatre in London where we'd played the miserable Taking Liberties "extravaganza" to a nearly empty and freezing cold building on February 21st.

But the Göta Lejon was sold out, and we commended the Swedish people for their obvious good taste in music for having bought tickets. We played a fantastic, tight set, and the audience loved us. It was like we had found our footing on the ladder of success, and we soaked in every second of adoration.

After the show, the record company took us out to dinner at a club where a former backing musician for Bob Dylan, maybe Rob Stoner, was playing with his band. We had been plied with rich food and alcohol, and we were inspired to heckle the band as we thought of ourselves more aligned to punk rockers than "older guys" like him. We also stole a huge pepper mill from the table, the location of which is now unknown.

The tour continued, and while the response elsewhere wasn't nearly as luminous as that of the Swedish audience, we were riding on the leftover elation from Stockholm all the way home to New York.

Our first show back in town was singularly underwhelming, and The dB's were faced with the reality that our hardest work was still ahead. But we always treasured that show in Stockholm.

When I went back to the Göta Lejon years later in the employ of Hootie and the Blowfish (with whom I've played keyboards and guitars for over 25 years), I told them I'd played there years before. Someone found a poster of our show there and gave it to me, a lovely souvenir of a fantastic night.

Peter Holsapple, The dB's

X/THE REPLACEMENTS, CLEVELAND 1980

Here's one of many "favourite show" memories. I was 14, and my favourite band was X. Matt Fields' mom (the "cool" mom with the monstrous vinyl collection) took us all in a van to see them on the "More Fun In The New World" tour. I think it was me, Matt, maybe David Wain and Scott Harbert, the guitar player for my eighth-grade band Immoral Minority. We were living in Cleveland, sitting in the back trembling with excitement, holding hands and singing every X song. The show was in an old theatre with built-in seating. The audience was sitting down very polite and adult during the opening act. I saw John and Exene standing behind the bass rig and immediately got out of my seat and walked to the very front of the stage to try and be as close as possible to my heroes, and maybe get their attention. The lead singer of the opening band, who were all sitting on stools, stopped mid-song, looked down at me, and shouted "Hey kid, waddaya think this is, a rock'n'roll show?" I was mortified and fled back to my seat. I remember thinking the band was pretty good, even though I was there for one reason, and one reason only. A year or so later, the album "Let It Be" came out and changed all of our lives (and music), at which point I realised the guy who had shouted me down was Paul Westerberg, the opening band The Replacements. In subsequent years I would get to work with John and Exene from X, and had a friendly acquaintance with Tommy Stinson (who can't have been much older than me playing bass at that magnificent show). But I've never met Paul and would probably be as in awe/terrified now as I was then. That was a damn good show.

Craig Wedren, Shudder To Think

BLACK FLAG/DOA, LA 1980

The way I looked at playing music as a kid, even as a teenager, I felt rock music was really exciting. I wanted to be a musician. I used to be a drummer but my buddy, Dimwit, God rest his soul, was a better drummer so I said, "Right, I'll learn to play guitar." I started that when I was about 18. It was a real charge – that energy that you got off the fans. And the more that you got out of them, the more that you gave back. They really feed into each other. Then when we got to playing punk rock around 1977, when we were 19 or 20, the energy was even higher because people felt that they wanted to go crazy – break the rules of society and be free. Music is a great expression of that and that's why I still love playing music because you get that energy back off the crowd. One gig really stands out.

We played with Black Flag in Los Angeles in Hollywood. The show was at the famous Whisky A Go Go. We had been down there before, playing LA with Black Flag, I think at the Hong Kong Café and so few people showed up that at the end of the show, we're 1,400 miles from home and we had just being playing a couple of shows and didn't get paid much. Chuck from Black Flag came up to us after the show and said "Well, we split the money evenly between the four bands. Here's your share, you got $8." Okay, that should take us about one-tenth of the way home with the cost of gasoline! So we went back home.

Later our manager said "Black Flag want you to come back down and do this show at the Whisky." This was two weeks later. And I said "We were just down there and we got $8 we pretty much starved." He said "No, no, no this will be good. They'll give you $175." Oh okay. This was 1980 and bands were getting paid nothing.

So we drove down, Chuck, Randy, Dave and I. We didn't have a van, so we crammed into this Volkswagen that I had. It was so small we had the bass case in the gap between the guys in the back and where the gear shift is. It was just crammed. So we haul down there – it takes 30 hours or so. We drive down non-stop.

We get there and Chuck says "It's great you guys came to do this, thanks so much – but we sold out the first show, so we're putting a second show on. And I'll give you another $175. You'll get $350 as we know we'll sell out the second show too." Great, great.

We go along and the place is packed. It holds 400 people or something like that. We do the show, Black Flag plays and then they go to empty the venue so the next show can start, and people can start getting in.

What happens is there's a mob of people waiting outside for the second show. And then there's a mob of punks that come out from the first show. So there's hundreds of punks at the corner of Hollywood and Vine or whatever corner the Whisky is on. About 700 or 800 punks on the sidewalk and an LAPD cruiser comes by. A couple of the guys from Black Flag and DOA are watching out from the windows and door of the club and a punk throws a beer bottle and it crashes on the fender of the police cruiser. And, of course, all the punks start cheering.

The cop car turns around and comes back. And a few more bottles start to fly. The police think better of two cops facing 600 punk rockers, so they take off. A couple more cars come by and of course they get beamed by beer bottles too. People are cheering and chanting and all that kind of thing because the track record that the LAPD had was really, really abysmal. Not just with punk rockers, but with citizens in general. Unfortunately, they had a really terrible reputation that was completely well-deserved. Forget about "protect and serve".

We're just sitting there waiting and the mob is just milling around. Maybe about 20 minutes later – people hadn't come into the Whisky for the second show yet – a helicopter appears overhead. LAPD were really famous for using their choppers to co-ordinate crowd control or whatever they're doing. Then from all four directions, about 30 or 40 LA cop cars come and block off all the streets from either end. And then about 50 cops come out with billy clubs. Nothing happens initially.

What happens finally is the head cop walks right by everybody and into the middle of the intersection. Everybody is watching. There's nobody throwing beer bottles by this point. The head cop looks at everybody then he puts a shotgun over his head and slowly turns around to make sure everybody sees the shotgun. Like: "Okay you guys want to mess with us 'here's what we have'."

At that point, when he finishes circling around, that must have been the signal. Because the police attacked and started wading into people. Of course, all the punks tried to escape down the side streets – but they were clocked off by these cop cars and with more cops arriving and a helicopter overhead co-ordinating what we would call the "police riot".

It just ended up being complete mayhem. Obviously, there was no second show. They next day the news was all over it "the first rock'n'roll riot since The Doors in 1966!" That type of thing.

It was just an example of the police going too far. And you know what, flip the calendar forward 40 years and there you are today.

Joe Keighley, DOA

BLACK FLAG, US

My favourite gig was the first time I saw Black Flag. I had been to plenty of hardcore shows at that point, but nothing matched the intensity of Black Flag. The whole band went off and played like it was their last day on Earth. Henry Rollins was incredible. When he sang it was like his heart was coming out of his throat. I left that show black and blue from dozens of stagedives, but I was sweaty and happy. Black Flag were a huge influence on me when I started to play in bands myself. They taught me to throw everything you had into the music and let yourself be carried away with the passion and energy.

John Porcell, Judge, Youth of Today, Bold, Shelter

THE ONLY ONES, NEWCASTLE 1980

One of the best concerts I ever saw was as a 17 year old at Newcastle's Mayfair watching The Only Ones. There was something about Peter Perrett that reminded me of Syd Barrett and I'd just heard "Another Girl Another Planet" on the radio. The guitar just stood out a mile, it sounded better than anything I'd ever heard and I had to get to see them. I remember watching the first part from the balcony left wing but soon needed to get down near the front. There was new wavers, die-hard punks, students, thugs. All kinds in the front crowd zoo, but I was skinny then and slid my way through to the front right and settled over at John Perry's end.

It was the white Strat that drew me in, looking a tad bashed like it had seen lots of gigs. The excitement in my young bones was unexplainable, John looked drunk actually, although in later life he assured me he wasn't. But whatever he was on certainly wasn't sabotaging his playing skills, as he played a blinder. I was watching like a hawk, totally inspired. The place was heaving and the stage was shaking and I kept wondering if his drink would vibrate off the top of his Fender Twin, but it didn't.

This performance sealed the deal for me. I took it away with me deep, it is still in me as I write. I needed to be there that night, just like a young warrior seeing the medicine man, we get changed forever. I could never have believed that three years from then I would be standing on stage in the same spot and the first person I thought of was John.

Fast forward 40 years and I end up doing a wee fun gig in London with John. It was so exciting to meet him. I never thought I would, I met an educated, sincere soulful man, with time for everyone. He liked his cricket and would answer every question about guitars I could throw at him. Anna and I were very taken with him. As a 56 year old, to stand and play a few tunes with John Perry took me right back to being a teenager and was a total honour.

A few months later, my band The Daintees played the venue under Chelsea Football Stadium and invited John as our special guest. He came along with his lovely partner Elvera. We learned "Another Girl Another Planet" and invited John up. We would not do that for many artists, but for John yes, it was the best feeling listening to him playing those great lines. And that evening, just like the first time I saw him, will remain forever in my heart. Thanks John. And hey, it's nice when your heroes turn out to be decent too.

Martin Stephenson, The Daintees

THE 4"BE2"S/MICRODISNEY, CORK 1980

The Kampus, the Arcadia Ballroom, opposite the train station of Cork city, 1980/1981, any Saturday you might pick. You will find a steady flow of Cork youngsters making their way to the colossal drafty ballroom which sat against a backdrop of granite rock on the Glanmire Road.

The headline act might surprise you. The show bands were still kicking around but not showing up at the Arc any more. 1980 was an eclectic moment in "alternative" music and the bands Elvera and Andy attracted to The Arc reflected this. Prince Far I, The Distractions, UB40, The Specials, The Fall, Culture, The Cimarons, The Only Ones, Hawkwind and the 4"Be2"s.

That last one is not so familiar. Well the band were the brainchild of Jock McDonald and John Lydon's brother, Jimmy, who did lead vocals. They were a punk funk group who revelled in lad culture and arguably created the template for the Happy Mondays who emerged seven years later in Manchester

On that autumn evening in the Arc, our band, Microdisney, were opening for Jimmy and Jock. The 4"Be2"s had got into a spot of bother on the previous night at the show in Dublin. Jimmy's brother, John, was along for the ride and to join in on a few songs. For one reason or another Johnny Rotten (Lydon) was coaxed into a confrontation and ended up in Mountjoy Prison.

The 4"Be2"s did not travel with back line and on showing up early evening for a soundcheck put in a polite request to use the support band's backline. We obliged, though I was nervous that my ancient AC30 (split head) might not survive the ripping the guitarist might deliver. All was good on the night. The 4"Be2"s enjoyed some healthy banter with the audience. They stumped and laughed and took plenty of swigs from cans of lager, which was teasing to an audience who had to make do with coke and crisps. The ballrooms were always dry venues.

The audience. Here we go.

The first few rows would be Cork's Daunt Square punks, in rain macs and gelled hair. Behind them would be curious students, in assorted used garments and badges. Behind them were the hippies, still bemused and trying to work out what the future might hold for them.

The 4"Be2"s on reflection were channelling PIL quite covertly, a recipe of dub and blitz rock, and a toasting hectoring vocal. I didn't come away from the evening with those thoughts – this is pure reflection and, let's face it, it's an examination of history.

It was a lovely odd moment in Cork's cultural history. A jumble of incongruous elements.

In the 1980s, UK music was a thriving industry and relatively minor acts could make a living from touring. There was a minor celeb culture created by a buzzing UK music press. The Arc was very much on the circuit at the time.

However, the city was provincial and nicely odd, and the audience brought that oddness to those shows which perplexed the visiting acts. These bands were used to the conformity of the club shows and the student union Ents gigs. Serious young people, formalised dressing, negotiated responses.

Cork was unique and maddening and a place with a living narrative. The city was trying to respond to change, but the drag from the tropics of west Cork provided a remoteness which was so curious and wonderful it should have been bottled. I'm sure these shows were unforgettable for the UK acts flitting in and out from Thatcher's traumatised 1980s Britain.

Sean O'Hagan, Microdisney, The High Llamas

THE PASSAGE, KRISTIANSAND 1981

Touring Scandinavia, we hit the bottom of Norway at the port of Kristiansand. It was a cute town of coloured wooden huts set in a rigid grid. Our gig was held in an all-comers venue that was part-restaurant, coffee shop, bar, waiting room, hotel, theatre, public toilet and concert hall, rather like those saloons in cowboy films.

We unloaded our gear through the front door, to find in the restaurant an American country-and-western husband-and-wife duo in Stetsons, singing maudlin songs to the slippery sounds of a steel guitar. There was no one in the restaurant but them. It turned out that our per diem meal was ready for us in that very place, and so we became their audience: verse after verse of gloom and melancholy to accompany our pizzas. We thought, "Gloom, melancholy? We can outdo you, y'all." Nice couple though. They told us that Kristiansand had a habit of catching fire, that Trotsky stayed there in the 1930s, and warned us that our audience would be very rowdy and very drunk.

And they were right. But the kids were open to our sounds, some throwing epileptic shapes while others shoe-gazed, and we found ourselves in the centre of a Norwegian-beer-soaked happening. After the gig, we towed our gear back through the front door to the van or at least we tried to. Stopping all movement there, apart from themselves, was a punter and a bouncer having a vicious fist fight. As soon as they saw us they stopped, patted us on the back, praised the gig, and keep the door open as we proceeded out between them. Once we had passed the door they returned to their berserk brawl, blood on the floor. Three or four times it was Biff-bam-pow! Great gig! Oof-aargh-krunch! Everybody left fulfilled.

Richard Witts, The Passage

BLACK FLAG, NEW YORK 1981

Peppermint Lounge

I got into punk rock when I was 12 years old. At first I was a big fan of groups like Kiss and Aerosmith, thinking that that was the heaviest stuff out there. But then I saw The Sex Pistols on a TV awards show and I realised that there was something much more going on. I couldn't really explain it, but it somehow spoke to me. It felt right and it made me feel like I wasn't alone. I began listening heavily to The Ramones, The Clash and The Dead Boys as well. Nobody in my neighbourhood seemed to like this kind of music. In fact they hated it, and began to hate me too. I started going into the city to CBGB's and to cool little record stores downtown. Most of the people I met down there told me that I had missed it all – it was over, punk rock was dead. But I still craved something fast, raw and new. Rockabilly, new romantic or that funk art thing that was happening at the time was not going to satisfy my teenage angst.

Then one night I happened to see a late-night TV special about West Coast punk and a band called Black Flag. There it was! Nastier and wilder and more in your face than any of the late 1970s punk bands I had been listening to. I had to see them. Their records were hard to find but I saw in the Village Voice newspaper that they were playing a show at the Peppermint Lounge in the city and I just had to go, even if I had to sneak out of my apartment and break my curfew. I went by myself and waited for hours until they were about to come on. In the lobby, I met some kids that had come all the way from DC to see the band, and they had all these cool badges and things on their jackets. They had shaved heads and chains for belts, cloths wrapped around their boots, but they were not skinheads. They had their own thing going on.

Finally, the band hit the stage sometime after 1am. The bass player, Chuck Dukowski, was pacing around in a circle like a tiger in a cage, banging his bass with his fist. Robo the drummer was playing this clear lucite kit, doing a slow but very tense drumroll pattern. The guitarist was making all these fucked-up sounds that I had never heard a guitar do before. The singer had on a flannel shirt and white tube sox pulled up over his blue jeans. He was shouting, "I am not a machine! I am not a machine!" over and over again. It was kinda disturbing, scary and noisy as fuck. I didn't know what was going to happen next. Suddenly the band kicked into a full-on blast beat, and the DC kids started dancing down low like slow skanking crabs and began to wreck everyone in this packed trendy club. There were a couple of guys there that I knew from the local scene that could clearly hold their own amongst this full-on creepy crawl invasion.

Black Flag sounded like no one else I had ever heard before. They didn't care to dress up in punk rock fashion. They were just who they were, these guys from Southern California who didn't give a shit. Every dissonant note was from the heart as if they would die doing it. It was a window into what was about to explode in my life and with my own band in that coming year – new way of moving, thinking, playing and living. Some of the DC guys I had met that very night would play in bands like SOA, Minor Threat, and eventually Fugazi. One of the dudes would even end up becoming the next singer for Black Flag.

Jesse Malin, D-Generation

THE KINKS, DUBLIN 1981

The mid-1970s is a time I associate with violence. Violence in the North, violence on the terraces, violence at the disco, violence in the home.

Punk rock was an antidote to all of that. When punk came along, it was the moment for me when the 1970s burst from black and white into colour. The media tried to paint this new music as some sort of threat to society but the kids knew instinctively that punk culture was an onslaught of the imagination against those fractious, conservative times. The flares and long hair of the boot boys was on the way out to be replaced by the pinks and greens and yellows and leather and safety pins of the young punks.

I was only 11 in 1977 so was far too young to be a punk and the arguments I had with my parents would've been about no longer having to wear short trousers rather than about nose piercings, but the spirit of punk had visited me and I was a believer.

Over the next few years, through the influence of the DIY culture of punk, music started to become something that happened on your street, in your estate, on your doorstep. There was a punk band from around the corner called The Threat who let us kids sit in on their rehearsals in the singer/guitarist's garage. There was an older boy called David whose family had moved back from England. One day David told me in his exotic English accent that he had joined a band called The Virgin Prunes. He also told me not to call him David anymore as his new name was Mary. Okay so. That was punk.

The New Wave that followed was more my time and one band in particular caught my imagination: The Jam. Before The Jam, I was really trading on my older brothers' tastes; they'd introduced me to The Pistols, The Clash, The Rats etc but The Jam were my band and their third album "All Mod Cons" was my musical coming of age.

It's hard now to put into words my feelings as a young kid but "All Mod Cons" spoke to me in a way that no record up to that point had. It was aggressive and spiky as you'd expect from a record of the time ("A' Bomb in Wardour Street"), but was also incredibly musical and lyrical ("Down in the Tube Station at Midnight"), and even reflective and sentimental ("Fly" and "English Rose"). What intrigued me most though was that the precocious singer/guitarist Paul Weller had written all the songs on the album. All the songs bar one, "David

Watts", which the sleeve of the album attributed to a Ray Davies. A bit of investigation led me to purchasing a 20 greatest hits of The Kinks. Although their music sounded quaint and vaudevillian compared to The Jam, it was obvious that "Mr Clean" from "All Mod Cons" was a punked update of "A Well Respected Man".

I waited in vain for The Jam to come to Dublin, but in 1981 The Kinks were playing the National Stadium and myself and a friend from school got tickets for what would be my first-ever concert.

The gig itself is a bit of a blur but some memories remain: queueing up outside the Stadium wondering if we'd be turned away for being underage; the local support act introducing themselves as The Kinks to the amusement of the crowd; Ray Davies teasing the mods at the front of the stage by singing fa-fa-fa-fa-fa-fa-fa-fa before going into a different song, although they did eventually play "David Watts".

What I took from The Jam and The Kinks was that the musical vignette was the greatest of street art forms. There was something magical to me about songwriters. Imagine writing a song. Imagine having your name after a song on a record. Now that was something to aspire to.

I eventually got a cheap bass guitar and formed a band with my best friend Gary. I had no musical knowledge or talent but I'd been brought up on the "give it a go" attitude of punk, so that's what I did. I remember our lead guitarist Liam asking me what I wanted from the band and from music. Despite my musical limitations I knew exactly what I wanted. "To write 10 good songs," I responded. I'm still playing music and at an age that would horrify any young punk, but the aim is still the same: to write 10 good songs.

Ken O'Duffy, songwriter

THE MEKONS, LONDON 1981

I have seen 1,000s of bands so this was hard. I was very surprised by my choice having been lucky enough to see The Clash, Nirvana, Johnny Cash and most of the bands that I have ever wanted to see. Although cross that I have never seen The Smiths, X-Ray Spex, The Slits and Magazine, I thought I would choose a gig like Pulp at Glastonbury in 1995 which is famous for how great it was (I still taunt my partner for going to see Tricky instead).

The gig I have chosen though is seeing The Mekons in 1981 for the first time at an unknown venue in London. My boyfriend of the time, as well as repeated plays by John Peel, meant I was in love with their single "Where Were You?" and desperate to see them play it in front of me. All I remember is dancing furiously in the front row and developing a bit of a crush on the floppy-haired singer Tom. I was so thrilled by the gig, didn't even mind the two-hour wait for the night bus home. Rather drunk and overexcited, not helped by my parents leaving me alone at home for the fortnight, I passed out in my front garden clutching the set list given to me by the band. Next morning about 6am I sheepishly let myself in my home and then spent the next decade going to see the Mekons and Three Johns as much as I could. Still wish I had that set list...

Karen Amsden, Hagar The Womb

POISON GIRLS, BELFAST 1981

Will the real Christ please stand up.

My excitement was palpable, catching the Saturday morning bus into Belfast city centre with my mates. It was just six days before Christmas.

On arrival we joined the procession of punks bound for the A Centre in Lower North Street where Poison Girls were playing.

Once inside I watched support acts Just Destiny and Stalag 17. I even managed a chat with singer Vi Subversa prior to them playing.

This was a daytime gig so all the windows in the venue were blacked out to make it dark inside. There were no pews, so before Poison Girls took to the "stage" (there wasn't one), I made my way right to the very front, and stood directly in front of Richard Famous, so that I didn't miss a note.

Even an irritating female, shouting for "Persons Unknown" after every song couldn't spoil my enjoyment. Eventually the band bestowed their most popular song on her and she was quiet. Halle fuckin' lujah. It was a moment to treasure, missed by persons unconscious slumped with glue bags on the floor.

This gig was an awakening to lots of those present and the political impact of this band still resonates today.

I'd been writing to Poison Girls on a regular basis. I'd instantly know their letters on my hall floor as they always placed the stamp on the envelope upside down.

However, I never ever expected to see them play live.

Punk rock. You ridiculously unpredictable brilliant bastard.

Sean O'Neill, Spit Records, writer, co-author It Makes You Want to Spit!: The Definitive Guide to Punk in Northern Ireland

POISON GIRLS, DUBLIN 1981

Lourdes Hall, Sean MacDermott Street, winter

Picture the scene. You're a 15-year-old schoolboy. You have formed a deep routed love of bands like Crass and Poison Girls. You find inspiration in their ethos, beauty in their cacophony, and you are starting to realise you're an individual rather than an outsider. And you know that you have to find a way to express your outlook on life and not be worried that others disagree. You don't think you'll ever meet your inspirations, and then the postman changes your world.

For me punk was a game-changer. The first music that I liked. The first scene I could identify with and the first influence that I allowed to shape my life. It was a realisation that things can happen on your own terms, that everyone else isn't necessarily right, and even if they are there's no blame in being wrong.

In 1978 or 1979 I had latched onto everything that Crass and their counterparts had issued. Unlike bands like The Clash, Sex Pistols, Buzzcocks or The Damned, Crass seemed to speak to me and seemed to represent feelings and opinions I hadn't realised existed. I didn't agree with everything that they said, but what they did say was so important and said in such a way that it didn't matter if you agreed. You listened, you read, you absorbed and you formed your own opinions. I had begun conversing with several of the bands from that scene, writing letters, asking questions, seeking information and always receiving a friendly and personal response. Hardly a day went by without the arrival of a package, a cassette, a fanzine or a record to my house that I would hoover up when I came home from school. But nothing could have prepared me for the letter received from Poison Girls on a winter's morning informing me that they were playing in my town in two days' time!

Poison Girls… my town… my invite… my dream come true to a certain degree.

On the day of the gig I found that none of my friends were allowed to go. My sister agreed to drive me there and wait in the car knitting (my Dennis the

Menace jumper) while I went to it. To a certain degree I can be quite shy so, as a 15 year old, going to a show in a local hall on my own was a pretty daunting thing. But in I went, paid my £1.50, took a free cup of tea and stood at the back of a cavernous church hall watching the characters and visually intimidating punk rockers socialise and interact with each other.

There was no doubt I was an outsider. There was no doubt I was one of the youngest people here. There was no doubt I was alone.

But equally, I felt like I was a part of this, not apart from it. I felt safe, I felt comfortable and I felt at home.

A few minutes later I spotted Richard Famous wandering through the crowd to get himself a cup of juice. I stopped him and told him who I was.

Bear in mind Poison Girls had been a top five indie chart band for several years. They had toured with Crass. They had sold 1,000s of records. They had graced the cover of Sounds. They had featured in the NME. They had been on television nationwide. They were a big band. So for the guitarist to stop to chat to me and to start off with "I'm so glad you got my letter" was something that was very special. We chatted about guitars and how I wanted to get a band together but was finding it hard to find people who shared the same idea as me. He told me to stick with it and when I had the right people there I would know it as there was no feeling like creating music on your own terms with like-minded people. I knew immediately that I had to follow this through. Sure enough, a month or so later I joined the first line-up of Paranoid Visions and have remained there to this day.

The gig itself was awe-inspiring. Sadly, a few years later I read that the band felt it was a bit of a cold and emotionless experience, but that wasn't my feeling. The warmth of the artists, the camaraderie of the audience and the sense of belonging changed me forever.

Peter Jones, Paranoid Visions, FOAD Records, Rotator Records

HANOI ROCKS, LONDON 1981

I played in a band called Hanoi Rocks. Our first gig in the UK was in 1981, at the Moonlight Club, a tiny bar somewhere in London. We had prepared for the tour with 40ft-long guitar cables, thinking that the stages in the UK, the mecca of punk, and rock'n'roll, must be big stages. The stage was the size of a postage stamp, there was maybe 10 people in attendance, lapping up their pints at the bar, and not really showing any interest in what was happening on that dark stage, or maybe they did but were too nervous to show it. We looked like five stray dogs in make-up, making the noise of a jumbo jet. We also realised we could reach them with our 40ft-long cables. Off the stage we came, to the horror of the beerlappers. Pints came down from the faces and eyes widened. We proceeded to kick them to get a reaction. The next gig was better.

Sami Yaffa, Hanoi Rocks

THE CLASH, NEW YORK 1981

In the summer of 1981, The Clash played Bond's International Casino in New York. And after the first show was oversold by greedy promoters the band agreed to honour every fan ticket and added more shows to make a total of 17.

Being 16 and eager to join the circus, I would go along to the backstage door and wait for Ray Jordan, band security, to appear and then put on my best "Please, sir..." look on my face (think Oliver) and he would shove me in the backstage door.

But not just me, there were other kids, familiar faces from outside the studio or backstage doors around the city. We were drawn to the band, and the band was fiercely loyal to their fans. We were invited into studio sessions and backstage areas with no caveats except to be respectful of the band as they worked or played depending on the situation.

So armed with my rudimentary film camera I would appear and try and join in. The Bond's gigs were a chaotic explosion of the group's performance through the lenses of New York support bands (Grand Master Flash etc.) and Sandinista representatives. Every night ended with a stage invasion after which the band retreated to the graffiti-covered dressing room to plot the evening's antics. Our lives were changed forever.

The punk rock school invited you in to see what you had to bring to the party and so later that year with the band in Electric Ladyland recording "Combat Rock" I dutifully called the studio and asked to speak to Kosmo Vinyl the band's representative to ask if I could drop by and take some photographs. He said sure and so, when I was waiting outside the studio and Joe Strummer appeared to start his day's work, he asked what I was doing and then summarily shoved me in the door. "Stop standing around, then!" he said, as if to say there's no time to waste. And that was it for me, the ipso facto beginning of a creative journey with Joe and Mick as my spirit guides, instilled with the feeling that if you wanted to create you had a responsibility to follow the truth and hold it up to the light. I try and live up to that everyday after nearly 40 years in the game.

I wish Joe was here to man the ramparts with us now, to fight for the NHS and against the fat cats who endeavour to control our destiny. Nevertheless the fight goes on.

Josh Cheuse, artist, designer, photographer

TAV FALCO'S PANTHER BURNS, NEW YORK 1981

In high school, I was cast in a school play. During rehearsals I got into a scuffle behind the curtain and socked someone on the nose. Sadly, that overreaction shut down the play, and I have felt terrible about it ever since. So, no more fighting backstage.

Let's see. Among other gigs was a 2am set at Danceteria in New York. Jim Fouratt booked Panther Burns in there direct from Memphis. Will Rigby came down from a dusty rehearsal flat in midtown to play with us. Jazz acoustic bassist Ron Miller played the Fotdella, Alex Chilton was flogging lead guitar, and I played my six-string Höfner violin-shaped guitar with the inboard factory fuzz tone. Robert Palmer, pop and jazz writer for the NY Times, whom I knew from Arkansas, joined us on squawking, free clarinet. In those days, the headliner went on at 4am in New York. In this instance, it was Joe King Carasco. Our set turned into quite an atonal art-damage incantation as no one in the audience who were riveted in disbelief nor musicians onstage quite knew what to expect. After it was all over, Fouratt came backstage and berated our performance as perhaps the worst-sounding affair he'd ever heard. Alex took issue with his acerbic remarks, citing the fact that no one had asked for his opinion and spewed such a sulphurous tirade at him that even a sailor would have blanched. But Fouratt went on to say there was someone asking to come backstage named Geoff Travis from some outfit in London called Rough Trade. That post-gig meeting resulted in our first album, "Behind the Magnolia Curtain", which we recorded later in the year in Memphis.

The famous Life Ball in Vienna was perhaps the most catastrophic gig (yet there were others of near-equal magnitude). After a very long European tour in the

1990s, we were booked onto one of three stages at 3am on this benefit gig for Aids research. Our nerves and the emotional morale of the band was under duress. The kind of music we play in Panther Burns is unlike anything ever heard at Life Ball, but that year Amanda Lear was the headline, which was exciting. She was fabulous! So was our band actually, but the organisers and stage crew did not think we were so great. Twenty minutes into our set, the MC came out to my microphone and announced the end of our show. I said, "I beg your pardon, but we are not done playing yet. Get the hell off stage!" He was a husky, black MC from the UK that Life Ball had hired. So I launched into a heavy fuzz-tone rendition of "Bourgeois Blues" from my first album. This is the song I use when somebody is trying to mess with my show, as I had done opening for The Clash in Knoxville in 1984. There we came two rat hairs within causing a riot with that song, but that is another story.

After about 15 minutes of fuzz-tone, the audience at Life Ball were going completely berserk! Actually I remember some people in the audience had come to Vienna from Italy for Life Ball because Amanda Lear was headlining. The Italians knew about Panther Burns, and they were cheering us on mightily. So the block-headed MC comes out again and gets on my microphone. At that moment, I yanked the baseball cap off his head and threw it out in the audience, and then I kicked him right in the seat of his pants. Instantly two stage bouncers grabbed and held me while the MC socked me in the face with his fist. They proceeded to drag me off stage. The blond groupie I had picked up in Hamburg on tour was horrified and would not speak another word to me. Next day, she took the first train back to Germany, and I had to fly to Madrid to appear on FestiMad with a big black eye that impressed everyone.

Tav Falco, Panther Burns

DISCHARGE/THE EXPLOITED/ANTI-PASTI/CHRON GEN/ANTI NOWHERE LEAGUE, LONDON 1981

There have been so many gigs with Chron Gen that were extra special, but the one that probably had the most impact on our future was our first London outing which just happened to be the Apocalypse Now gig at the Lyceum on Sunday, May 24th, 1981. I'd seen many bands at the Lyceum as a fan and was in awe of the place. We had built a good following in the Hitchin/Stevenage/Luton area and were gigging hard, but this was a different level. Our fee was £70 and we had a proper contract for the first time! The line-up was Discharge headlining, then Exploited, Anti-Pasti and Chron Gen. Another unknown band (called The Anti-Nowhere League) were on first. We organised two coaches and a friend borrowed an old ambulance which was our tour bus for the day. We were bricking it. I couldn't eat my nan's legendary Sunday dinner through nerves. With any organised outing like this, the whole day is brilliant; waiting for the tour bus to arrive, loading the gear and then cracking open the beers as we set off for the Lyceum. I will always remember walking around the empty theatre. It was epic! We got a soundcheck which was an experience in itself – everything was so slick and organised. The doors opened and The Anti-Nowhere League did their thing, with Animal wielding a studded axe. Our turn came and we nailed it! It was the gig of our life so far. There were over 3,000 people in the audience and the travelling support did their bit to generate an amazing atmosphere. We got a great reaction from the crowd and came off stage with a natural high that is like no other. Two months later, the Apocalypse Now UK tour was on the road, coinciding with the release of our first EP – "Puppets of War". The remainder of 1981 and 1982 got pretty busy after that.

Glynn Barber, Chron Gen

KILLING JOKE/AZTEC CAMERA/UK DECAY/CHARGE, LONDON 1982

A storm was brewing. None of us knew it at the time, but dark clouds had been building within the band while even their regular fans remained oblivious. Killing Joke had been gathering an enthusiastic following over the previous three years, with UK punk's second wave in full swing, heading up the charts in the punk and alternative press. The group had been holed up in Conny Plank's studio in Cologne working on their third album, "Revelations", and feelings were running high. A Peel session in December 1981 had given a hint of the new material: the now familiar tribal drumming, thundering bass and excoriating guitar that earmarked the Killing Joke sound, Jaz Coleman's grim humour and biting lyrical tirades mocking and accusing in equal parts.

There were four bands on the bill – promoters Straight Music were fond of multiple line-ups, often choosing to put some radically different groups together, presumably as a ploy to widen the pool of potential punters. Unfortunately, in those more chaotic times, that also meant ramping up the chances of a violent clash between different subcultural factions.

Of course, Killing Joke being Killing Joke, all of the above would come together to create the perfect storm. Maybe Jaz Coleman's oft-cited dalliance with the forces of darkness was playing a hand in proceedings – certainly the singer's personal troubles were coming to the fore, as he failed to turn up to a BBC television appearance three days after this gig and was eventually tracked down a few weeks later holed up in Iceland awaiting the end of the world. The Falklands conflict was about to take the UK a couple more minutes closer to midnight, and there was an ominous atmosphere surrounding the gig. As the crowd filed into the Palais the queue seemed to go on forever, which should have set alarm bells ringing somewhere – numbers were well beyond safe limits. As the auditorium became more and more packed, temperatures, and tempers, started to rise.

First up were Charge, who had just released their second single "Destroy The Youth". They were incredibly loud, though their glam tendencies and guitarist Stu P Didiot's preference for wearing stockings and a short skirt set them apart from most of the UK82 crowd. Second act UK Decay were building a solid following, with their classic single "For My Country" positioning them closer to the post-punk/proto-goth crowd than their contemporaries in the burgeoning hardcore scene. So far, so good. The atypical Killing Joke audience, broadly in tune with the post-punk ethos of the time, were sympathetic enough to the opening acts and the mood, though still dark and threatening, hadn't yet spilled over into violence.

All that was set to change with the third act on Straight Music's post-punky variety bill. Alongside Orange Juice and Josef K, Aztec Camera were at the forefront of the "Sound of Young Scotland" proffered by Postcard Records – a triumvirate of jangly new pop acts celebrated in the NME for their "fragile and vulnerable beauty" and making inroads in the national charts. The mismatch was stark – between the brutality of Killing Joke's thunderous war dance and Roddy Frame's delicate melodies, and between the London hardcore punk crowd and these smartly dressed new indie kids on the block. It didn't help matters that the gig was by now running extremely late, and the packed crowd were in no mood to have to wait through another support act before the main event. Aztec Camera took the stage to a hail of gob the like of which I hadn't seen for some time. It was painfully obvious that this wasn't the kind of audience they were used to playing to, nor was this the kind of reception that they were comfortable with. They struggled on through two or three hesitant songs as the gob rained down like Niagara Falls along with an accompaniment of glasses, bottles and other missiles. Their set lasted less than 15 minutes and they were off.

By now, things were getting pretty ugly and the safest way to protect yourself in the packed crowd was to simply go with the flow and defend your own territory, physically if necessary. Killing Joke took the stage and launched into "The Hum". The audience responded enthusiastically and mayhem ensued – it felt like being thrown into a tumble drier full of angry hedgehogs. This wasn't entirely unusual at Killing Joke gigs, but the sense of frustration and discomfort inside the venue made it particularly acute here and now. Funnily enough, a French television crew were filming the show. They can't have known what was going to hit them – quite literally – as the gig went on. Second song, "The Fall of Because", was a fan favourite and it set the crowd into an even more furious frenzy.

When Killing Joke launched into "Wardance", all hell let loose. The barriers surrounding the cameras came crashing down, with the cameramen disappearing into the melee. Jaz Coleman's reaction – "That's the spirit" – only exacerbated things further, while desperate French technicians tried to pull their stricken colleagues and expensive equipment out from the crowd. The band played on – showcasing half a dozen songs from the upcoming "Revelations" album alongside older favourites. "We Have Joy" was a darkly ironic celebration in the circumstances, "Tension: and the blistering "Pssyche" seemed to reflect the energy of the crowd, with set closers "Change", "The Wait" and "Unspeakable" drilling the point home.

Battered and bruised, the audience filed back out into the cold and wet February night unaware that Killing Joke would soon be thrown further into disarray and change was once again afoot. Jaz Coleman disappeared after the following night's gig in Brighton, the group fracturing on the eve of their classic third album release, eventually regrouping without bassist Youth. It was to be another 26 years before the original Killing Joke line-up were to begin working together again. Always teetering on the brink of collapse, Killing Joke were always a thrilling ride: the alchemy of that original line-up always ensured an exhilarating balance between brilliance and chaos.

Footnote: A few high-quality clips from the French television footage can be found on YouTube and are well worth tracking down.

Russ Bestley, designer, writer, The Art of Punk

_____ DUBLIN, JANUARY 1982

"FUUUCCKKK OFFFF."

The singer, defiant, roars into his microphone. It's the "gobbing". He is covered, head to toe. In gob.

The tickets are a surprise birthday present. Favourite band. Our first gig. 17. We meet out front, the place is buzzing, and we don't really know what to expect. It's always been second-hand. Until now.

Records and radio. Peel on a Sunday night or forensically reading the likes of Melody Maker, Sounds, the NME and sometimes even Hot Press. Then there are the opinions of that close friend. Vinyl played in his parents' front living room. Encyclopedic in his knowledge. I listen. Mixed tapes made and shared. Learning then much beyond the pale of my middle-class housing estate and school. Many of the foreign bands, however, seem to always moan about how it's "too expensive to come and tour in Ireland" and, "not worth crossing the Irish Sea". Meaning we are largely left with gigs dominated by showbands, country and western or folk, which, as we all know, only your parents or squares listen to, because it's square. (The post-punk London-born sons and daughters of Irish migrants would soon demonstrate our ignorance of that legacy.)

"Should we go in?"

Bouncers check our tickets. Keeping the purple-coloured stub with the band name and we're in. The noise. Simply so loud. My whole body. A cliché, but my heart is pounding like never before. Now feeling almost external. That bass. Up through the soles of my feet, my legs and into my complete being. The opening band, already on and that's when we see them. Spitting. The crowd right at the front, non-stop, spitting at the lead singer. Their revulsion. Their rejection. He is drenched. The band carry on, a fusion of rock and funk, opening for the new wave band. Straight away, I'm thinking, who thought that was going to work?

"FUUUCCKKK OFFFF."

Looking around, punks, kitted-out devotees, including us, of new wave, cold wave, a few hippies and others. It's hot, it's dark, it's humming. Sweat. Then I notice a mother with her daughter. Both punks. Daughter, maybe 15. This is it. A revelation. Dublin, January 1982 and, for a moment, I try to imagine my mother bringing me to this gig.

That opening band finishes. Stifled applause and shouts of abuse, in retreat, the band slinks but the singer strolls.

"I can't believe we're here," she says. And finally they're there, just back from a tour "of the continent". All exotic. Getting to escape this city, the island.

Then lead guitar and a familiar repetitive two-note riff and it feels like the roof lifts off. Erupting, the crowd pogos and flies and roars, soaring in recognition. Elation. The release. A volume of sound now in my ears, my body, which I have never experienced, until this moment. This moment. Full of boundless pent-up, fuck-off, whatever possibilities. Band plays. Singer charismatic. No lull. No let-up. Never stop. For the first time, pure euphoria. This release. Communal. Looking at each other. A communion. I don't want to be anywhere else.

Mark Curran, researcher and educator studying the impact of predatory global capital

THE CURE/ZERRA ONE, EUROPE 1982

I had just arrived in London.

I got Robert Smith's address through a friend who worked in the audio business.

I wrote a letter to him… yes, an actual letter! I said something along the lines of "You don't know me. My name is Paul, I'm Irish and I've just come over from Dublin. I'm trying to put a band together, but I don't know anybody in London and as you're the person I respect most in music I thought I would write to you." There was more to it than that, but it was along those lines. Whatever I said must have resonated with Robert as he called, and we had a great chat. As you can imagine I was overawed when speaking to him, but I was trying to remain as "normal" as possible so as not to put him off. He asked how he could help and said "if you manage to get some songs recorded I would love to hear them".

I didn't get in touch for at least a year. By then Zerra One was born. It was a two-piece with backing tapes. Guitarist Grimmo (from Dublin) and myself on keyboards and vocals. I waited until we had some home demos of a few songs and I dropped off the cassette to a studio where The Cure were recording. He told me to call him the next day. I was so nervous dialling the number as the recordings were very basic, primitive even. Robert came on the phone, and again I remember it so clearly, I even know what pay phone I was in. He said

"Paul Bell, these are amazing songs."

Shortly after this, Robert asked if we would like to go on tour with them. Obviously I said yes. He then asked how would we travel, did we have road crew and where would we stay? I explained that we would travel in Grimmo's car. We didn't have any road crew so we would set up and take down our gear ourselves. I said we would either use cheap B&Bs, or if we couldn't afford it, we would sleep in the car. To which Robert declared "Okay, that's it. You're doing the tour."

He continued, "You will travel with us in our tour bus. You will stay in the same hotels as us. You'll have the same catering as us. You will have a backline roadie, and use our lighting, monitors and front-of-house sound guys. Oh and you will get the same per diems as we do on the road. Plus you will get paid a fee for playing each night."

After I had picked my jaw up off the floor, I said "Robert, that is amazing and we would love to do it but even if you could give us the tour we would never be able to afford the same hotels or crew as you."

He said, "This is the last time we will speak about this. You will not have to pay a 'buy on fee' to do the tour. You will travel in the same bus as us for free, stay in the same hotels as us for free, get all the catering and backstage drinks and food for free, get your own road crew for free and on top of that you will get the same PDs as us and a fee for performing each night. Do you want to do it?"

Meals! You must remember we were both on the dole in London and living in a squat. We sometimes had to steal bread, milk and eggs from shop deliveries at 5am so the idea of having professional cooks catering for us from the moment we would arrive at every venue until the moment we left that night was mind-boggling, even more so because every meal was amazing.

On the UK tour, we used to hang around chatting and having a few drinks with the band and crew after each show. On one of these nights when everybody except Robert, Grimmo and I had gone to bed, Robert took out a bag of tapes of the tour so far and said, "If you don't mind I would like to listen to Zerra One." Even through my hazy brain I could tell he had said those words, those actual words "If you don't mind I would like to listen to Zerra One." Grimmo always had a ghetto blaster with him so Robert put a cassette of that night's show in it and pressed play. After a few minutes he turned around to me and with a very sad look said, "This is not what you should sound like." I said I thought it sounded really good.

Robert replied "It's good but it should sound better. Our sound engineer is not getting the subtleties or crescendos." The sound man they had detailed to us was their own sound guy. The Cure paid him a bit extra to do the sound for this mysterious, unknown Irish two-piece!

Then I heard the sentence that for me confirmed I had way too much to drink and it was time to get some much-needed sleep. I presumed I really was hallucinating.

"Could I do the sound for you?"

"Robert, before I answer, are you being serious?"

"Yes," was his one-word reply.

"Will you allow me to do your sound for the rest of the tour, providing I don't fuck it up that is?"

"Obviously yes," I answered. "Of course, we would love you to do our sound."

"Okay, that's it. I'll start tomorrow. We can record it. If you don't think it's good then we will leave it but if you like it we can continue."

I have to ask him the big question: "How exactly will this work?"

As quick as a flash, he said: "Let's try this. When we arrive at the venues I'll do our soundcheck first. Then I'll go out front as your sound engineer and soundcheck Zerra One. When it's time for you to go on stage I'll do your sound. There's 30 minutes between bands so I have enough time to get backstage and get ready for us [The Cure]".

I'm now looking at him as if he's mad and find myself saying the words, "That sounds great but how would it work when there's 3,000-5,000 people in these venues? How are you going to do our sound and then get backstage? You would be absolutely mobbed."

He's now smiling even more widely, "Well I've thought about that. What I'll do is wear a very nondescript coat and some kind of cap or hat with my hair pulled up into it. No eye shadow or lippy. I'll get one of the road crew to walk inconspicuously alongside me from the backstage so I can get to the mixing desk in the arena. Then when you're finished, I'll go out the front of the venue and around the outside to the backstage door."

He was really pleased with his plan. I was gobsmacked. All I could say was: "If you really think you want to do that and it's possible then it would be great having you doing our sound".

And so it was to be.

For the next 16 dates in the UK and another seven weeks in across Europe, Robert Smith, the lead singer, guitarist and songwriter from The Cure did the sound every night for the unknown Irish two-piece Zerra One.

It's one of those stories if someone else told me I'm not sure I would believe them, but it's true. Every word!

Paul Bell, Zerra One

THE CLASH, BOSTON 1982

In September of 1982 I escaped from New York City to attend Emerson College up in Boston, Massachusetts, to study acting. Right away I saw that The Clash were in town playing the Orpheum Theatre but of course as Boston was a college town the show was absolutely, positively sold out. Regardless me and a bunch of my juvenile delinquent/ troublemaking punk/skinhead friends went down to the venue to hang around and see if we could sneak in. As the band started playing, we could hear the opening chords of "London Calling" drifting out from the venue and onto the sidewalk. Dejected we were just milling about trying to figure out our next move. At that moment, the road manager for The Clash, the infamous Kosmo Vinyl, approached us and asked (actually it was more like he demanded) why we weren't inside. We told him our situation and he told us to follow him. He walked up to the people that were running the front door and launched into an intense tirade demanding that we all be let into the show for free because "These are the real people that should be inside seeing The Clash, these are our people." After he threatened to pull the plug on the show, they let us into the venue and we proceeded to tear it up and have a great time. It was an incredible night of music and camaraderie and I'll never forget it for as long as I live. To this day when I have a screening for one of my films or if we are playing an Antidote show, I always go outside right before the show starts to see what juvenile delinquents might be loitering about and get them into the venue. It's fucking important to me that they are in the show. Like Joe Strummer said: "Without people, you're nothing."

Drew Stone, Antidote, filmmaker/musician

ATTILA THE STOCKBROKER, NEW ZEALAND 1991

December

New Zealand was the one other country apart from the UK where my debut album "Ranting at the Nation" had been released in 1983: it had had a lot of radio play and I'd been getting sporadic letters and visits from Kiwis ever since. While in Australia I'd been hearing positive reports from over there about the pre-tour publicity – big headlines "Attila on the Rampage" in the national New Zealand Herald and "Attila Invasion of New Zealand" in Wellington's Dominion newspaper being two – and I'd done stacks of radio interviews.

But even so, I was in for a shock. I arrived in Auckland on December 17th, picked up the mandola, cleared customs and wandered towards the arrivals area where I was meeting David Eggleton and Otis Mace. There were a couple of TV cameras waiting at the entrance point: must be someone famous on the flight, I thought to myself. The next thing I knew, this bloke (TV music reporter Dylan Taite it turned out) was in my face with a microphone: "Attila the Stockbroker, welcome to New Zealand!" I was absolutely flabbergasted. There was another TV crew there to film me, and I had a quick chat with them before being taken to a bus and interviewed for the national television news while doing a kind of punk sightseeing tour of Auckland.

Then it was on to the Galaxy Theatre in the Old Customs House building (quite a big place) for a gig that was so packed that I was told people broke down the fire exit doors to get in. I'd brought as much merch as I could take on the plane and it all went at that first show! It was like being a pop star. Utterly bizarre. Later I saw myself on television – someone must have videoed the piece – and read the New Zealand Herald article: everything was rather put into perspective.

I was on the national news following an item about a dispute between two neighbours who couldn't agree which one was legally responsible for cutting down a dangerous tree straddling their properties. And immediately after the very large piece about me in the paper, there were about 16 pages of fat sheep prices. (Does that mean no one likes thin sheep in NZ? That seems a bit unfair...) But there was no doubt that the interest generated from that album release eight years previously had, if anything, grown over the years, and I was very happy: as a DIY poet/performer, to travel to literally the other side of the world and get a reception like that really meant something to me.

Attilla The Stockbroker

THE SID PRESLEY EXPERIENCE, LONDON 1983

It was the summer of 1983, The Sid Presley Experience had been booked to play at Andrew Czezowski's Fridge in Brixton (in its original location above the row of shops across the road from the notorious Brixton police station). The venue had also been the site of the legendary Ram Jam club back in the 1960s.

Also on the bill that night were Pogue Mahone and both bands were only just beginning to get some attention. As we were loading in, I heard a voice calling out "Hey, Del!" from one of the Pogue Mahone number; I've always been crap with faces and my lack of recognition obviously showed. "It's me; James from The Mixers." Then it dawned on me, it was indeed James Fearnley; we had both played guitar in a band called The Mixers a couple of years back, the same band that had been formed by my old mate Geoff Deeks, who had also sold me my 1960s ex-Ritchie Blackmore Fender Strat.

After the soundcheck, a couple of us went out to a nearby off-licence, where we ran into Keith Smith, well-known around Brixton and Herne Hill as one-armed Keith, the former boxer who had lost his arm a few years previously, running from the police on the electrified railway lines near Herne Hill station. Keith had gone totally wild after that incident, and it was no surprise to find him and a sidekick helping themselves to a large crate of lager, which they then brought into the back door of the Fridge. They proceeded to get totally wasted. Some were already questioning the wisdom of bringing them into the gig… but they ended up going into a stupor, and eventually being seen out by the bouncers, though it was more luck than judgment that the situation didn't deteriorate too much! (Last I heard of Keith a few years ago, he was involved in a project to help youths from going on a similar path to self-destruction.)

The gig went well, despite the meagre attendance of only 30-40 punters, and the GLC-imposed noise-limiter cutting out the PA system a couple of times. It gained The Sids our first glowing live review in the mainstream music press.

A little more than a year later both bands were paired together again, this time on New Year's Eve at a sold-out ICA, with Pogue Mahone now signed to Stiff records and with their new moniker The Pogues' (Irish for "The Kisses" being considered better for polite society and radio than "Kiss My Arse"). A couple of weeks later in January, the two bands were paired together one more time, on Chanel 4's legendary music show The Tube. The soundcheck at Tyne Tees studios took place the day before; we had driven up in a van overnight, whereas

The Pogues were flown in from London on the morning of the soundcheck. After we had finished ours, myself and drummer Kev Murphy ran into a totally legless Shane MacGowan in the green room; as he stumbled around he was imploring me and Kev to help him, as the rest of his outfit had abandoned him there. He claimed he'd got pissed on the plane as he didn't like flying, and we spent the rest of the morning plying him with black coffee and getting him in a fit enough state to perform.

The Sid Presley Experience at the time were being courted by a number of labels, including ZTT who were riding high with Frankie Goes To Hollywood and The Art Of Noise, and did indeed have meetings with them where they were enthusing about what they wanted to do with us. Unfortunately the bad vibes in the band were growing out of control, leading to the split a few months later, at the end of a hugely successful "Jobs For Youth" tour, sponsored by the Labour Party, with Billy Bragg, and a young Phil Jupitus as his alter ego Porky The Poet.

The Pogues, however, went on to live out the fairytales of New York and beyond.

Del Bartle, The Sid Presley Experience, The Godfathers, The Unholy Trinity, The Citizens of Nowhere, Credible Hulk Productions

SERIOUS DRINKING, DUBLIN 1984

The Trinity College gig was one of those great nights that seem to come out of nowhere. Band and audience were on the same wavelength. we felt we had a lot in common and made the gig together. It was the end of a journey that started with a drive from London to Scotland, an overnight Guinness-drinking marathon ferry ride to Dublin. And an early morning drive to Belfast. Please don't ask me to explain that piece of logistical genius but needless to say I've felt better before a gig than I did that night at Jordanstown Polytechnic. We arrived after this epic journey about midday and of course no one there was ready for us and no one knew what to do with us or where we were supposed to stay. Who'd heard of a band turning up early? Words like polytechnic reveal that this was long ago and a very different era. Britain and Ireland were very different places. It was only a year after Margaret Thatcher and Gerry Adams had narrowly escaped assassination attempts. The memories of the hunger strikes were still strong. The Good Friday/Belfast Agreement, the Celtic Tiger and Cool Britannia unimaginable dreams. The Jordanstown gig was also notable for the fact that Jake Burns, yes that Jake Burns, was in the audience.

Courtesy of a Cossack Vodka, two for the price of one, promotional night, by the time we played our last song. most of that audience was unconscious. That may sound like hyperbole for comic effect but is in fact true. After a promising start, the end of the gig was marked by desultory applause from about three people who presumably had missed the promotion. Most were slumped, heads on tables apparently oblivious to any external stimuli less powerful than mains electricity. Jake stuck to lager and seemed to have behaved himself. I have to confess he wasn't a diehard fan who travelled far and wide to see us. I knew him back in London and he happened to be in Belfast that weekend and thought it would be fun to come to our gig. "Hilarious" was the word I think he used!

After that I remember a hungover visit to the Giant's Causeway, a gig in Coleraine and a long and winding road to Limerick. Pre-satnav, we stopped at a pub near the Border asking how long to get to Limerick. From the reaction of the regulars to our short hair and English accents I don't think they got many visitors. Limerick obviously was not a regular destination for the locals. After some debate and we were given estimates of between two and six hours to get there. We departed with sighs of relief in the van, and probably the pub, as we crossed the Border into Ireland. We drove along high-hedged roads barely wide enough for our transit van to get through, stuck behind ancient Morris Minors with top speeds far more appropriate for the roads than the one we wished to travel at. Struggling with our rudimentary road map marked with Irish towns written in English and local road signs with names written in Irish, the road seemed long, winding and relentless. I think it took about seven hours. It might have been three but it felt like seven anyway, and that's the bit I remember.

To be honest, I've little memory of Limerick, not that it was bad or good. I just don't remember! Next morning on to Dublin, a warm welcome from the start from the guys at the student union which helps. Onstage everything seemed to click, the audience knew what we were about, had heard us on John Peel. They were the right kind of rowdy! Boisterous without being bullies, a great energy and it was a delight to be part of it. You can't really predict these things, sometimes you play well and no one cares, sometimes you are terrible and everyone loves you. Sometimes it comes together, and you've got a crowd that gets it. This night was one of those. No pictures, recordings or videos just memories – mine are happy, that's good enough for me! Backstage and beyond! A few drinks and myself and Andy the guitarist found ourselves out in Dublin with Sean and

Paddy Foy. When the pubs and bars shut (shut in the sense that they wouldn't let us in!) and we were invited back for a night cap, we of course accepted having no idea where we were going to end up. In the course of our meandering late-night odyssey, Paddy got called over for a chat by a garda. Andy and I stood at a discreet distance wondering how this was going to pan out but all was well, after a chat Paddy rejoins us, telling us that the copper had arrested him the previous week for some drunk misdemeanour and was asking how he was doing! Dublin the big city and big village. We emerged the next morning after some whiskey and an awful lot of tea having chatted the night away. Music politics, philosophy, history, all sorts had been covered. A truly wonderful night. Great craic! We left Sean and Paddy that morning feeling we'd made great friends and knew more about the world than we had the previous day. One of the joys of playing in bands of a certain size is finding short cuts to sides of cities, towns and people that you couldn't imagine otherwise. Sometimes the music helps open people's hearts and they let you into their worlds for a brief precious moment. This one has stayed with me for 35 years.

Pete Saunders, Serious Drinking, Dexys Midnight Runners

THE RAMONES/BLACK FLAG, LOS ANGELES 1984

Boy, oh, boy. An incredibly memorable show for me was November 17th, 1984. The Ramones/Black Flag concert at the Hollywood Palladium. Uh… can you even believe this line-up? This pre-L7 rock show was a genuine highlight because I'd been requested on stage for the Black Flag song "Slip It In" to assist with backing vocals (little did I know that the Palladium stage would be my home for more upcoming events). Never in my days had I graced a stage with an audience that big before. So I was experiencing stage fright and shock. It was also a magical moment due to the fact that, while onstage there, I remembered that my parents danced to "big band" music at the Hollywood Palladium in the 1940s. That gave me a warm and fuzzy feeling. The Ramones/Black Flag show made history as well because there were police in riot gear waiting for the punk rock crowd outside when the concert let out. Chief Gates' LAPD (those gratuitous menacers) had it out for Black Flag and their followers. The cops were ready to crack some mohawk-adorned skulls. You can see the famous documentary photo of the marquee with the police like stormtroopers by photographer and documentarian Gary Leonard by typing in the date and venue in a search engine. Later, on September 27th,

1992, L7 would play with Joan Jett, where we were her back-up band on a couple of songs at the Palladium for a Rock for Choice benefit concert. Saw many a rock show at the Palladium and L7 performed a number of times there, as recently as January 4th, 2020, for a rockstar-studded benefit show… Our very last live gig to date. Hats off to the Hollywood Palladium! Hope it makes it through the loss of gigs due to the pandemic <sigh>. Hats off to the medical personnel and carers everywhere… Sending love and strength.

Suzi Gardner, L7

THE GUN CLUB/THE CRIPPLED PILGRIMS, WASHINGTON 1984

It's tough to go through a catalogue of what has to be well over 1,000 gigs and pick just one I could peg as the best, so it's probably easiest to go with the first punk show: The Gun Club at the 9:30 Club in DC, probably 1984. More than likely, it wasn't the best show I ever saw, but it was notable for a couple reasons. First, it was in the old 9:30 Club space. Before it moved to swankier, larger, and much less smelly digs uptown, the club was a hole in the wall, rats in the alley, and an unmistakeable stench that even after having played a number of gigs there myself years later, I could never get a straight answer about. As a teenager, I felt like I was being initiated into a secret society, bathed in the sweat of other young punks (and given The Gun Club's audience and crossover hard-edged Americana, older punks) and the rotten stink of the club percolating up through the floorboards. The Crippled Pilgrims opened, and I instantly fell in love: not only were they a great band, but they were local, barely older than me, and their mere presence there showed me that a dream of wearing a guitar on stage wasn't just for rock stars or old freaks like Jeffrey Lee Pierce: it was right there, if I could only get a band together and write some songs that weren't awful. I was riveted by the Pilgrims, especially when their lead singer, Jay Moglia, distributed handfuls of Amtrak pamphlets by flinging them in the air: this was nothing like what I had witnessed at my earlier concert-going experiences seeing Van Halen or AC/DC at the enormous Capital Centre. This was not a rock concert. This was real, raw, in person, in my face. The Gun Club were probably great – I really don't recall their performance very much – but the seed was planted. This was where I wanted to be.

Bill Barbot, Jawbox

HÜSKER DÜ, IOWA CITY 1984

On Sunday night, December 2nd, 1984, I found out what loud meant. I was 22 and Hüsker Dü was playing at Robot's, a legendary loft where underground punk shows could be seen for less than five bucks in Iowa City. It was a bitter cold night, but as I walked up the stairs one long flight up, it got hotter and noisier until I got closer to the door that led into the loft. Once inside, I was smacked by a wall of cigarette smoke, sweaty bodies and the smell of spilt beer on a giant loft floor packed with every other freak I'd seen around the University of Iowa campus. I was alone, so I twisted and turned my way through the crowd to the front right before Hüsker Dü started playing. The trio was set up at floor level. I wound up next to the bass player, Greg Norton, with his impeccably waxed, handlebar moustache and his tall Peavy bass amp.

Long before this night, I'd played Iggy Pop's album "New Values" so loud that I blew a speaker in my father's big, boxy console stereo. I'd felt my pants vibrate at a Kiss concert; I'd even been close to the bright, guttural blare of stock cars roaring by on a dirt track, but this loud was a new kind of loud. It was a loud that still serves as the reason why I often ask people to repeat themselves if they talk in a soft voice to this very day. It was a loud that was so loud it made the air turn to gelatin. It suspended us like fruit in a bowl of congealed Jell-O. That's what happened to the air in the room: it congealed. Add to that a big deep bass throb pulsing through it all, and you have a clear idea of the Hüsker Dü loud. My ears were immediately sent into hiss and fuzz mode.

A sweaty mass of us danced spastically under a spray of metallic yelping that propelled us forward and back, up and down. The derangement might have been from the joint someone handed me, but most certainly it was from the volume and speed, like a locomotive crashed into the room at a very high velocity, and we all clung to it for dear life. The floor under us wobbled like a stiff trampoline with 300 of us pressed together on a bouncy loft floor in the middle of Iowa. I lost the back of my T-shirt. It got ripped off in the swirl. A picture of my exposed back exists somewhere: I've seen it– there I am in a sea of steaming people standing around dazed after the show.

Todd Colby, Drunken Boat

THE SMITHS, CORK 1984

Savoy, May 20th

I was 14 and went to the concert with my classmate Joe. It was his birthday so his mam bought tickets for us. I had only been to the Savoy once as a child for Little Red Riding Hood Panto previously and I couldn't believe The Smiths were coming to Cork. The band had a special affinity with Ireland as a result of all their family connections so they came over to play shows in Belfast, Dublin and Cork in May 1984

We had seen footage of a live concert from Derby on TV in early 1984 and we were totally sold on them. I remember being quite nervous when I got into the show as we seemed to be much younger than a lot of the others there who must have been all of 17 or 18! I was wearing a tartan shirt and this older fella came over to me and said "You aren't at a f**king Big Country concert."

We moved into the throbbing crowd near the front to avoid being noticed anymore. Support on the night was The Frank Chickens – two Japanese girls – I still remember they had a song about a canary. When The Smiths came on the crowd was swaying and the first song was unforgettable: "Still Ill". Every song played on the night was fantastic. I don't think Cork florists had ever done so much business.

The crowd went mental, culminating in a mass stage invasion during the encore. Morrissey threw his shirt into the crowd and it was ripped to pieces. I was hooked for life on live music. A classic Cork moment was captured on the live tape. This fella was shouting out "Jimmy… Jimmy... Jimmy Marr" to get the guitarist's attention when the guy next to him says "His name is Johnny ya langer!" Went home on a high and myself and Joe formed our first band called Ceremony as a result.

Morty McCarthy, Sultans of Punk FC, Pharmacy

THE JESUS AND MARY CHAIN, LONDON 1984

The Three Johns Pub, Islington, October 23rd

I remember this gig for so many reasons: it was a last-minute decision to go, the nights were drawing in and the miners' strike was still on and there was a miserable and depressed atmosphere all about. At that time, music itself felt uninspiring – the long summer that had been dominated by Frankie Goes To Hollywood and the ubiquitous "Frankie says…" was leading us up a cul-de-sac: for all the rhetoric, there didn't seem much difference between Frankie and the icons they appeared to want to overthrow. Most indie kids, most indie bands were skint and on the dole and at the height of Thatcherism seemed resigned to their fate.

Enter stage left, then, The Jesus and Mary Chain (I'm not sure there was a stage at the Three Johns). I had a white label copy of the first single – yet to be released – in my pocket in the trademark Creation paper sleeve and an open mind about what I was about to experience. There were about 30 people in the room, most of them from Rough Trade whose offices were just around the corner. They played a short set – lasting just 35 minutes – working their way through the limited repertoire of songs they had at the time, "Taste The Floor", "Upside Down", "Never Understand", adding in cover versions of Vic Godard's "Ambition" and Syd Barrett's "Vegetable Man". It was an aural and almost physical assault of manic intensity and performance that introduced their feedback-drenched sound for the first time. We were all stunned, and it seemed as if indie might have a future after all. The set ended and, perhaps predictably, chaos ensued and an argument flared up, not for the first time, over how the band had (mis)treated some equipment they'd borrowed.

There was something about the night and the band. Band Aid was just around the corner and we were all being told to care, yet The Jesus and Mary Chain didn't seem to care about anything. They were an antidote. And it didn't take long to catch on. Following an ecstatic review in the NME, the band became notorious. Ironically, the Three Johns gig was a warm-up for a Creation European tour, which they embarked upon the next day. So, the band had no idea of the furore they'd created until they stepped off the boat back into the UK and found a copy of the NME.

There were queues down the Old Kent Road for their next gig at the squat venue, the Ambulance Station, where far too many people tried to enter on the night. Controversy seemed to dog them, often stoked by the band themselves or their management. Punch-ups, riots, foul-mouthed tirades followed, all obscuring their brilliance, which would come to the fore the following year on their debut album, "Pyschocandy", a copper-bottomed classic and many critics' candidate for album of the year.

I'm glad I saw the show, but more than anything I'm glad they nudged indie along. Many important bands were inspired by them and followed in their wake.

Neil Taylor, author, C86 and All That

THE RAMONES, DUBLIN 1985

Growing up near the National Stadium in Dublin meant that we went to gigs as soon as we worked out how to sneak in. Usually this meant pestering the touts to give us tickets while assuring them that they weren't going to sell any more. Other times it was a case of simply running through a door as the support band left the building. We were confident that once inside the security wouldn't notice a small band of pre-teens wandering around a seated venue and that we had desperately wanted to see BB King, Gerry Rafferty, Dave Edmunds or The Wolfe Tones. What kept drawing us back? Initially the adrenaline rush of getting in but this was supplanted by a chance to see live music. Ultimately though it wasn't my music. I didn't have an older sibling to allow me sample their record collection and their musical tastes. That came in 1978 with Tonic for the Troops, the second album by The Boomtown Rats, swiftly followed by All Mod Cons by The Jam and Rocket to Russia by The Ramones. The contemporary punk, new wave and post-punk sounds became enmeshed with my teenage sensibilities. The sounds, politics and the overall raw excitement of it all burrowed in and never left.

The Ramones played the TV club on Harcourt Street on June 24th and 25th,1985. I had missed their previous gigs in the State in Cabra and the Grande in Phibsboro. This was their Too Tough to Die tour supporting their album of the same name from the previous year. It was their eight LP and the most critically lauded for over five years. This meant nothing to most fans since all of the albums were great.

The music was tougher and more influence by the American hardcore punk sound than their previous releases had been. The venue was packed. The band started with their customary 1-2-3-4 intro before each song .What did they play? It was difficult to say exactly, because of the sheer velocity each song was played at and the all-enveloping volume of the music. The crowd on the floor formed an amorphous moving mass of sweaty, flailing bodies. As any great punk rock gig should be. The sheer physicality of the sound was impossible to resist. It felt that almost everything you wanted to hear was included in the set. How many songs did they play? An internet search will say between 28 and 31 but that didn't matter. The crowd was pulverised to a joyous standstill.

Afterwards the audience spilled out of the venue, rapturous, sweat-drenched with post-gig tinnitus still ringing in their ears. They would be followed soon after by the band heading back to their hotel. As The Ramones emerged, all of the punks who had been sitting on the steps outside Gilbey's bonded warehouse (Later the POD) all stood up and broke into a round of applause .The band stopped ,waved and then were gone… until the next night.

The next day the band had an instore signing session in Comet Records which was then in Chatham Street. The crowd inside and outside of the shop had nearly all been to the gig the night before. They were augmented by punks sitting outside some of the adjacent shops sniffing glue. The band, led by Joey, who had notoriously poor eyesight ("can't see a fucking thing, blind as a bat" as one of the bouncers at the gig later told me), ambled into the kebab shop adjacent to the record shop first before they were directed next door by a relieved owner. Most of the crowd had or bought the "Too Tough to Die" LP or the most recent single "Bonzo goes to Bitburg". However many had brought every piece of Ramones vinyl in their collection, posters and, in one case, a silver baseball bat that Johnny, a big baseball fan, was happy to sign. I got my LP and single signed and asked Johnny "How come you're not deaf yet?" He replied "I dunno."

The next night, the band burned through another ear-deafening set that was equally impossible to defy.

The next day, a friend who had received a blow to an eye during the gig went to the Eye and Ear Hospital only to be met by a number of the people from the previous night's gig who were there with their ears still ringing.

Like any truly great gig, the feeling and buzz never really leaves you, even if the fine detail has been lost. That gig was also the perfect storm for me insofar as the tour arrived at exactly the same time as I had been plying the grooves of the LP and it was exactly the thing that I needed to hear at the time. It's a feeling that still resonates today at gigs 35 years later when a great band comes along at exactly the right time.

Eugene Lee, NHS worker

HÜSKER DÜ, LONDON 1985

Camden Palace, May 14th

Some bands physically resonate – it's palpable – like a current running the length of your body and emanating from your core like an electric aura.

Get me in a club with a great band and like-minded fans and I feel like my inner circuit board has just lit up.

Hüsker Dü – Bob Mould, Grant Hart and Greg Norton (Minneapolis/St Paul natives – note: also home of my beloved Replacements) – played London for the first time. The band had – rather strangely – agreed for the gig to be recorded for broadcast on the Live From London programme.

I can't rightly recall how I actually ended up going. Exact details are lost in the shadows of time but I think I was accompanied by Virgin publicist Nicole Fitton. There was most certainly a guest-list situation. It might have been a show put together my good friend Mick at the Asgard Agency.

I'd been listening to Hüsker Dü for about two years – "Everything Falls Apart" (1983), "Zen Arcade" (1984) – and the (then) latest "New Day Rising" (January 1985). I knew what I was getting into. Nicole did not. Acoustics in the Camden Palace had always been notoriously bad, no lie. Let's just say I left this gig with blisters in my ears. It goes down in my personal history as one of the loudest shows I had ever attended – a spot they still might hold – perhaps exceeded in decibels only by Tool or Motorhead.

What did I get for this? Complete transcendence – finding and latching onto the intertwining shimmering melodies in Mould's guitar is like mainlining the best drug in town. They were explosive. Even with the dreadful acoustics in the room, you could feel the monstrous talent.

There is a level of pure poetry in Mould. He understands melody, he writes soul-baring lyrics that connect with our collective consciousness (we are all sad, lonely assholes, looking for connection, understanding and acceptance). It was 50 minutes of pure, unadulterated joy for all who witnessed the spectacle. Hüsker Dü were like a category-five hurricane of sound – bludgeoning us with shimmering melody and grace. The tears on my face were not from a physical pain.

I left that show feeling cleansed – purified. I subsequently saw the band perform many times (Hüsker Dü, Sugar and Bob, solo). All brilliant.

Perhaps the hand of time has highlighted that first gig for a reason. It still glows like a long-burning ember of the musical maelstrom that I experienced that night.

Catherine McRae, art director/creative services manager, Virgin Records, UK

FIVE GO DOWN TO THE SEA?/ACTION PACT/THE POISON GIRLS, LONDON 1985

Thames Poly, Woolwich, southeast London, 27th July

Thames Polytechnic was a brilliant venue in the mid 1980s. Many great bands played there, including The Mekons, That Petrol Emotion, Sonic Youth. Indeed even The Jesus and Mary Chain supported us in their early days. However, my most memorable gig was one of the last played at the venue.

In those, simpler times, we often travelled to gigs by bus, we'd use the amps and stuff of the "main band"', so a few guitars in hand and we were ready to go. It had a classic set-up of bar at the back, stage at the front and dance floor in the middle. I remember the crowd being much "punkier" on the night but in there was also the usual smattering of oddballs and skinhead weirdoes like ourselves.

I can't remember much of our set, which was probably the norm for me at the time. Donnelly probably ranted a bit and did his thing, while we struggled to keep it together at the back. After we played, it was compulsory to repair to the bar and enjoy the rest of the evening and try not to lose the guitars. (We did leave a drum machine at the bus stop one time, but that's a different story.)

The Poison Girls were a good band, I remember liking them. There may have been a fair share of light-hearted, albeit drunken banter coming from the crowd, including ourselves. All in the best possible taste, surely. We thought nothing of it.

As we were preparing to leave we noticed a flurry of activity, a gang of guys came at us from both sides and CLUNK, I was out for the count. (I can confirm you actually do see stars.)

I remember a few of us being in an ambulance – we were on our way to what may have been Greenwich District Hospital. I was expecting all the nurses to look like Barbara Windsor – they didn't – but they caringly stitched us up and we were out in a few hours. It seems we were attacked by a gang of lads who broke up paving slabs and beat us over the head with them. It was scary, not least for Anne, who was with us, and was very pregnant at the time.

A few days later we received a call from a very well-known punk band wanting to apologise. They had thought we were fascists apparently, with our short hair and our shouting.

To use an old joke, I did NAZI that coming, CLUNK!

Ricky Dineen, Five Go Down To The Sea?

GOVERNMENT ISSUE/THE DEAD MILKMEN/UNIFORM CHOICE, CORNHUSKER 1985

Quite simply, Government Issue, The Dead Milkmen and Uniform Choice at the Cornhusker in 1985. This is actually the show that is depicted on the cover of Screaming For Change. UC were still like big brothers to me at the time and GI was an emotional touch-stone for a weird kid like me in a way no one else ever could be. Both singers lent me the mic so many times that night, I suspect it is where I made the decision once and for all to truly commit myself to singing hardcore.

Dan O'Mahony, No For An Answer, Carry Nation

THE EXACTONES, USA 1985

I'm Going to Make a Movie Before I'm Dead: An Ode to The Exactones

I lived at my parents' house in the summer of 1985, after my first year at Yale University. I had applied to Yale on a whim, never expecting to get in, but when I did it was like winning the Establishment lottery. I just wasn't interested in claiming my prize. I was told I could do anything I wanted if I focused on it – a career in law, international business, investment banking – but I didn't want the paths that were open to me.

While my classmates on the mainland were spending the summer involved in respectable internships, I worked a shitty job at a Pizza Hut so I could earn money and devote my energy on making music with my high-school band, The Exactones, that would later move to Boston and become The Dambuilders. This excerpt, from a longer work in progress, is a story about a gig we played that summer:

The room was small, tightly packed, thick with Gudang Garam smoke. A throng of local skate punks sized us up dismissively as we hauled our gear towards the makeshift backstage. The first band had just finished a blistering intimidating set.

"Thanks for coming out tonight. Next up…" said the band's bassist, his snarled lip shifting from wry smile to full-blown sneer as he drew out each syllable for effect, "is thee eg-ZAC-tones."

We took our positions on stage, facing inward, crouching like wrestlers bracing for the onslaught. Hearts pounding, nervous feet tapping. If we were going down, we were going down together.

We started with a minute or so of loud feedback – saturation over a single major chord, while Keoki ripped through sped-up Keith Moon fills. When his crash-cymbal wash faded, he looked at each of us, clicked his sticks together, and the entire band lurched in for the intro. Myron hammered the opening guitar chords while Oobob shouted into the mike, the first verse launching into the anthemic chorus: "Everyone hates me/I have no friends/I am a loser/ AND A BUM …"

1-2-3-4 BOOOOOOM!!!! The audience erupted into something completely unexpected: wall-to-wall slamming.

We didn't plan this.

Fearful of losing them for even a second, lest the vibe shifted into ass-kicking mode, we segued through the first four songs without stopping, then took a short break, pausing long enough to catch our breath, to shift gears. The potentially awkward pause was filled with what we least expected: actual applause.

This was going really well.

After managing to get the audience on our side, we chose to play a faux lounge jazz song about golf we wrote in high school. We could have played more punk rock songs, but we had to be true to our dorky roots in some way. We knew we were playing with fire.

Myron strummed silky, reverb-soaked major seventh chords. Keoki slapped the snare with cross sticks. Mas noodled on a meandering wet-dream riff as I thumped out a soft-soap bassline. "Oh yes, it's lovely … out on the golf course," Oobob crooned, launching into a verse about a sex-addict golf-pro.

"I flirt with the girls (oh) and flirt with the guys (oh)/But my golf comes first and his driver comes second…"

Oh.

The biggest and scariest-looking guy in the crowd started an ironic disco dance, which morphed into a jokey fuck-you rendition of a square dance plus the funky chicken. Others followed him in an impromptu line dance around the front of the stage. Were they making fun of us? I wasn't completely sure.

"When I'm old, I want to return to the golf course…" Oobob leaned into it, defiant, knowing what was to come next. The dancing and overall energy seemed to shift, from mocking sarcasm to something more sinister.

"... and hit the orange golf ball cause I can't see ... I can't see ... I can't see!"

The backbeat building: "I hit the orange golfball 'cause I can't see/I can't see/I can't hear/I can't hear!!!!!" Oobob was screaming now, possessed like a drug-addled Saturday night street preacher on Kalakaua Avenue.

"I CAN'T TOUCH/I CAN'T TOUCH/I CAN'T SMELL/I CAN'T SMELL/I CAN'T BREATHE!!!"

Keoki and I were on top of the beat – pushing the band forward, increasing the tension. Myron and Mas hit their distortion pedals, creating a wall of noise as the fuck-you line dance shifted to a line slamdance and then into pure cacophony, bodies in motion, throwing each other from one end of the stage to the other. Oobob stood on Myron's amplifier shouting "I'M GOING TO MAKE A MOVIE BEFORE I'M DEAD!!!!" We huddled against our amps, feedback squealing, while Keoki thrashed out a bombastic arena-rock ending.

I climbed up on my amp and jumped on the final note, ripping the cable out, pulling me backward in mid-air. I stagger forward, fearing the momentum would send me careening off the stage into someone's teeth or on my ass.

All eyes on me. Open mouths, awkward silence and...

I somehow manage to catch my fall and stand up. Oobob raises both fists in the air. Wild applause and shouting.

Victory!

Despite the relief of not only averting an ass-kicking and/or splitting my head open, but making a brief, genuine musical connection with an audience of potential haters, we had the sense to not overstay our welcome. It didn't change the fact that we were outsiders. We made a graceful exit just as the last band finished their set, lumping our gear out of the hall, into the truck and the Kalihi night.

On the drive home, in the cargo bed, Myron, Keoki and I celebrated with leftover cans of beer. That night we accomplished something beautiful. I felt a combination of adrenaline, euphoria and something else that I couldn't quite put my finger on. Whatever that feeling was I knew then and there that I was willing to chase after it for the rest of my life. I took a swig of warm Primo, looked up at the stars and thought, "Fuck everything else, *this* is exactly what I want to do with the rest of my life."

Dave Derby, The Exactones, The Dambuilders

GREEN ON RED, DUBLIN 1985

No matter what anybody tells you, the 1980s were not good. The likelihood is that whoever does tell you that the 1980s were good was not there. Or born for that matter. It was grim. Furthermore, the music was not good. Yeah I know there was great, great music in the 1980s but the daily ambient assault was serious GBH to the psyche. Not least because of the pseudo-sophisticated gated-snare sound. That gated snare was everywhere. The 1980s were particularly not good in Dublin. Dublin music was shit. All the more so for being constantly told that it was all brilliant and that everybody was the "next U2".

It took the 1990s for that to change when the effects of American hardcore and Van and Bob produced two extraordinary and mutually loathing scenes that arguably produced a mass of the most enduring and little-heard music to come out of the country. That's another day's work. Back to the task at hand.

Incoming international bands of any interest or inspiration were thin on the ground. It felt like months passed before somebody crossed the water to make noise. I'd been to a bunch of gigs at that point of course. Lizzy and U2 in Slane in 1981 and The Stones in 1982. And in the Ivy Rooms on Parnell Street. My own Velvetsesque Psychedelic Fursian garage band even played a few supports there to a great local Hawkwind-influenced gang out of St Anne's Park called Zero Zero. Heading to the Buttery to an underground international band felt different. Exotic. Cool. The real thing. Finally.

I first came across Green on Red on the BBC2's Old Grey Whistle Test doing "Keep on Movin'". A blast of neo-psyche country we would call it now. I thought they were pretty cool and soon after when they were billed to play the Buttery in Trinity College, I took the opportunity to pop my small international-gig cherry. Not sure if I'd ever been through the gates before and I had to walk back and forth over the cobblestones on the front square a couple of times before I found the entrance. I was early nonetheless; eagerness having got me to hop an early 42 from Artane.

As I walked into the sparse room, there was a soundcheck in progress. A singer in a puffy north American anorak doing a few lines in to the mic. Whoever these were, this support act were honestly the most uncool-looking band I had ever seen. They finished the check and got off. A short while later in the jacks the singer was beside me at the urinal:

"Hey man who are you guys?" "We're Green on Red..." "You're not the singer." "Ah Dan doesn't do soundchecks. I'm Chris the keyboard player." "Ah-okay-grand-fairenough-have-a-good-one-see-yee-later..." "Thanks see yah man."

I ended up sitting on the PA at the edge of the stage in front of Chris Cacavas's Fender Rhodes. He nodded over and I felt right at home and welcome. A couple of times across the night he tossed me a can from the plastic bag he had at his feet under the keyboard. This was the coolest thing ever and also I'd spent my last coins on a single drink earlier. It felt special.

The room was amply peppered with obvious scenesters and the undeniably cool people I'd seen at racks in the good record shops in town: Freebird upstairs on Grafton Street. Basement X downstairs on Burgh Quay. Golden Discs on Liffey Street (where I bought my first Velvet Underground and Patti Smith albums it should be noted). So this imprimatur from the band was most welcome.

Some tedious guy kept shouting "Neil Young!" at the band; an attempted slur on their slight stylistic debt to Canada. This was some edgy chap who clearly had never listened to much Neil Young because Neil Young had long hair. He became more belligerent as time went on and was ruining it for everyone until a couple of people put him straight. I have a vague recollection of being tangentially involved in this process and nodding conspiratorially to a few individuals across streets and bars months later in the city as a result. I think I got another can after this too... I was feeling pretty proprietorial about this band by this point.

None of my friends liked them. My punky friends thought they were too... Neil Young... and they were too raw for my rockist friends. I heard the Velvets and Dylan and a bit of hardcore and X from LA and yeah Neil Young and the singer who didn't do soundchecks™ was troubled and smart and the words had flecks of the American crime novel, beatniks on the highway and probably great literature I didn't recognise and I'll never get around to reading. Chuck Prophet's guitar playing was special and you can still hear that on his own solo records and gun-for-hire side-man work with big names all over the States to this day. Cacavas is still making great music too. He moved to Germany and Europe is his scene now.

Anyway, after the third can of drink, it all gets a bit hazy and it's time for me to go back across the river and up the Malahide Road again. To this day the thought of that fucking gated snare still makes me ill and angry and resentful.

Daragh McCarthy, The Babysnakes, The Mighty Avon Jnr

THE POGUES, DUBLIN 1985

As a teenager growing up in Dublin during the early 1980s there was – and still is to this day – nothing like seeing a live band. I was very fortunate to see hundreds of Irish and international bands ranging from The Golden Horde, Something Happens!, Stars of Heaven, The Blades, The Clash, REM, The Smiths, Jeff Buckley and The Go-Betweens to David Bowie, Aztec Camera, Dexys Midnight Runners and The Ramones (the TV Club gig was the loudest gig ever!) to name but a few. The international bands often used Dublin as fine-tuning "warm-up show" before embarking on their UK and European tours. You always had the same faces at all the gigs and it became a real network and lifelong bonds with kindred spirits were formed in the mosh pit. We were all equally delighted to see acts that we had read about in NME, Sounds and Hot Press come to play small shows in our fair city. We gave them the warm welcome they craved and lots of the bands say Irish audiences are the best. It's because we could not believe our luck to see such brilliant acts in our little country. It was the least we could do – everyone's a winner!

Some of the bands who played in Ireland had a real affinity with us Irish, because they had Irish ancestors and we all felt proud to hear their Irish surnames and Irish influences. One such act Declan McManus, aka Elvis Costello, was playing the Stadium in 1984. His support was a London-Irish band called The Pogues. This six-piece band (pre-Philip Chevron RIP and Terry Woods) gave a captivating performance with a mix of punk rock songs with an Irish traditional twist which blew my mind. As is often the case with support bands, they won the audience over, and from that evening on The Pogues became the soundtrack for my teen-to-adult life.

Having seen the Pogues in excess of 150 times globally, including countless St Patrick's Day gigs, one particular concert really made a lasting impression on my Pogues journey. That was their first headline show at McGonagles in March 1985.

McGonagles (the old Crystal Ballroom, where my parents first met at a dance over 60 years ago), like the TV Club, the SFX , the Underground, the Top Hat and many great venues where you could see bands nightly, was the scene for one of the most incredible wild concerts I have ever witnessed.

This magical mix of punk rock was like nothing I had ever witnessed before. They had incredible energy and evoked a romanticised view of a London coupled with the melancholy of immigrants leaving Ireland for England or America. This mindblowing show featured Spider Stacey on tin whistle and beer tray which became his trademark until later years when health and safety rules interfered with the art! "Waxies Dargle" would never be the same again live once the beer tray was retired! A hot sweaty gig packed to the rafters with the black-painted walls dripping sweat, the whole dancefloor was a mosh pit. The gig was complete with my idol Elvis Costello who was at the back of the venue. As it turned out, he was working with the band on their follow-up album to "Red Roses For Me".

I look fondly back on those innocent carefree times of life in Dublin. Music is the lifeblood of the city and I am fortunate to still work in music 30 years later in London. Thank you Pogues

Orla Lee-Fisher, music fan

THE CRACK, BRIGHTON 1986

I've been to plenty of life-changing gigs: Culture Shock at Treworgey Tree Fayre, RDF at the Last Bus Shelter in Amsterdam, both in 1989. Levellers played with those guys many times in those days. I was present at Culture Shock's final gig at the Fulham Greyhound which the police stopped and turned into a riot, I even almost played bass for RDF at Stonehenge one solstice. All great times. I could go on about all of them. But the gig I've chosen happened before all that, and without it I'm not sure I'd have been there for any of those awesome shows.

In the mid 1980s I'd seen The Waterboys play "Fisherman's Blues" on Channel 4 show The Tube. That was my introduction to the power of acoustic music, and I loved it – but their records had sounded nothing like that, so I became determined to find someone who did! Thankfully I didn't have to look very far. Turned out there was a local Brighton band who were playing turbo-charged Irish folk music with incisive, sociopolitical lyrics. They used to be called The Bliffs but now they're The Crack. (They would later become the mighty McDermott's Two Hours).

Anyway, as someone coming from the punk scene but disillusioned with it, I thought I gotta check these guys out! Even the folks talking about them in the pub were the guys I wanted to be with – post-Beanfield traveller types and anarchist squat kids. I was making my first tentative moves into the squat scene then – and fancied the girls I was breaking into empty houses with like crazy. It seemed like the perfect gig!

So on a hot summer's night in 1986, I made my way to the seafront arches and the old Zap Club, paid my £1 entry and got ready to see The Crack. First thing

I noticed was the venue was packed. Heaving. I'd played in a couple of local bands and this was unheard of. The band clearly had a dedicated following. Anyway, I got myself good and lubricated at the bar then pushed my way to the front as the lights went down. I think the band opened with "Dirty Davey" (a song The Levellers would later cover) and immediately the crowd went wild, pogoing for all they were worth cos there was no room for anything more sophisticated! I was too self-conscious to move properly but was going up and down with the crowd by osmosis. The singer/songwriter, Nick Burbridge, was eyes closed at the mic, delivering heartfelt tales of modern angst over Tim O'Leary's demonic fiddling. Tim has a way of playing that's completely visceral; you can't help but dance – it's like some supernatural power way beyond traditional musicianship.

About four songs in, after I had been buffeted around by the crowd up the front, a beautiful girl came and asked me to dance. I obliged and she proceeded to strangle me for the rest of the show, still jammed in, bouncing up and down – it was brilliant! Nick and Tim inches away, forward-projecting for all they were worth, bass and percussion thumping through the Zap's tiny PA. It was life-changing for me. I decided there and then that a. The Crack were my new favourite band and b. the next group I was in would use the power of acoustic music to sing songs that actually meant something. Full commitment stuff. Anyway, the gig was amazing. I bought their demo tape on the way out and headed off into the night to tell all my mates about it.

Still one of the best gigs I've ever attended and definitely the most important in terms of the rest of my life. So, thanks for The Crack.

Jeremy Leveller, The Levellers

WILKO JOHNSON, DUBLIN 1986

The Baggot Inn Dublin. I don't know how I ended up at this one alone. I knew a fistfull of semi-pro blues guitarists. That's how it was on northside Dublin in the 1980s. But alone I was and my first time at the Baggot Inn. A long traipse across town on a weeknight.

The Baggot was the top aspirational tier for a couple of generations of Dublin rock bands. The next step before moving to London to try it all there. Later owned by Jack Charlton, the beloved Irish soccer team manager and more importantly a founder member of the Anti-Nazi League in 1977 – a fact which should be repeated loudly and often.

The entrance to the venue was a side door down a lane and when you paid for your ticket you were almost immediately in the narrow space in front of the stage. They had definitely oversold it and when I got in, the room was already packed. And still they came. I think everybody was taken by surprise by the number of punters. Apart from usual pre-show expectation, there was a definite shared feeling of "This is effin' unbelievable!"

The Baggot had disappointing grey unfinished plaster walls, deeply unpleasant Irish pub toilets of the time and black fixed steel-frame bench seats you had to slide in and out of. The houselights were stark bare bulbs and the stage lighting rig was "minimal" too. I miss it.

I pushed through bodies at the front of stage and jostled for a drink at the dripping bar (hoping not to be refused), looking around at the assembling mass for the possibility of a familiar face. I was one of the youngest kids in this room for sure. But I didn't feel like a kid. No way.

When they came on stage, the Italian bear of a drummer Sal Raimundo looked wonderfully out of place behind the ephedriney, black-pant, twin goggle-eyed assault of Wilko and Watt-Roy. That pair were scary. Wilko looked like he might be having a bit of fun with us with the vibes but Watt-Roy defo looked like he would nut you one. They looked a bit pleased and surprised themselves at the number of us too. I assumed there was some internecine edginess between the punk types and the rockers in the room but from the first rhythm and blues note out the fucking window that went. We all erupted like mentallers.

This was definitely what I would later learn to call a pit. No threat, no violence, just some kind of rock'n'roll comradeship and mutual amazement at what was going down. Any edge had evaporated instantaneously. Happens in metal too.

I was well aware that Wilko was a legend on guitar and that his rhythm/lead scratch was an extraordinary feat but, as a young bass player, I had eyes only for Watt-Roy's frets and fingers. Any views I got of Wilko were solely from my peripheral vision. I would swear I never took my eyes off Norman all night. Same as years later watching Iggy with another Watt on bass… This was my first time to see an undeniably classic bassist up that close and this was transcendent straight-ahead power. On it. Swinging his guitar from side to side as he hit the mic for back-up. He was no Jaco Pastorius. "Ere, Jaco," being the derisory epithet of the day in the rehearsal rooms of Dublin when you attempted to add a third note to your playing. Course then when Watt-Roy took a solo later, he blew us all away.

I was hanging out for the old Dr Feelgood track "Twenty Yards Behind" with its great conceit which I still try to live by to this day. In the end, I don't think it was in the set that night. He did play "Back in the Night" and "She Does It Right" from his Feelgood days which were also on the just-released first proper solo album "Ice on the Motorway". What great songs he has written in addition being a guitar hero.

I wasn't going to stay in that melee all night. I would retreat to the bar but neither was I going to miss out on the madness. In I went. The narrow front-of-stage space was a viscous undulating mass of sweating rock comrades having their mind blown.

Getting in, getting out or getting to the jacks or back to the bar or anywhere, you had to let yourself be moved along this intestinoid tract without prior purpose. Let the ebb and flow shift you along until you were deposited out whichever side you hoped to get. A kind of Taoist moving without moving was what was needed here.

I've seen Wilko and Watt-Roy a bunch of times since and without fail the pit is always fraternal and mental and I am no longer the youngest kid in the house and no longer in the pit. Enduringly Watt-Roy is still the man. The only foil for the Canvey legend. The kind of gig that stays with you for days.

Or years indeed.

Daragh McCarthy, The Babysnakes, The Mighty Avon Jnr

THE VERY THINGS, LONDON 1986

Stallions, Falconberg Court, November 3rd

From the cutting room floor of an unmade B-movie, The Very Things take the stage. Each member a sinister manipulation of neatness, sartorial scars in the creases of their white shirts and black ties. The stage was a derisory few inches off the floor: a mockery of elevation, a broken high-heel. From this low perch, the band began to boom.

A few brilliant frames out of synch, the singer sports an ambiguous cravat. He has the charisma and poise of the young Orson Welles. Or his understudy. Or his stunt man. The band builds a wall of clicking guitars. At last the authentic sound of Egyptian surf music! Bass and guitar play parallel runs, doubling down on a televisual force before racing off on separate scenic trajectories. Slick drum-fills punctuate the sturdy construct. The Shend delivers words like someone expelled from elocution school or who progressed through its modules too quickly. Part Lord Haw-Haw propagandist, part deranged crooner.

"The Bushes Scream While My Daddy Prunes" is a title that tells its own tale, fuelled by Twilight Zone and Outer Limits insight. In "Down the Final Flight", the guitar becomes a machine for Morse code, tapping out a frantic signal in a sonic blur. Message received. Loud and clear. Close to the venue is a bar whose steps may have been emblazoned with: "In London everyone is different and that means anyone can fit in." Before the gig, I sat on these steps with a pint. A human fire hazard.

The Very Things are cinematically cool. They make everything darkly amusing. A ravaged disco dancer leans against a glass pillar of live fish. The water glows against his hedonistic head as they launch into "World of Difference" with its sampled intro: "You know I used to drive a rollercoaster. Delivering nitro? Yes. Were you killed? Uhuh."

The Shend lights a cigarette. After a final drag, he flicks it in a magical arc to land before the audience. A bar of molten steel. The venue becomes a smelting plant. The Shend points to me and the glowing cinder. He wants me to put it out. This could be the Great Fire of London. The end of the world. I freeze. He shuffles down. Gravity is at play. He brings his shoe down upon the cig. He smiles. Disaster averted. A moment trapped in arson eternity.

The next day I journey from my above-the-Bedford abode in Balham to Riding House Street where I am studying film and TV. I find a typewriter. It is a theatrical prop as I bang out my review: The Very Things (live at Stallions). A young man of boundless ambition, I make no photocopy. I race through rain to the New Musical Express office and deliver the sole typescript with biro corrections. All deadlines are existential. The next Thursday, over a tooth-white cup of tea in a greasy spoon in Tooting Bec, I sit with the NME. One more sip before I open it. Expectant. Weary. Knowing the review will never get published.

John Fleming, writer, Irish Times journalist

LIGHTNING STRIKE, US 1987

Soho, London, June 1987. I'm in a band called Lightning Strike. We have been playing small local gigs, nothing special. I'm Dave, the singer and guitarist. I'm 20. With me tonight is Eddie my best friend and guitarist. We met at my first day at secondary school. Also, in the band is Jon on bass, Teb on drums and Sten on keyboards and percussion. Sten was a bass player but we recruited him in anyways. He was the only one of us not from south London. He was from Rhyl but squatted in Brixton.

Me and Eddie were going to see Straight to Hell at the cinema but had the times wrong so popped into the Intrepid Fox for a pint. We'd never been in this pub before. The music was loud and rockin', the barmaids were wearing red rubber dresses and there was a parrot on the bar. I was immediately smitten by a 6ft-tall Swedish girl – Celia was her name. I returned to that pub every lunch time for a week. Then I met Kevin Daley: The Mouth.

Kevin run the pub with his partner Trudi. He had managed another London band, Twenty Flight Rockers. We had seen them a few times and they were cool. We talked Kevin into coming to see us at rehearsal. He turned up with Arron from the Fox. He sat there while we played him some songs. "Faster," he said. We played them again. "Faster," he repeated. Faster we played. He looked up and nodded. We had a manager.

We rehearsed as much as we could and wrote some new songs. Kevin knew some young and exciting clothing designers. New leathers and personalised jackets followed, along with T-shirts from Boy and boots from Johnsons. Bullet belts and chrome braces completed the look. A mixture of biker meets Vietnam special forces was the look. The sound? Rap 'n' roll. The Clash/Sex Pistols meets The Beastie Boys. Before long we had an agent and were playing places like Klub Foot, the ICA and our local, the Marquee. We would often do walk-ons there. We'd run across the road from the pub and jump on the stage before the main band, play three songs then leg it back to the Fox.

We were picking up lots of music press – NME, Melody Maker and Sounds were always at our gigs. One day during an interview at the Fox, the Old Bill stormed the pub looking for someone with a gun. Kevin had bought me an M16 water pistol for my 21st. I'd left it on the dresser by the window. Someone opposite had seen it and dialled 999.

We had lots of record company interest, but no one wanted to offer more than a singles deal. Capitol Records were very interested, and we burst in one day with a handwritten contract. The head of A&R signed it and put us in a studio to demo. He then got cold feet and wanted to send people for the tapes. We recorded that all-night session with baseball bats at hand.

One day in October, a friend Craig Duffy came to see us at the pub with his American girlfriend, June Hony and her friend "Jane Friedman". Jane was Lou Reeds "sweet Jane". Craig worked for John Curd. John was a major promoter and, like Kevin, a real character. After seeing us play live, wheels were put in motion to take us to New York in December. Jane and June booked us 14 shows in two weeks. We sold everything we could, begged and stole the rest and along with Jimmy the Hippie our roadie and Normski our photographer we flew to NYC.

We had no instruments when we landed. Me and Eddie bought two $100 guitars which were duly spray-painted and customised. The rest of the backline was borrowed. We rehearsed in a studio in New Jersey before heading back into the city.

We played the Cat Club and there we met Mark Eichner, a young A&R man from RCA. He raved about loving the band and wanted us to be his first signing. We bummed some cash off him for food and said we'd see him at the next gig. We left the club and went to a flat in the Bowery where we were meant to be staying with a bloke called Louis, a shaven-headed New Yorker with a thick neck and a gravel voice. The flat was just up from CBGB's and numerous crack houses. New York in December is cold, especially if you had a mohawk like I did. We started to crash when it kicked off upstairs. Louis was having a mad episode with his girlfriend. There was talk of a gun in the apartment. That was it; we split and found an all-night diner and spent the rest of the night drinking coffee while Normski snapped away thinking maybe his mum had been right when she said "Are you sure you wanna go to New York with those white boys?" Jane and June met us. We were split up, some went back to Jersey and stayed in a Winnebago outside the studio. Normski and I went back to June's in the city.

We spent the days selling our T-shirts, so we had money for food. Nights were spent gigging. We played places like the Lone Star, the Gas Club and the Pyramid. RCA were at all our gigs along with SBK. SBK were a publisher, the top man's son wanted to sign us, but we weren't too keen on being his plaything. We did a radio session which we recorded at CBGB's. This was great but strange because we recorded during the day when it was empty. We managed to squeeze in another of our infamous "walk-ons" at the Cat Club in front of Zodiac Mindwarp. They weren't too pleased as they were doing the gig for their new record company. Oh well, all is fair in love and war.

We were spending a lot of time at RCA. They had food and gave us records. Jimmy would then sell the records to someone we knew who had a shop. This provided us with petrol and cigarettes. One afternoon Jimmy was giving my mohawk a trim in the executive toilets when the head of RCA walked in. His face was a picture. He stormed into Mark's office demanding to know why some bloke from London was having his hair cut in his bathroom.

Our next gig was at the Ritz. Mark was there with Simon Lowe, an Englishman who was head of A&R. We were supporting The Butthole Surfers. The Ritz was a great venue, 2000 people crammed in. The place was rocking. Mark paid for the gig to be filmed. I remember Matt Dillion being there. We were getting closer to that deal we could feel it.

Our next gig was a weird biker venue. We were downstairs in the dressing room. I must admit I always found a dressing room with a dildo on the floor like this one a bit off-putting. We were all tired, hungry, skint and on edge. Tonight, all of RCA were coming. Then in walks some women. A real New York space cadet. "Who wants to fuck me?" she said. "Anyone but the n***er," she added pointing at Normski. I looked up, "There ain't any n***ers in here, now fuck off!"

The gig kicked off. It was rammed. Hot and sweaty like a good night at the Marquee. Full of punks and skins with a smattering of Hells Angels and of course RCA records at the back. Next thing you know the woman from earlier; is on stage on her back, naked from the waist down. She is being manhandled by a group of skins. The punks don't like it. We don't like it. The guitars come off and we wade in trying to stop the melee but having to throw a few punches to defend our honour. The woman is manhandled off the stage by Kevin and Jimmy while Normski snaps away. The gig continues. RCA watch on sheepishly.

One more to go. The return to CBGB's. This last gig we were on after midnight. We plotted in the van after soundcheck. We knew SBK were coming to this one. So, for four hours we sat and watched the crack dealers do their deals. Every so often someone from the building would throw a bucket of boiling water at them. They'd run out of the doorway onto the sidewalk before returning. We watched stretch limos pull up and score, street girls, pimps and junkies all looking for their next hit. There was a pushbike chained up to a fence. Some bloke walked past then returned with a scaffold pole. He spent 20 minutes breaking that chain before leaving with the bike, the chain and pole.

Then SBK arrived in their stretch limo. We went into a cafe next door. I was not impressed. I had a hot chocolate. It came with cream on top which I blew onto the table. We agreed to sign with them. We went next door and smashed CBGB's throwing any T-shirts we had left into the crowd. Playing on the same stage as The Ramones and Blondie we felt at home.

The next day we were going back to London. We were all in Jersey in the Winnebago. Mark and Simon turned up. It was a Sunday. They were desperate to sign us. They had heard we were going with SBK. Mark had been with us from the first gig. He had loved the band and wanted us to be his first signing. Fuck SBK. A handshake was made. "Right Mark now get us to the airport. We have a plane to catch."

Dave Earl, Lightning Strike

GOD TOLD ME TO DO IT/BAD DRESS SENSE, LONDON 1987

For lots of reasons, the first Bad Dress Sense gig stands out from the hundreds that I've played over the years as being a bit special. Not only was it the first one I'd played outside of Ramones covers bands in my home town, but it was the first I would ever play with a band for which I'd written the songs and it was my debut gig as singer/guitarist. Some 30 years later and I still can't really do either very well, let alone both at the same time, so imagine how shaky I was in 1987. I was a bit nervous to say the very least – and with good reason as this was not going to be a gentle introduction into the caring sharing world of DIY punk rock.

Jason and Paul, the two other guys in the band, had got us a gig at an infamous squat in London called the Blue House, supporting a lovely bunch of nutters known as God Told Me To Do It. They were a confrontational band who were always stirring things up and doing exactly the opposite to what you were expecting. They'd got themselves in the tabloids a few months before when they squatted the Libyan embassy and for this gig they'd decided to upset the punks by hiring a stripper to come along and do her thing. I assume just because it would piss the audience off. As you'd expect, when word got around, the DIY grapevine was not amused and retribution had been promised. There was going to be a ruck. Into this stepped Bad Dress Sense for our first gig.

In the end it went off really well. I have very dim memories of dusty concrete rooms, a weird playing set-up with almost no lighting and a few crusties jumping around and falling over while we played. I remember sharing the backstage area with the stripper and her minder. I swear he had a wooden club with nails banged into it. I remember being petrified for most of the night and watching Paul and Jason's body language for the tiniest advance warning that things were about to kick off. In the end nothing happened; it probably was never even on the cards. You know how these things go. But I didn't know that at the time and by the end of the evening I remember feeling ecstatic that we'd got out of there alive and with a debut gig under our belt that could have gone a whole lot worse.

I also remember thinking that this was what I wanted to do for the rest of my life.

Ed Wenn, The Stupids, Big Ray, Bad Dress Sense, Sink

THE CELIBATE RIFLES, DUBLIN 1987

McGonagles

The story apparently was that they had borrowed the money from a friend who owned a shoe shop in Sydney and just took off on a world tour. A fairly adventurous thing to do in those days. A lot of their shows were only being set up with weeks, days (or hours) notice as they made their way across Europe. As far as I know they played all over the States and Asia on that tour too, and were back in Dublin again a year later – for another knockout show in the Underground on Dame Street. I guess there must've been other bands on this kind of completely independent jaunt back then, but not many who made it to this neck of the woods. For various reasons not a lot of touring bands hit Dublin in the 1980s, and Ireland felt pretty peripheral back then – so a small-time punk rock band from the other side of the world playing McGonagles was a novelty, a rarity, and a cause for excitement, regardless of whether you'd heard any of their records (which I hadn't).

They were basically a party band borrowing heavily from the Stooges and Radio Birdman, with a major emphasis on speed and frantic riffing. I've seen a lot of bands use that template since, but on this particular night this was entirely new to me, spotty and agog in front of the stage. Also it was the first time I'd heard a wah-wah pedal being used with the appropriate abandon and conviction. They embodied everything that was great about the Australian layabout ethos (as my teenage self imagined it anyway), coming across as open, up-for-it and not in the least po-faced. They were dressed for the beach (with the exception of the lead guitarist who was wearing spandex – another first for me at the time!) and the only thing they seemed to take seriously was the uncomplicated transference of high levels of rock energy to everyone in the room. Their singer – Damien Lovelock – was an onstage study in not giving a shit, and, offstage, turned out to be a friendly, sweet and properly inspirational guy. Next day the band of school buddies I played with at the time immediately set about figuring out a weak and pedestrian version of their absolute cracker of a set highlight, "Back in the Red". "What a way to see the world," we thought, impressed at how they made the whole thing seem like not a big deal. Obviously it's a punk rock cliche to say this, but it certainly seemed that if these messers could pull this off, anybody could. Dynamite show – good times!

Michael Connerty, Female Hercules

THE RAMONES/THE CELIBATE RIFLES, CHICAGO LIKELY 1987

The Rifles played a show opening for The Ramones who we very much liked. We played well to a large crowd and held their attention as much as anyone can a Ramones crowd. We saw and met the band and had it ended there that would be a great night. That being my first time in Chicago, as a blues fan I had to go see some. Dave had a couple of friends there so I managed to convince them to go see some blues.

We found a venue where Magic Slim was playing. He had a three-piece band, he sang and played a Fender Jazzmaster. He was a tall fellow and he made it look small, but what a guitar lesson. Great tone understated and then not when needed. They played with gentle but firm energy and just knew and felt how it should be. I was in awe of his style and way. I learned from listening to him what I was trying to do with 20 notes he could do with one. An uplifting and humbling experience but it rocked and was fun at the same time. How great gigs and music can be – tone, space and spirit leaving you better for it happening.

Kent Steedman, Celibate Rifles

THE DOUGHBOYS, REGINA 1988

My favourite show ever is one I didn't attend.

It sticks with me to this day, 30 years later. I think about it every few weeks. I don't know why it struck such a chord with me but we don't choose these things. There was no term for FOMO in the 1980s but it's one of two experiences I missed out on in my musical journey.

The first is going to see The Pogues at Reading and Leeds on the "If I Should Fall From Grace With God" tour. I was there, I saw the skinheads with face tattoos, a goth girl had made up her face to look like she'd been beaten and was playing the sympathy card begging for spare change, some burnt out anarcho-punk offered me hash.

I caught New Model Army but didn't care. I had the whole festival experience within an hour of being there. I had to leave before my favourite band went on because of shit train schedules. I was hugely disappointed but not entirely crushed as I really didn't like the song "Fiesta" and the Christmas song had taken over the world so I felt like my beloved Pogues had been co-opted by normal people. If this had been the "Red Roses for Me" or the "Rum Sodomy and the Lash" tour I think I might have skipped the train home and slept in a field. That one hurt but it didn't gut me.

The lifelong regret was missing a band from Montreal called Doughboys at a basement house gig in Regina, Saskatchewan, Canada. It was their first tour. The singer John had broken off from Asexuals to start Doughboys and their brand of punk rock included melody and harmonies. This was mind-blowing to me. It was everything I wanted in a record.

I was in eighth grade. I'd seen Iron Maiden and Kiss but heavy metal was behind me, I was fully into punk rock. I mean really, really deep into it. Some friends of mine told me Doughboys were playing a basement gig at a house where some kids actually lived on their own! I asked my dad if I could go out but it was on a weeknight and he said no. I'd never not been allowed to go out before. I didn't know how to process it but this was the one he was going to hold his ground on. I pushed him on it but he refused to allow me to go. Despite being a punk, I still had a good home life and still listened to my parents so I stayed home.

That show became legend and for the rest of my life I wish I'd been at the house party gig by Doughboys. I have been lucky enough to become friends with the singer in real life and we go for breakfast every once in a while but I long for that house show more often than I like to admit. I saw the band every time they came through town after that but it was always in a crowded club full of kids and not with the core group of 20 punks from my town.

David Bason, Barfbag

THE ANGELIC UPSTARTS, BERLIN 1989

Tempodrom, September 9th

It's a dark September night in West Berlin, the air is filled with tension mixed with a strange sense of exaltation. I'm 20 years old, this is my first gig on the continent and I'm playing at an anti-fascist festival with festival headliners The Angelic Upstarts. Support is from local band Jingo de Lunch and fellow travellers The Blaggers (Blaggers ITA).

We're on. Fuck! The biggest crowd I've ever played to up until now was 600 or 700 (and that was in Hamburg the night before). The crowd tonight is 7,000-strong and the mere fact of being here set against the background of recent political upheaval in the Eastern Bloc all helps create a charged atmosphere, ready to explode and which will result in the city bursting apart at its seams.

Less than six months earlier I'd been sitting at home in Dublin with no job, no qualifications and little in the way of prospects. A simple twist of fate had brought me to London where Chuck Taylor, a work colleague, had told me that the Angelic Upstarts might be looking for someone to play bass for a couple of gigs in Germany. It had sounded almost too good to be true.

It was only when he said that we'd be leaving for Germany in a week's time that the reality kicked in. Major panic, I got a lend of a bass and spent every spare minute going over the songs, playing along while listening through the earphones of a cheap copy Walkman.

The day of reckoning came and we piled into singer Mensi's jeep to make for the airport. The line-up was: Ronnie Rocka, guitar; Brian Hayes, guitar; Mensi, vocals; Max Splodge, drums; and yours truly on bass.

Night one was in a squatted venue in Hamburg, rammed with the usual motley crew of punks, skinheads, left-wing radicals and music fans. A local biker MC acted as security. I looked on incredulously as one of the bikers brought a bin liner filled with baseball bats into the dressing room in the event that trouble ensued.

Luckily the gig went without incident and when the drummer Max turned around at the end and said "You played a blinder mate", I inwardly breathed a sigh of relief.

In those days Germany was divided into East and West as was Berlin. The city was like a small discoloured jigsaw piece surrounded by East Germany and encircled by a 155km-long concrete barrier, the infamous Berlin Wall. As our small convoy of old Mercedeses ground to a halt, we handed our passports to the stern-faced border guards, tightly controlled armed checkpoints providing the only means of entry from West to East.

We dropped our stuff off in a big squat we were staying at in Kreuzberg and headed for the venue, a massive circus tent located in the inner-city park known as the Tiergarten.

I don't recall a whole lot about the gig itself except that playing on that stage was like an out-of-body experience (up to this night I'd only played a grand total of 10 gigs ever). I simplified the bass line on one of the songs, a reggae number "I Understand", asking Ronnie after the gig if it had sounded alright, he nodded and waxed lyrical about an echo-drenched guitar solo he'd played during the same song. Lesson number one, nobody cares what the bassist is playing!

After the show we adjourned for refreshments to a punk bar, The Pink Panther, still buzzing after a successful gig.

Some two months later, on November 9th, the fall of the Berlin Wall took place. Germany's social and political topography changed once more as thousands of East Germans, who up until then had been forbidden to travel, poured into the West. That night captured a moment where punk, hope and a sense of possibility all came together. The rest as they say is history.

I dedicate this piece to Chuck Taylor, Ronnie Rocka and Matty Blagger, not forgetting the brave frontline staff of the NHS and their Irish equivalent the Health Service Executive (HSE).

"A Pakistani waiter
An Orthodox Jew
A homosexual writer
I couldn't be you
A Nigerian doctor

A nurse from Taiwan
My dad's a Muslim cleric
I couldn't be you

Stand together, all with me
Fight the Nazis, we believe
Anti-Nazi is what I am
That's the way I stay
Till I Die"

Dave Linehan, Aidan Walsh & The Screaming Eagles, Hooligan, Foreign Legion,
The Blue Carpet Band

FUGAZI, DUBLIN 1989

When asked to write about my favourite gig, my initial thought was that's easy: Fugazi, McGonagles, 1989. I then thought about that time and the constant stream of gigs week after week. That's definitely not to say they were all good or even memorable but there is a lot to choose from. I loved so many of the gigs and, being involved with the Hope Collective, I often got to spend time with the bands which gave me another experience that was unique. I wish I had known this at the time though. As with any time I'm asked about Hope, I have to admit I didn't realise how special it was and how it would shape our lives and that we would still be talking about it 30-plus years later. It never felt to us like there was a movement or that anyone would be influenced by what was happening in the Hope Collective but that's how every movement happens I suppose. So, it's hard to talk about the gigs without harking back to the friends we made, the weekly Hope Collective meetings over tea and biscuits, the planning of gigs, venues, posters and who does what. It truly was a great time.

It's easy to talk about the gigs that stood out and of course I would have to say Chumbawamba in the SFX, No Means No, I LOVED Snuff and Senseless Things and, of course, the band that started it all for me, Not Our World. This is the tip of a very big punk iceberg. But if I have to pin it down, it has to be Fugazi in McGonagles. I don't remember experiencing a gig with so much energy and tension and stress. Stress brought on by the fact that the band missed the ferry, this message was brought to us by Niall's dad who had to drive into McGonagles to let us know as we were pre-mobile phone. It's hilarious to think about that now. So as the venue was hopping and Not Our World had already finished their set, Fugazi waltz in with amps and guitars in the air as they part the sea of people and make their way to the stage. It was literally a last-minute arrival and they managed to set up and take to the stage.

I remember standing on a ledge at the side of the venue with my best friend and sidekick Valerie and waited and waited. It was my first time to see them live and I can easily say it was the most incredible gig I have ever experienced, and it was an experience… the sound exploded and the crowd loved it. There was the usual stage diving and banter from the crowd that always winds Fugazi up, amps were almost knocked from the stage and the sweat was dripping down the walls. I felt like I had witnessed something special.

The amazing thing about this gig is that this is what started all the magic that became the Hope Collective. Ian McKaye gave back most of the money they were due to be paid and said "Do something with this." I think it's safe to say we did.

Miriam McGuirk, promoter, Dublin

SOUL MUSIC AT THE LONE STAR CAFÉ(S)

It was an odd shaped venue, the original Lone Star Café in New York City. When you walked into the club the bar was on one side and the stage directly opposite it, with a high bench like table and chairs, just in front of the stage side and not much room between. There was a balcony up a sweeping staircase to some fine Texas dining up there.

I was in NYC somewhere in the late 1980s at the tail end of a US trip, harvesting tapes for my company Ace Records. I loved NYC as I didn't have a lot of business there, so this allowed for some RnR of both varieties. To that end I picked up the Village Voice and it turned out Bobby "Blue" Bland was playing the Lone Star the next night. Much to my surprise I couldn't raise a crowd, so I just went down there on my own, after all I was there for the music, not the socialising.

Mr Bland was carrying a full band, five horns and a complete rhythm section, who also handled any backing vocals. The band were in full uniform, though I noticed as the young trumpet player at the end of the line swung round, his jacket was safety pinned at the back. I guess he was last in and that was the jacket they had for him. But they were playing all the Joe Scott charts and sounding very right, with Bobby in great voice. You couldn't miss the guitar player, as he looked like he had just breezed in from Malibu with surfboard under his arm. Unfortunately, surf was definitely not up in that part of the East Coast. But he had a fine looking guitar and could play it, though initially as a rhythm player. Next number and that featured a Wayne Bennet-style lead break and as it approached Bobby uttered the classic words, "play it for me white boy". The kid froze at first and then started building a solo. Bobby moved to the back of the stage, put his arm round his shoulder and brought him to the front. The solo took off.

Next thing a large black woman joined the crowd at the front of the stage as Bobby was offering the mic to the audience. She took her opportunity and took off with the most remarkable, bravura performance, that almost literally brought the house down. Bobby just stared open-mouthed, acting like a microphone stand as she ripped through some remarkable soul wailing – what a voice and who was she?

Shortly after I arrived and quite some time before show time, I met this couple from out of town and we got talking – not that I wasn't from even further out of town. He had a small camera and took a lot of shots when the band came on. As we were leaving, I gave him my card and asked if he could send some prints and I would send him a couple of Bobby "Blue" Bland LPs. He did and I did. So my stay away friends missed out on a remarkable night of rhythm and blues music and I had a ball.

Wind forward to 1991 and the Stax/Volt box set had just come out and I was back in town and as it happened back in the (new more conventional) Lone Star Café, for three nights of sweet soul music courtesy Carla Thomas, Eddie Floyd and on the third night Sam (of & Dave) Moore, all backed by Booker T & The MGs. I had contributed quite a bit to the box, so was invited along and did not turn that invitation away. Stax book writer Rob Bowman, the great mastering engineer Bill Inglot and discographer Peter Gibbon, later of Ace, were all there with me. They turned the house each night and we sat on. The third night, Saturday was the big one, with a live broadcast on ABC television during the first house. Also Sam Moore was added to the bill as was – wait for it – Phil Collins. To be fair to him, his presence probably contributed a lot to getting on TV. He got on stage and a bit off-mic as he did understand the company he was keeping. I was standing at the back as he did a quick tribute piece to camera and disappeared off into the limo. Because of the TV, the show was start/stop as they slotted in advertising breaks, but the next break was a guy coming on stage and saying the president (Bush Jnr) has just had a heart attack – a cheer went up from the back. It was a scare......

At the big table down the middle sat the Warner/Atlantic top brass. At a break, I went to the loo, big US stalls, and next thing there's this big guy standing at the next urinal. I looked round and there was Ahmet Ertegun and behind him two bodyguards. So they emptied the place for a sold out second show. Somehow we hung on to a table in the corner. With the TV and executives departed, the musicians relaxed and the whole performance level went way up, with Eddie Floyd and Carla Thomas in full flow and the MGs' groove as good as it gets, if not better. At the end Sam Moore came on. He was walking with a cane and sat on a high stool. He did some Sam & Dave, and then went into Otis's "I've Been Loving You Too Long". As Sam hit the line "You were tired and you want to be free", he dropped onto his knees, the cane went one way, the stool the other and the entire audience went through the roof, grown men were weeping.

So, a tale of two Lone Star Cafés and two remarkable nights of soul music.

Roger Armstrong, Ace Records

BAD BRAINS/SICK OF IT ALL, UTAH 1989

Every single CBGB's show was off the hook. When we started getting a rep we could tell things were different, you could just feel it. We knew things were going well when CB's called to ask us to play instead of us begging them to let us play. I got to our own Sunday matinee show and there was a line around the block. I couldn't believe it. I couldn't even get into my own show. I had to wait in line with my bass in hand. Nobody knew me there yet so I couldn't cut the line, I just had to wait it out and when I got to the front they were like "Oh, sorry".

Then we went out on tour with Bad Brains. It's hard to think of a good show story from that era because we were out with Bad Brains so every show was incredible. It was the Quickness tour and they were at their peak. We played in Utah and, for no reason, HR came out at soundcheck with a trumpet. He started playing trumpet during soundcheck but never played it in the set. So after his trumpet practising he had a Cheech and Chong-sized joint in his hand. It was bigger than a cigar. The roach was probably an ounce of weed. He finished with the roach and just threw it on the floor. We were straight edge, not for any reason, not part of the movement but just trying to not be drunk and high. But all the roadies were scrambling for it on the floor because it was a huge amount of weed that he threw away.

Richie Cipriano, Sick Of It All

STEVE DREWETT, PYONGYANG 1989

World Festival of Youth and Students, North Korea

My most memorable gig must be playing solo in Pyongyang, North Korea, in 1989. I actually played this 13th World Festival of Youth and Students because Attila the Stockbroker, who was originally approached, was dismayed to find that the dates clashed with his pre-arranged tour of Canada. Attila asked them if they could change the dates of their festival so that he could do it, they replied in the North Korean equivalent of "You're joking right?" Anyway, much to my gain and my eternal thanks, Attila suggested that I would be a perfect replacement to do the festival. From this point on I was going to play the most bizarre and wonderful gigs of my life. It was the largest international event held in North Korea at that time, and I became the first western rock musician to play there.

The Koreans invited musicians, poets and speakers of all shades of the global political spectrum to appear at the festival (though mainly from the left) which was to take place in brand-new Olympic stadiums with accommodation in brand-new Olympic villages (of tower blocks). They had built this entire infrastructure in a bid to host the Olympic Games in 1988 but they failed to win it. It went to their southern counterparts and enemies, and so was held in Seoul. So, North Korea therefore astutely decided to use these pristine sporting facilities to host a world festival.

Due to the global nature of the event, it was to take a week to fly all the participants in, and a week to fly them back out again, plus a week [Eight Days – Beatle time] for the festival to take place. I was so lucky because I was one of the first batch to fly in and one of the last batch to fly out, so I was there the full three weeks.

I found all of the Korean officials to be very helpful and friendly. While I waited for the festival to start, I took walks around the city and into adjacent woods without anyone stopping me or challenging me. It was, of course, obvious that the same freedoms did not extend to the Korean people. That is another story. I could tell many stories of my time there, but I have to be brief.

The gig programme for the festival was kept vague, saying something like the People's Theatre on Thursday (I'm making this bit up, it's just an example) will feature a range of music from Europe, no names of artists.

The way you secured your gigs was different too. In the morning a representative would arrive at your accommodation block at 9am and ask who would like to play today. I would then say me, me, me, with my hand in the air like I was back at school. They then took my name and said, "We will come to pick you up at 2pm." So no matter how much partying you had done the night before, if you wanted to make the best of your time there, you had to be up early to get the gigs.

At 2pm sharp, I loaded my Cube amp and Fender Esprit guitar into the minibus and climbed on board to be taken to the theatre I was to play. My interpreter was a really nice guy but his English was not perfect and we also had a real culture clash, in that normally easy concepts to relate to someone in charge of artists at a concert, became stumbling blocks, as he was not familiar to terms like "soundcheck" (well not in English at least).

So we arrived at the back of this massive theatre and I soon found that I could not make myself understood enough to glean what time I would be required to do my sound. At times like this, I'd just relax and go with the flow to see where it took me.

In a land of "full employment", the theatre was overstaffed with helpers, all in charge of very specific things. When I realised that I needed an extension power lead to enable my amp to be plugged into a very distant power socket, none of the crowd of people around me had "finding extension power blocks" in their job description, so they located the guy in charge of "finding the people charged with the extension finding". So, while the hunt was on, I busied myself with getting my gear sorted as much as I could. It was a huge theatre stage, which made my little combo amp look even smaller. There was little other equipment around, just a microphone and stand, my amp, my guitar and a chair. I was intrigued at how big the auditorium was, but the curtain was down so I couldn't tell.

I still couldn't make myself understood as to when the soundcheck might be. No one seemed be in a rush and there was so little on the stage, I half-expected that more artists and their gear were still due to arrive.

Finally, the man in charge of finding people had found the man in charge of finding power extensions and, after a wait of a good 30 minutes I plugged my guitar in and adjusted the volume. Everyone then gesticulated that I move over to the mic. I timidly moved over to it and said "one, two, one, two" which was carried out at enormous volume to the unseen auditorium and echoed around the huge space beyond the curtain.

I played a section of a song and sang to make sure that I could hear everything, and then stopped and put the guitar down. Now everyone near me was saying

"Okay? Okay? Are you okay?"
I was saying, "Yes, yes, everything is fine. What time am I playing?"
To which the reply was "You okay? Okay?"
"Yes all is good," I said.
I tried again, "What is the onstage time?"
No answer. Puzzled looks.
"When am I playing?" I asked, strumming an imaginary guitar.
"Yes, you okay? All okay?" was the reply.

One of the theatre workers was standing between me and microphone, pointing at the mic with one hand and guiding me over with the other. I came to the conclusion that although I was happy with the sound, they apparently were not, and wanted me to do it again presumably so they could adjust what they wanted to adjust. I picked the guitar up again, turned the amp on and walked towards the mic.

At this point, I was gently prevented from getting any nearer, as a traditionally dressed Korean woman seemed to float by me and stood at the mic, staring at the back of the theatre curtain.

What happened next, I will never forget, it was one of the most wonderful and bizarre moments of my life. At this point, the curtain began to rise and, like a magician had pulled back a cloak to reveal something that hadn't been there before, I found myself staring at well over 1,000 people sitting in their seats silently. I don't know how long they had been there, but longer than I had been in the building and that was now getting to be close to an hour. They had been obediently sitting in silence while they listened to my confusion on the other side of the curtain. They had not issued a murmur. I was stunned. I hadn't had a chance to get stage fright but now I was expecting to just start performing from cold.

Luckily, as I was being introduced by the traditional Korean MC, I had the forethought to grab my recording Walkman and set it to record on the chair to my side. I had to be able to prove this!

The reception was absolutely fantastic. Although at first I thought they were expected to clap or get into trouble, I later reasoned that these people could never leave North Korea to experience other cultures. And so who would <u>not</u> want to sit in a theatre to see and hear things they had no previous experience of?

There was also the clapping! There is clapping and clapping, and you can tell the difference if it is forced or if it is joyous. I will never forget these people, and I feel, they too, will never forget me.

Steve Drewett, Newtown Neurotics (In the year of our plague, 2020)

SOULSIDE, EAST BERLIN 1989

In early 1989, while the Iron Curtain was still standing, my band Soulside played an illegal show in a Protestant church in East Berlin before going to Poland. It was a very special show at the time because, according to a Polish friend who I met on that tour, punk rock was totally forbidden in East Germany and a lot of punk kids suffered a lot under the Honecker regime. Because we didn't have work visas, we had to go into East Berlin without our instruments along with the tourists.

We met a young kid with dreads who came to take us to the show. First, he showed us mimeographed leaflets with translations of our lyrics, which he had made for the people coming to the show. Next, he took us on a breathtaking ride on the commuter train. This was where tourists were not supposed to go and it was above ground so we could really see the city. There were WWII-era bullet holes everywhere we looked, especially around the windows of the buildings. We got off not too far from the centre of town, which was pretty close to the east side of the wall. Then we walked toward the church. There were soldiers with rifles around since we were so close to the wall, but our guide explained to us that since the show was in a church, there was immunity as far as enforcement against the show.

The soldiers watched us, but didn't move out of position. The neighbourhood was lush, which was a pattern all around the Eastern Bloc, since there was a lack of development after WWII. As we approached the church, we could see that most of it was bombed out. Much of the lot the church was on had been overgrown with bushes and the trees had gone wild. There were remains of walls where there had been extensions of the church.

As we went over to the place the show was, we started to become part of a small crowd that was waiting outside. The language barrier was more intense than in West Germany, but we tried to mix in and communicate as best as possible. It was apparent that many of the kids around us were drunk. The first band was playing so we got to see what their local scene was like. I would say the music was very arty, sort of like The Talking Heads meets The Melvins. We played on their instruments and amps and I remember having a challenging time getting the sound to stop from cutting out. Their amps were rigged transistors and one of the guys had to keep redoing the wiring.

After the show we went to our guide's house for dinner. It was great to spend as much time with them as possible. We made it back to West Berlin at night and I remember the guards at Checkpoint Charlie giving us the eye for coming back so late as tourists. Since the Berlin Wall came down six months later, the show and the experience of travelling there was forever etched in my mind. Seeing how punk/DIY culture spread even behind the Iron Curtain before the internet was pretty amazing. It was enlightening to see these kids doing the same thing as us – with much less resources, but with the added passion to compensate.

Bobby Sullivan, Soulside

NAPALM DEATH/EXTREME NOISE TERROR/BOLT THROWER/CARCASS/INTENSE DEGREE, LONDON 1989

ULU

You'd be forgiven for glancing at this line-up and thinking you'd picked up an extreme metal zine by mistake, but way back in 1989 this gig, aptly named "A Night of Rock'n'Roll Armageddon" was the one of the pinnacles of the then furtive UK hardcore punk scene. Unlike its US counterpart, the UK scene had been born from the legacy of UK 82, anarcho and crust bands that moved in Crass and Discharge circles and pushed their musical power and lyrics to the very point of decimation. Sure there was a slight thrash metal influence (most of the bands on that bill are firmly entrenched in metal circles these days) but back then this was the largest gathering the UK hardcore scene had witnessed. This scene was, in all its glorious extremity, finding support in the most unusual of places, John Peel acting as its chief ambassador. He'd been playing and inviting in for sessions many of these bands for the last couple of years and championing their sociopolitical, sonic terrorism across the nation's airwaves on his nightly BBC show. This in turn had caught the eye of the music broadsheets which had been devoting more and more column inches to this underground phenomena of the extreme, dubbing it Britcore. Which all ended up at this gig and its public broadcast on national television. Anyone remember SnubTV? It was the mildly alternative music show that boasted a weekly teatime slot on BBC2 and was the brainchild of the unintelligible Frenchman from Eurotrash, Antoine de Caunes. The show devoted a whole episode to UK hardcore and was centred around this gig. What they filmed wasn't pretty.

Five bands for a meagre £3.50 was a snip even back in the late 1980s so expectedly the show at London's ULU is a sellout and punks, thrashers, crusties and indie kids alike are shoe-horned into the confines of this 600-capacity venue to witness the band on everyone's lips, Napalm Death and their all grinding, supporting cast. Earache Records, which were born of and at the forefront of this movement, had laid on this showcase of the extreme and the expectation was high in the air. Mansfield's Intense Degree were up first and capitalising on their 1988 debut "War in My Head" and a Peel session of March that same year. They are the least metallic band on the bill tonight. Their superfast hardcore more in the vein of stalwarts Heresy proving the perfect, adrenalin kick of warm up this gig needed. Up next were another band fresh from dropping their debut album and being taken to John Peel's bosom, Liverpool's Carcass. 1988s crudely produced "Reek of Putrefaction" had already been heralded an underground classic with its blitzcore grind and medical textbook lyrics. They even shared a guitarist with headliners Napalm Death in Bill Steer. Dreadlocked front man Jeff Walker growled and snarled like the deaths he sang about were his own, as songs like "Genital Grinder" saw the first stage divers of the night leap like lemmings into the assembled throng.

Carcass are the most metallic band on tonight's stage, their riffing and lyrical subject matter pegging them into a pioneering seat in the brave new world of grindcore. They are rewarded with an increasingly violent pit. Next up were the Games Workshop-inspired, Coventry crust-thrashers Bolt Thrower. Their debut "In Battle There is No Law" hadn't been an Earache affair but had been released the previous year on Vinyl Solution records after they were once again championed by none other than John Peel. With a sound that was as much Discharge and Crass as it was Slayer, their raw guitars and stupidly fast rhythm section was also moving into grindcore territory. Also, like Intense Degree, they boasted a female bassist, something of a rarity in the testosterone-fuelled world of extreme music but a door which the punk mentality of their collective backgrounds had opened.

Unlike Carcass before them, who were a wall of intense speed, Bolt Thrower's sludgy crust-metal breaks offered respite from the blast beats. The crowd by now was at capacity, the squashing horde offering ample support to the occasional stage divers leaping for victory. Main support tonight were positive veterans of the UK scene Extreme Noise Terror. This Ipswich quintet were conceived in 1985 and boasted two vocalists for that added harsh vitriol and are widely considered the forefathers of this genre and its subgenre crust-grind. Their roots are unashamedly crust-punk but, they had evolved and were veering toward grindcore with their short, sharp, political ragers that became a blueprint for the movement in its formative years. With all this in mind, ULU starts to turn to mayhem and there are practically queues stage left and right for divers to launch themselves into the increasingly chaotic pit. Cameramen are now starting to look over their shoulders as moshers barge towards them as they try to document the unconventional image of ENT and the crowd reaction alike.

However, nothing could prepare the Snub TV crew, security guards, venue staff and to an extent the crowd for Napalm Death. They were fast becoming one of the most infamous bands in the UK. Their 28-track debut album "Scum" had propelled them into folklore, where people not even remotely associated with punk or metal had their curiosity aroused by the band dubbed the "fastest band in the world". Their debut may have dropped two years previous but the media hype on Napalm Death was growing feverishly. As soon as they hit the stage, it all erupted. The orderly stage-side queue of divers looked for new launch pads and the PA was scaled on each side, three or four people atop at any point, then swandiving into the vortex of bodies below. Fire hoses were sprayed upwards, trying to topple the lemmings. Chaos was reigning while Napalm Death's soundtrack to oblivion played as its backdrop. The whole night began to feel like a Boeing 747 hurtling out of control towards the ground as chunks of the PA fell beneath the climbers, crashing onto the heads of the sardine-packed crowd. The Death managed to maintain course during the carnage and after it was all over everyone spilled out into the crisp February night.

This show was arguably the pinnacle and end of a scene. Vocalist Lee Dorian left Napalm Death not long after and they elevated into the metalsphere along with Carcass and Bolt Thrower who would become death metal behemoths in their own right (and still are to this day). Intense Degree faded into obscurity and the lone hardcore punk survivors Extreme Noise Terror would lose vocalist Phil Vane with his untimely death in 2011. But for this evening, as documented by the BBC, Britcore lived, roared, conquered and became extinct in a blaze of primeval glory.

Miles Hackett, Dry Heave Records

PIG IGNORANCE/SHRED/THERAPY?, DUBLIN 1990

I've been wracking my brain trying to figure out what gig was my favourite and what to write so I decided to write about the background of how I got to experience and help out with the gigs that I have such fond memories of. When thinking about it, I realise I was the same age as my now four young adult kids!!!

I got involved with the promotion of these gigs purely by my friendship with Mir and Niall McGuirk. I suppose a lot of the time I was the third wheel so to speak, but I was never made feel like that. The punk scene was new to me, but I was always made feel so welcome at the Hope meetings in Niall's. Over many cups of tea and lemon puff biscuits, we would decide who would go to the printers up by Trinity College and who would get the job of promoting the gigs by hanging the posters and placing the flyers in the many record, book and coffee shops around Dublin.

My memories of these gigs were sitting at the door of the venue with Mir greeting the gig-goers, many of whom had become lifelong friends, handing out information on different causes that meant a lot to us and saying "no" to the many journalists who tried to blag their way in saying Niall had put them on the non-existent guestlist!

I could say the gigs I remember most are Green Day or Fugazi or No Means No. Yes these were exciting big name bands with packed venues, but the ones I remember best are the ones that meant more to me.

One of these gigs was Pig Ignorance, Shred and Therapy? at the Attic upstairs in the White Horse. My younger brother and his friends were allowed to go, so that was a bonus. It was a packed gig full of energy, people dancing, floor bouncing as was the norm in the Attic venue. A sense of excitement around Therapy? filled the room. This gig was a benefit for a cause that had affected but not dampened the spirits of our good friend Niall, so we were glad it was a success.

That's my short memory of one of the many gigs that Hope Promotions gave us back in the 1980s and 1990s when there was little else for us to do. Money was short but these gigs gave us a never-ending love of music and a sense of belonging to something we could believe in. And now, through our memories and love of music, we may be able to help a little with this great cause and get us through this troubled and unsettling time.

Valerie Kirby, promoter

BLYTH POWER, BERLIN 1990

August 11th, 1990. Blyth Power and Salad from Atlantis are touring in an evil-smelling van. The tour has so far taken them through Holland to Aalborg in the north of Denmark, then to Berlin via a hair-raising overnight drive during which it turned out that the innocent youthful guitarist left to drive through the transit route was unaware that there had ever been two Germanys and that Berlin was smack in the middle of the other one. Thus he deviated from the transit route and we had found ourselves lost somewhere behind the Iron Curtain without visas. Fortunately, no one cared anymore, but a couple of years previously he would probably have got us all shot.

From Berlin, we headed back west, where we came to Hamburg, and having failed to fall foul of the VoPos and neo-Nazis in Berlin, we unexpectedly became embroiled in local politics in there instead.

"Crikey! The Jerries are counter-attacking!" As our front line wavered and began to retreat, I turned and loped, half-doubled, back the way I had come.

It had all looked so promising at first. Flora, the venue, was a big squatted cinema, well-organised and well-looked after in the manner of most German anarchist establishments. The food was excellent, and the bar sold no alcohol in a responsible attempt to spare the neighbours the worst excesses of homegoing revellers. We were impressed. We had completed our soundcheck and were relaxing, waiting for Salad from Atlantis to do theirs. The first indication that all was not well came when the sound engineer began to take down the microphones and stow them away in a locked case: then a succession of serious faced autonomen began to stockpile pick-axe handles by the door. Across the hall, a bespectacled youth in baggy judo whites was limbering up against a concrete plllar, bottles slipped into pockets and a crowd began to gather inside the door.

"What's happening?" I asked.

"Some Nazis", I was informed. "They come to attack the house." I digested this: right-wing agitators were on their way to attack the venue, presumably with some determination, given the precautions that were now in hand. What was I going to do about it? Something smashed outside, voices shouted. The crowd at the door streamed out into the street and I followed them through the sally port, eager to see what was afoot.

The conflict was still at stone-throwing distance. Figures at the street corner, at the end of our building, were hurling rocks and bottles. I couldn't see how many of them there were, but our side seemed to be growing in numbers as the efficient anarchist grapevine did its trick. I followed our chaps along to the corner to see the Nazis retreating up the road towards their HQ – a local bar whose proprietor allegedly harboured a grudge against Flora. We seemed to be holding our own as the battle wavered up and down the street, neither side getting close enough actually to engage, but the barrage of stones becoming increasingly determined. I bent down and picked up an expended piece of rubble, weighed it thoughtfully in my hand, made up my mind and then hurled it at a hairy-looking chap, whose allegiance could be readily determined by the direction in which he was hurling his stones. It hit him. Enthralled, I bent down and picked up another and flung it as hard as I could up the street. It bounced off the side of a car and skidded between the feet of a denim-clad stranger. I fell to with a will: as fast as the spent missiles rolled to a halt around our feet, we hurled them back again. Everyone seemed to be having a great time.

Suddenly a fresh wave of leather and hair surged out of the enemy stronghold and charged towards us. "Crikey, the Jerries are counter-attacking!" flashed through my mind, as we fell back around the corner. They chased us to the steps of Flora, then broke off, partially as a result of a fresh barrage of stones, and partially because the riot police were now gathering at the far ends of the street.

A fresh sally went out from Flora, and all of a sudden we seemed to be charging up the street yelling "Nazis Raus!" and flinging anything we could find at the advancing enemy. I could plainly see them coming – one man was carrying a huge axe, which scant seconds later, and 30 yards or so further on, I passed lying abandoned on the ground. The judo expert dropped it down a ventilator grill, taking care to leave no fingerprints. Our rush gathered momentum. In my enthusiasm I picked up a discarded bottle and hurled it overarm, like a cricketer or an Airfix toy soldier with a hand grenade. It went spinning wildly away to the left and burst against the wall showering some of our troops with "friendly fire".

"Divvy!" shouted Jamie, running past with a handful of concrete fragments. Overhead, anxious motorists were shouting from upper floor balconies as the battle overran their vehicles. Non-motorists and those high enough to be well clear of stray missiles jeered and egged us on. One or two hurled refuse. The riot police – of whom I was far more afraid than the by now far outnumbered Nazis – didn't seem about to intervene.

About 10 yards in front of me, a boiling mass of limbs and threshing pick handles marked the target. There was a crash of breaking glass and then dense clouds of black smoke began to pour out of the enemy den. This final act of destruction seemed to signify full time. We made our way back to Flora and sat defiantly on the steps, while the riot police packed away their picnic hampers and went home.

I never tried to convince myself that there was any justification for my actions that day. I wasn't "caught up" in the event or "carried away" by it. I was in full, sober control of my faculties, well-aware that I was behaving irresponsibly. The fact that I enjoyed it all immensely only makes it worse. Moral of this story: people who live in glass houses should move, because the world is full of evil children with no respect for other folks' property.

Joseph Porter, Blyth Power

SLAYER, NOTTINGHAM LATE 1980s; TOOL, NOTTINGHAM 1993

What was your favourite gig? This has to be one of the difficult questions to answer really so I'll break it up into a few different sections. I think I'll start to try and answer from an audience member's point of view first as going to see a band as a fan. There's quite a few that stick out but the memorable ones all seem to be from my younger years. I mainly used to go to the Rock City in Nottingham starting from my late teens in the late 1980s and early 1990s. At that time, I was well into my thrash metal. Slayer had just released "South of Heaven". I had listened to "Reign in Blood" to death so as soon as I heard that Slayer were coming back to tour the UK to support their new album, I had to get my mate (as he was old enough) to get tickets.

Dave Lombardo's kit looks sooo huge on the stage and he literally used the whole thing. All you could see was views of his stick thrashing away above his kit. Tom Araya looked like a giant with Kerry King and Jeff Hanneman each side of him, heads down, playing guitars like men possessed. It was fucking brutal and ripped my face off and I loved every second of moshing and stage diving like it was going to be my last time.

The second section would be "band I never heard anything of but blew me away". The date was May 22nd, 1993, and I was going to see Rage Against The Machine and a band called Tool was supporting. This was again at the Rock City in Nottingham. Having no expectations whatsoever, we walked in before the support band had started. On walked a strange nervous-looking man wearing just hillbilly thermals. He proceeded to transfix everyone in that venue and sucked us all into his weird and wonderful mind. The rest of the band played amazing tunes alongside the lyrics from Maynard Keenan. The next day I ordered "Undertow" and listened to it non-stop and Tool went on to be one of the largest bands around at the time.

Steve Pod, Vanilla Pod, Menshevik

THE DICKIES, CARDIFF 1990

Well, everyone like myself at a not-so-tender age has a memory bank full of prestigious gigs one can call to hand. The axiom of "we may be old but we got to see all the cool bands" certainly has some truth to it. Through sifting the sands of my own memory one recalls finally getting to witness The Dickies when they visited the UK on their Just Say Yes European tour in September/October of 1990. I never thought I would ever get to see this band. There were my adolescent heroes in 1979 when I was merely 13. I had been aware but missed the banana boat when Dickiemania had hit the UK the year before with "Banana Splits" making noises in the charts and the rip-roaring "Incredible Shrinking Dickies" hitting the stands. But just as soon as I belatedly began to fill up my shelves with all their silly-coloured vinyl, news hit me that Chuck Wagon, the guitarist/keyboardist/saxophonist and whatever else you handed him had offed himself, signalling sure signs that my newest favourite band were not going to be putting out any more records, let alone touring anywhere in my vicinity.

It took a 10-year wait, a l-o-n-g time in any teenager's life to read the news that they would be arriving in a matter of weeks. By this time I had already served my sentence in a few bands, and was currently playing the drums for local Newport lunatics The Cowboy Killers. A gig was planned on their schedule to play my hometown of Cardiff on October 3rd, but being the fan that I was, I cajoled a mate or two (one of whom drove!) to share this momentous occasion with me by seeing them in Bristol the night before. True to form and luckily for me, they were fucking red-hot, or I would have had some explaining to do to my pals. An hour's worth of Dickies' songs had left me with bruises, cuts and tender ribs after battling my way to the front and getting squashed up against the stage. I had got to see The Dickies! The following day, feeling like shit, I figured I'll take it a bit easier that night and experience the band from a safe distance. That was until a message was left on my answering machine informing me that the promoter for the Cardiff show had flaked out and the gig was cancelled... But Simon Phillips, Newport gig promoter and all-round good egg, had taken the initiative and organised a replacement gig for them at Newport's TJ's club. Would we like to take the support slot? Errrr... yes please! Forgetting my pains from last night, I got my arse up there sharpish and managed to spend a bit of time with the band before the gig started.

I don't remember too much about how we played that night, but it was a full house with bodies flying everywhere when The Dickies fired up for probably their most intimate gig of the tour. If anyone reading this knows what TJ's was like in those days, I don't need to explain myself. Everyone had a blast, the band had a blast and rumour had it that it remained the best gig they played on that tour. (No wonder they returned to the scene of the crime when they came over a few years later.) The Dickies had been given no guarantees as to how much moola they would get from the show. Less than 24 hours' notice had been given to sort it all out and to advertise, but troopers that they were, Simon and the Newport brigade handed over 800 quid to The Dickies. This was way more than I think they expected, considering the door price of £3.50, and we walked away with £150, the most dosh I had ever had in my hands from playing a bunch of stoopid fucking songs. Of course there was five of us in our band so it wasn't a king's ransom when we divvied it out.

The big prize of course was to share the stage with what is now one of the oldest surviving punk bands. I saw The Dickies many times after that and played support again to them only recently with my band Bad Sam on their Primordial Ooze tour, but that Tuesday and Wednesday night almost 25 years is still fresh in a now old man's mind!

Kip Xool, Cowboy Killers, Bad Sam

BUZZCOCKS/CELIBATE RIFLES, GOLD COAST 1990

The Playroom. Iconic coastal venue. The Celibate Rifles were playing with Buzzcocks on their first reformation tour here. Place was full and full of energy. Was a popular area for us anyway, surf crowd. Upstairs dressing room and separate stage from the punters.

We started playing and it was as usual wild and crazy. I remember it being a particularly tight show from our perspective. We were in a good one. The Playroom had I thought one of the best-sounding stages anywhere we had played, for our style of music at least.

As an aside, The Celibate Rifles are the most physically demanding thing I have ever done, pretty much every time we played. Climbed mountains, surfed once upon a time, fire-walked, played sport, bushwalks in wild places, played with other fine musicians – nothing came close to that intensity and energy required to play a show with the Celies.

Toward the end of the set we started playing I think "Electravision Mantra", maybe last song but details outside of sound and playing are of little importance in that state for me. The song has a longish intro that builds into the verse. At some point in that intro, a fan came flying through the air and crashed into me. This was not a random stage dive, it was a horizontal impact just below my guitar into my legs. Very fortunate it did not majorly damage my guitar, me or him that I know of. I recognised him as he got up and then dived off, over the monitor, into his six-foot-plus mate who I also knew.

We finished and, once rested, I went out front to hear a bit of Buzzcocks and saw the two culprits. So I went up and asked what that was all about (probably not that politely) as it was not the easiest thing to deal with in the middle of a song. The tall one replied "I was having such a great time I had to pick up my [substantially shorter] mate and throw him at you." It's not something I would ever do myself but it was the only response that couldn't be faulted in the moment, stupid and sorta dangerous but funny and characteristic of the madness that we saw often from the stage looking out at our shows. They were forgiven as only minor damage to my guitar and me ensued.

Kent Steedman, Celibate Rifles

THE HEAVY METAL KIDS, LONDON 1990s

The Stick of Rock, Bethnal Green

I could have chosen so many "that was my favourite gig ever" moments. Some standouts were Rose Tattoo at the Army & Navy in Chelmsford. Their first UK gig in 19 years and literally on the floor of a boozer with only a handful of people in attendance. I remember when the guitarists stepped forward to do the backing vocals, we all took a step back! It was that powerful. Madness at Finsbury Park the first time they reformed was a cracking day out. All the Ska gigs in the late 1980s with the Riffs and the Hotknives as we felt we had our own little thing going on. I could choose pretty much every "first time" actually as they were all special. The first time I saw The Business, New Model Army, Test Tubes. The only band that still make me go in the pit, Subhumans – just reminds me of being at school and angry about stuff! All the psychobilly gigs at the Klub Foot. Ask me each day and I'll have a different "favourite gig". I was just about to settle on Chas & Dave in Morecambe but then actually Chas played at my wedding and I'd get lynched if I didn't say that was better! So I'm going with The Heavy Metal Kids.

HMK were fronted by Gary Holton (also an actor who appeared in ITV show Auf Wiedersehen Pet). I was too young to have seen the band first time round and Gary had sadly passed away so I was resigned to the fact that I'd never see them. I'm a big fan and, apart from my own band, they're the one band that I collect. I've got every foreign pressing, white label and obscurity I can find. I'd heard the stories from friends who had seen the band originally. Including the members of Sparrer who actually played with them in the early days. Max Splodge was also Gary's best mate and they lived together and I loved hearing the stories of their various antics. As you can imagine with Max, they were hilarious but the one thing that always shone through every story by anyone who ever came across them was how charismatic Gary Holton was.

He was an old school entertainer who owned the stage. His acting skills were apparent as he strutted in character, posturing and captivating the audience. They were pre-punk and even Johnny "Rotten" Lydon paid them credit and admitted nicking Holton's image! Apart from a few numbers, their music wasn't even heavy rock so it definitely wasn't that that won the punks over. But they had attitude in abundance and influenced many and are often overlooked in the trendy "history of punk" books which concentrate on bands like the New York

Dolls when the Heavy Metal Kids were far more "real" and influential to London kids forming bands.

Cock Sparrer to this day come on to stage to "The Overture" which is the instrumental from their seminal album "Kitsch".

So when I heard they'd reformed, I had mixed emotions. Finally I could get to see the band and hear the songs. But how could they reform without the original singer on whose reputation the band had subsequently entered folklore?

The Stick Of Rock was owned by Steve Bruce (Cock Sparrer drummer) and I used to play there a lot with my band at the time. That was how I got to know him and how I ended up in Sparrer 28 years ago! When he said he'd booked the Heavy Metal Kids I just knew I had to go. Watford Jon (best mate and Argy Bargy singer) refused to come as he thought it was sacrilege them playing without Gary and would be really naff. The band took to the stage and the replacement singer (a guy called Dave who was also in a tribute band called Those Glam Rockers) absolutely smashed it. To start with the band sounded like the fucking record. Powerful, well-played. These guys were seasoned professionals who came from an era when bands were signed to labels and it was a career. In the original rhythm section of Keith Boyce (drums) and Ronnie Thomas (bass), you had the ultimate backbone of any band. Untouchable. But when Dave started singing I closed my eyes and it sounded as good as Holton would have done. I was blown away. I actually called Jon midway through and said "Listen to this! I can't believe you haven't come, ya fool!" (He then went to every HMK gig after that and we became good friends with Keith and Ron.)

Not only did it sound amazing but Dave had charisma by the bucketload. Half-singer, half-stand-up comic, he had us all pissing ourselves with his onstage banter. "The Cops are Coming" was especially theatrical and by the time the false arms came out during the cover of "I Who Have Nothing" (changed to "I Who Have Ffffuck All"), the small crowd in attendance all knew they'd seen a very special gig.

Okay – it wasn't the full original line-up but it was still a great show. And more importantly they were great songs that were finally getting an airing again which was fully deserved.

I actually went on to play a few gigs together with them but after one got smashed up in St Albans. I think that was the end of that! But I still remember a good night out with good people. To hear good songs that era of The Heavy Metal Kids was fun and I remember it all started at the infamous Stick of Rock in Bethnal Green.

Daryl Smith, Cock Sparrer, Argy Bargy

NIRVANA/SONIC YOUTH/BABES IN TOYLAND, READING 1991

Playing Reading Festival in 1991 was my favourite gig Babes in Toyland played. Babes were living in a flat in Wood Green, near Southern Studios in north London. Hanging out backstage with Iggy Pop, Sonic Youth, Dinosaur Jr., Nirvana and Silverfish was a celebration in itself. There were also a bunch of other folks hanging out backstage: Mudhoney, Courtney Love and Iggy Pop's son Eric. Everybody's friend, Dave Markey, was filming a documentary called 1991: the Year Punk Broke. Iggy Pop and band used Babes backline, because apparently, they didn't bring any of their own.

To think it was 29 years ago is unreal, but it seems just like yesterday. Viva viva rock'n'roll!

Lori Barbero, Babes in Toyland

THE MUMMIES/THEE HEADCOATS CALGARY, EARLY 1990s

Guy and I ducked out after a Fugazi gig one night in the early 1990s in Calgary and went over to see Thee Headcoats play. The Mummies were opening up, but we had no idea who they were at the time. We were just both big Billy Childish fans.

The place was small and I think a biker bar. There were certainly mostly bikers there. Definitely not the place to be by the looks of it. Yet, as we all know, life usually runs in the converse of expectations. When The Mummies hit the stage, they hit with such force and commitment that everyone's mind was playing catch up with what they were seeing. Four totally disgusting-looking fully-costumed-in-filthy-rags mummies were beating their instruments to death and whipping through killer garage tracks one after another.

Everyone in the room got into it in one way or another. After a while one of the drunk biker women went to the bathroom and wrapped herself in toilet paper mummy-style, and came out and stood in front of the stage giving the band two birds. This made them even more jacked up.

As the singer rocked his Farfisa back and forth hanging from the water pipe above the stage, the organ gave way and he came crashing down with his arm breaking between his body and the keyboard. He kept playing.

After the set, Thee Headcoats couldn't really do much. I've seen them and loved them, but that night they dissolved into a mess and eventually broke up on stage when the drummer took the only working microphone and used it as a drumstick.

Billy Childish quit and walked out of the club. It seemed like a reasonable response. We were all wiped.

Brendan Canty, Fugazi, Rites of Spring, The Messthetics

RAMONES/ASEXUALS, MONTREAL 1991

Gabba Gabba Hey

One of the more memorable opening slots of our gruesomely extended career at the forefront of the Canadian punk/hardcore scene was the night we opened for the all-mighty Ramones. The legendary front man of the US equivalent of The Sex Pistols, Joey Ramone was hard to ignore during soundcheck. Tall and pear-shaped, clad in black leather and purple glasses, he lurked around the front row of the stage with a girlfriend. Strangely, I don't remember much about the other members of the band. Joey drew your eye like a magnet. I do remember we crammed our gear into the postage stamp of remaining stage real estate, as the Ramones crew refused to strike their gear after soundcheck. The road crew was rattlesnake mean and cussed us out from the side of the stage to not go over our 30 minutes. I think our singer cut our set short to 20 minutes because he was understandably intimidated.

When The Ramones finally emerged from the minuscule subterranean dressing rooms of the Rialto theatre, from which the Asexuals were banished, Joey comically walked out into the back alley. I was shocked at the classic Spinal Tapness of Joey needing a roadie to redirect him toward the stage. The Ramones played a tight and great set, but I couldn't help thinking the tunes sounded rushed to the extreme.

Years later, after I had relocated to Los Angeles to start another band called La Motta, I was lucky enough to accompany a veteran roadie friend of mine to a pool party at Johnny Ramone's house in Laurel Canyon. Johnny greeted us warmly at the door of his cozy hillside bungalow and searched out a blue sharpie to autograph the predominantly blue eight-track "Rocket to Russia" tape I'd brought (Gabba Gabba Hey – Johnny Ramone). We were entertained by The Stray Cats jumping off the roof into the pool, tunes from poolside speakers disguised as Flintstone-style rocks, and a kid making fun of Joey's looks in his swim cap. To a freshly minted Angeleno, this star-studded pool party made quite the impression: Pearl Jam, Sound Garden, Vincent Gallo, The Stray Cats, and Johnny Ramone? Life is good in California, long live The Ramones. "I Don't Care" was one of the first tunes I learned to play on guitar, two-finger style, and the impact of the Ramones is hard to overstate.

Sean Friesen, Asexuals

RECITAL, WEST SUSSEX 1991

Unlike my peer group I was never in a band. Well, except for being an accordionist in a Levellers/Tofu Love Frogs-inspired Irish folk group called the Merry Folksters, which would travel around the country in my little black Mini. Yep, that includes the four members plus banjo, fiddle and accordion crammed into a tight space, alongside camping equipment, food and lots of alcohol. You see, I never learned how to play the guitar or drums but instead, from an early age, started to play classical piano, getting my grade eight by the time I was 16. I don't know why I played the piano. I came from a working-class "non-musical" family who, except for my singer-songwriter Uncle Roger, rarely listened to music. School was a bit of a no-show for me, as was college, and I wound up in a dead-end job packing in an electronics factory, before getting into the West Sussex Institute of Higher Education (the lowest of the low, beneath a university and polytechnic) to study "classical" music. I knew my grade eight would get me somewhere in life. So, alongside listening to the Subhumans, Crass and Extreme Noise Terror, I was being introduced to the likes of Luciano Berio, Luigi Nono and Karlheinz Stockhausen. Little did I know at the time of Penny Rimbaud's love of classical music and especially the work of Benjamin Britten.

The course began with a recital, and there I was in ripped-up jeans, open para-boots and convoy cut with long smelly dreads, matted together by beeswax and neglect (I couldn't be bothered to get them done "properly" by a friend). I was like a crusty cross between a band member of Deviated Instinct, a new age traveller and a model for one of the cartoon characters you find on Doom

LPs. So far the recital had been the usual flute and violin sonatas, wind pieces and the odd four-chord pop song. And then I step up to the piano. Most hadn't heard me play, and for what it was worth, I didn't think I would come out with anything decent anyway. And then I did it: played the first of Lennox Berkeley's "Six Preludes for Piano", a short but virtuosic piece lasting one minute 30 seconds. For me, it was a blast of sound, reminiscent I thought of Extreme Noise Terror's "Murder" or Napalm Death's "Multinational Corporations". The piece sweeps through a merciless rhythmic pulse of jabbering arpeggios and short melodic figures, ending on a discordant broken chord that is held hovering by use of the sustain pedal. After a minute and a half I stopped. And turned around to a momentary look of shock and silence from the audience: and then applause. And that gig sent me on my way towards a musical "career" that balanced my playing of music by the likes of Franz Schubert and Hugo Wolf with the subcultural and academic career of writing about Crass and anarcho-punk. Good days.

Mike Dines, writer, co-author Punk Pedagogies: Music, Culture and Learning; and The Aesthetic of Our Anger: Anarcho-Punk, Politics, Music

NIRVANA/MUDHONEY/PAVEMENT/L7/TEENAGE FANCLUB/BEASTIE BOYS, READING 1992

A gig that was a bit of a milestone for me was Nirvana's appearance at the Reading Festival 1992. I had first heard them the previous autumn, on a college radio station while travelling in California, and they had pretty much reawakened my interest in music. So I was very keen to see them live. This was also to be the first time I had been to the Reading Festival, so a double first!

My partner's 18-year-old nephew Patrick was also keen to go. After checking that the dire weather hadn't caused the whole thing to be abandoned, the two of us caught a train to Reading and bought tickets on the door. The comedy tent had blown down in the gale force winds, and the thick mud churned up over the previous few days of the festival made it hard to get around. As all the bands we wanted to see were on the main stage, there was no shelter from the lashing rain. I remember looking at my watch and seeing it was still 10 hours to go before Nirvana's set, as my teeth started chattering.

I enjoyed Pavement, L7 (tampon throwing and all) and Teenage Fanclub and watched Bjorn Again and The Beastie Boys as they were Patrick's choice. Then it was Mudhoney, who I was a fan of, but couldn't help being amused by the crowd throwing clods of mud at them. They didn't appear to see the irony though. Nick Cave seemed to go on forever, but finally Nirvana appeared, Kurt Cobain in a wheelchair in what looked like a white dress and wig from the rather distant spot we were in. I was unaware of the speculation as to whether they'd even turn up so thought it was a rather random thing to do, but they soon got going, powering through the familiar songs. The wind made it hard to make out much in the way of detail, so I dived into the crowd to get nearer and managed to lose Patrick, but could make out what most of the songs were. For a while, I forgot I was shivering and sinking in the mud. Gems like "Smells Like Teen Spirit", "Drain You" and "Come As You Are" were magic for the first hour or so, but after that it got a bit hard to make out what they were doing, but at least we managed to regroup and catch a train back to London at the end.

Looking back, I'm so glad I managed to see them, as they would soon be no more.

Gaye Black, The Adverts

INSIDE OUT, DUBLIN 1992

Inside Out (Detroit) at Charlie's in Dublin 1991. This was a matinee show, the place was so packed (easily 250 kids) and we were sleep-deprived, travelling from Spain to Ireland in 55 hours. But it was insanely great and drummer Cathy passed out backstage from the heat. Afterwards, so many kids asked for our autographs, the owner said we rivalled Fugazi in that regard. Pretty kickass!!!

Lynda Mandolin, Inside Out

BLACK 47, HOBOKEN 1993

My first band leader, Wexford's Johnny Reck, said to me, "Kirwan, there's only two things you need to know in this business, get paid and get out alive – not necessarily in that order!"

Sound advice that continues to work. It does call for judgment though and that judgment can often be clouded by fatigue, the companion of every touring musician.

No matter, the bandleader must call the shots on stage. You're the one who can see what's going on, and ultimately you're responsible for the safety of those who come to see you.

But you're far from infallible; in fact you're usually hepped up from adrenaline and often dealing with security people who have little knowledge of crowd psychology.

Moshing can be exhilarating but there's a brutal narcissistic aspect to it that has always troubled me. Once at Vassar College, of all places, I saw a slight young woman hurl herself into a group of beefy football types who had commandeered the front of the stage.

Security stared on nonchalantly as she hurtled around in the thick of the fray. Suddenly she was struck by a swinging elbow and vanished. No one seemed to notice, particularly security. I watched the spot where I imagined she fell and after some moments caught a glimpse of her being trampled upon.

I panicked – screamed and cursed at the moshers and eventually security ambled forth and formed a circle around her. An ambulance arrived and she was rushed to hospital. However when we called by later, we discovered she had slipped out without leaving her name.

A happy ending, one hopes; unfortunately for me the gig was recorded by our sound tech who edited my ravings into a hilarious 60-second rant. Never had the F-word been used so frequently in the space of a minute.

Occasionally too you have to stand up to someone of undoubted authority, as happened at the 1993 Spring Festival in Hoboken. We had driven through the night from a late show in Ohio to find that the small city was bursting at the seams with fans – every band's dream.

Towards the end of our set, a well-dressed gentleman materialised on stage. I ignored him as best I could, assuming that security would cart him off. Funny how that magic mix of fatigue, adrenaline and Jameson's can blind you to reality.

During the climax of our song "James Connolly" as band and audience silently stood to attention, fists thrust in the air, chief of police La Bruno finally managed to identify himself, and ordered me to cease, desist and get the hell off the stage.

With political passions aroused, I knew this might have caused a riot, so we ignored him and finished up with a lively paean to a pregnant girlfriend back in Ireland.

The chief was not amused – he shut down the bars, declared me forever persona non-grata in his city, and sent the 30,000 revelers packing out of Hoboken and into legend.

A mere trifle compared to our encore at the Academy on W 43rd Street on St Patrick's Night 1996. A gun was fired but such was the onstage band volume the sound barely registered; still the nitroglycerin-like smell cut through the enveloping fumes of tobacco and weed.

Talk about crisis! The place was jammed, with only one obvious exit. At the soundcheck, I'd noticed a number of emergency doors that opened onto the street. But with such a boisterous crowd, who would notice them?

A procession of security and promoters arrived onstage imploring us to stop playing – and do what, cause a catastrophe as the panicked audience attempted to squeeze through the only open door? We had to keep playing though unsure if the shot had been fired at us.

It was a long five minutes before the side doors were opened and a calm announcement made to vacate the premises.

It's still a harrowing memory, for a policeman – an avid Black 47 fan and lovely young man – had accidentally shot himself; to cap it all, two of our family members were wounded by the ricocheting bullet.

We did get paid and got out alive but St Patrick's Day has never been the same.

Larry Kirwan, Black 47, writer, Green Suede Shoes

HARD-ONS, LATINA 1993

In 1993, the Hard-ons played in Latina, Italy. It was an all-ages affair organised by local punk kids, inside a huge ancient place of worship.

Apparently some head monk had to approve the gig first. On one hand, the monks want cash flow through venue hire but they can't just let any immoral riff-raff waltz through; after all, it is a sacred place.

Hard-ons' lyrics had to be translated into Italian and submitted for appraisal in order for the show to go ahead. The Hard-ons lyrics, on the whole didn't come close to The Mentors or GG Allin but they weren't exactly The Seekers either. The youthful promoters got together and produced a phoney set of positive lyrics, all about the benefits of being kind to the infirm, being polite to one's parents and the like, and the head monk swallowed it hook, line and sinker. Nowadays a monk can go google "Hard-ons" and I guess that's what they do now.

The gig was off-the-hook. Some 500 sweaty Italian kids filled the joint and it was brutal from the get-go. There was some steam being let off well and truly. The mass of bodies pulsated and the whole night we were worried about the PA stack tumbling to the ground from all the pogoing, dancing, stage-diving and general hoop-de-do.

Our last song was the opus "Suck And Swallow". During the improv feedback-drenched freakout, I turned my gaze to the side of the stage and I saw him. The head Franciscan monk, in his well-known and conspicuous attire (brown hooded robe and thick rope around the gut), was standing there with his hands on his hips like an angry teapot.

"Suck! Swallow! Suck! Swallow! I saw my baby walking down the street. Suck! Swallow! She had a gut and sores on her feet! Suck! Swallow! I said baby if you're all alone…" And so on went the lyrics.

The monk had steam coming out of his ears. Had he been wearing a bow-tie, it'd be spinning wildly. I'm sure his English wasn't that bad.

A young man jumped up on stage. He ran all the way by my side. He stood momentarily next to the monk, about two feet away from him. All within seconds, he then launched himself into a massive rampaging stage dive, the magnificence of which caused a stage invasion from youngsters who were generally overcome by the energy of a live punk show. Everything got accidentally unplugged. It descended into utter chaos as all good punk shows do: end of show.

We all looked at each other. We all turned and gazed at Friar Tuck. He was angry as fuck. He didn't know what the hell was going on but he knew it wasn't in keeping with his god. I am an atheist, but I was scared.

Raymond Ahn, Hard-ons

COCK SPARRER, LEONCAVALLO 1994

It was 1994, Cock Sparrer did their reunion, new album and tour in Europe. I was listening to them for many years. I never thought I could see them live. They were announced at Leoncavallo, one of the biggest and more important music squats in Italy. Finally, in the beginning of the 1990s, streetpunk and oi! music was starting to be accepted in the squats (called in Italy "centri sociali" – social centres), thankx to the Sharp (Skinheads Against Racial Prejudice) crews born in Italy in those years. The Sharp crews were finally starting to have a dialogue with the squat movement (strictly anti-racist and anti-fascist), to manage to set up some oi!/streetpunk shows there, to show finally to all the people that oi! music and skinhead didn't mean fascism/racism. That night the fascist boneheads tried to boycott the event, with some aggression on the road between the train station and the Leoncavallo squat. In the venue, thousands of punx, skinheads, rudeboys and rudegirls, coming from all of Italy and also from other countries, were waiting for the great Cock Sparrer gig.

It was a great event, the public response was amazing – the first official big oi! event in an Italian squat. A big emotion for me, a concert that will be forever tattooed in my heart. After that event, full of enthusiasm, I started organising some big oi!/streetpunk events in the squats of my region, bringing bands like The Business, Red London (in Vicenza at the Ya Basta squat) and Angelic Upstarts (in Venice at the Rivolta squat). The Cock Sparrer gig was really important for the Italian anti-racist/anti-fascist skinhead/punk scene. It was the beginning of a new era for the oi!/streetpunk music in our country. And besides, a big satisfaction for me with my band Los Fastidios, a few years later, to be able to share stages at important European festivals with Cock Sparrer, was a dream come true. Love music, hate racism!!!

Enrico, Los Fastidios

ALEJANDRO ESCOVEDO, TORONTO EARLY 1990s

Ultrasound was the club on Queen W in Toronto that I had been booking. I had started a good working relationship with an agent at Mongrel Music based in San Francisco. The roster was really interesting and very cool and he had an act from Austin Texas called Alejandro Escovedo that he needed dates for. The history of this artist was fascinating – he'd been in a punk band called The Nuns, and another critically acclaimed act called Rank and File. Alejandro had a new record out called "Gravity" and I quickly fell I love with the songs: they tore at your soul.

His show was booked on a Sunday night which was the death knell for almost any show as people in Toronto were absolutely lame about going out on Sunday night.

Generally because they partied hard on Saturday night. The band drove up to the club in a small van, as a three-piece: Alejandro, with Susan Voelz on violin and a chap called Frank on cello. We chatted during soundcheck and I found them to be just really lovely people. You get a pretty good instinct for people when you deal with so many characters every day.

No matter how hard I had tried to sell people on seeing this act, there was no getting anyone out on a Sunday night. A grand total of close to 10 people showed up. But what a gorgeous, intimate show the band put on for this lucky handful of people. It was wonderful and such a special performance. I felt like I had just witnessed something unique. Alejandro took time after the show to speak to everyone and I know he made new fans.

They made very little money that night, so I invited them to stay at my apartment to save them some money. That became the beginning of my nearly 30-year friendship with Alejandro. I have since watched his fan base build rapidly on his returns to Toronto. I have watched when he's been joined on stage on several different occasions by Bruce Springsteen. I have watched some of his children grow up, I have gone to his weddings. I have seen him overcome a debilitating illness.

He is one of the best songwriters that I've heard, an incredible storyteller, a charismatic band leader. He's so innovative in his performances and he's been critically acclaimed for many, many years. He's a musician's musician. He has written and performed a play, and is writing a book. He is a kind and thoughtful person and also a sharp-dressed man who delights in going shopping with me when he comes to town.

That first show was incredibly special. I have been lucky enough to be part of presenting so many of his shows in so many different formats, from singer songwriter to full on punk rock. It's always an intense surprise. I'm really proud to call him my friend.

Yvonne Matsell, promoter, Toronto

ALL/CHINA DRUM, LONDON 1994

I've been going to gigs since about 1990 and even though I've been to hundreds of gigs over the years, it's some of the earlier ones that have stayed with me the most. On that basis, if I had to narrow it down, my favourite was probably seeing

All on their Breaking Things tour at the London Powerhaus in 1993 or 1994 with support from China Drum. All (and The Descendents) were pretty much my favourite band in the world in the early to mid-1990s and I made the trip down from the north to see them. I grew up in a little northern town where punk gigs simply didn't happen. I only had a small number of friends who shared similar musical interests and getting into Manchester for gigs (the nearest city with any kind of notable punk activity that I was aware of at the time) was difficult. Getting to London was even harder. So this was a big deal for me even before I got there.

With memories affected by the passage of time and the beer consumed on the evening, some of my recollections are slightly blurred. I don't remember all the songs that were played, I don't recall any specific onstage banter or quite what happened in the latter stages of the night but I remember it as the first time I really felt part of a "scene" in any definite way. Aside from my few local friends, I just assumed there were only a handful of people in the UK who gave a damn about the bands I loved. But here there were hundreds of them all singing along and running into each other as All ripped into their opening song. I spoke to loads of people that night. All strangers who loved the music I loved. I stayed in touch with some of them for a while and often saw them when I went back to London over the following years.

It all sounds bit cheesy now, but I was young(ish) and naive about how big the scene was in the UK. As such, it was a defining moment for me and my love of punk outside of just listening to records in my bedroom. Additional high points included having a pre-gig coffee with Stephen Egerton and talking to Karl about our shared love of cartoons and bands like The Chemical People and The Hard-Ons. Also, the inclusion of some of my favourite Descendents songs in the set and meeting a young and slightly nervous Chad Price. This was the first time they'd played the UK with Chad on vocals and, apart from the songs on the new LP I'd ever heard him sing before. So I didn't know how well he'd handle the songs Scott and Dave sung on record. Clearly, I needn't have worried. Chad and the band took it all in their stride and blew me away. I saw All play London again in 2014 and, while that show was also great fun, the first time I saw them always sticks out as one of my fondest gig memories.

Scott McLauchlan, Brassneck Records

SHANE MACGOWAN AND THE POPES, PINKPOP 1995

The day started auspiciously enough. I was still in the first throes of heady excitement from touring in The Popes, fronted by one of the most raw and viscerally pure poets ever, Shane MacGowan. The notion of entertaining the masses at Holland's Pinkpop festival at the hellishly early time of midday didn't diminish my enthusiasm at all as the band convened downstairs after what was a mildish night of reacquainting ourselves with our old friends, Amstel, Grolsch and Bavaria. My lasting memory of the evening was Shane buying a huge hash cake. You know, the kind that they cut individual slices out of. Then he ate some of it before going to bed. All seemed well.

Surplus to requirements for the first song of the set, I waited at the side of the stage, tin whistle in one hand and fiddle in the other. My musical compadres launched into a cover of "Cracklin' Rosie" with typical ceili-punk gusto. Shane's timing seemed out at times, but maybe this was a nod to the rhythmic flexibility of Charlie Parker's playing. After all, Shane was a jazz aficionado, in addition to having an encyclopaedic knowledge of pretty much every strand of popular music. He never ceased to amaze me in that respect.

After sitting out the next one as well, I bounded onto the stage for "Greenland Whale Fisheries". Off we went. Shane missed his cue. He came in seconds later, in a different key, a perfect fourth below what the band was playing in. I was a big fan of experimental music at the time, but this seemed to be a bit too exploratory. It was certainly shaping up to be an interesting gig.

As we continued with bewildered looks on our faces, Shane further deviated from any semblance of the song we were playing, with his vocalisations progressively sounding like someone muttering to himself. Was he okay? What was causing him to lose his way like this? Why the hell was I wearing Rupert Bear, white-checked trousers when everyone else was in black? All of these questions went through my mind as I looked out into the audience. I saw a congregation instinctively reacting to what they were hearing, which meant much jumping around and general going nuts in a glorious way. It was a beautiful uplifting sight, jolting me out of my confused state – a timely reminder that music's not about perfection. It's about embracing the very inexactness of what can happen.

Which was just as well as by Christ did the inexactness continue. By the time we started "Dark Streets of London", Shane was shaking violently, seemingly clinging onto the mic stand for dear life. His manager Charlie MacLennan came on stage, his voice booming "What's wrong with ye?" over the PA while the juggernaut of our collective persevered. It was certainly the most bizarre re-enactment of James Brown's legendary stage exit routine I'd ever seen, but there he was, leading Shane off, while the crowd went apeshit. I flitted between hoping that Shane was going to be fine, and thinking that must have looked amazing out front, considering the reaction it got from the great unwashed.

Backstage afterwards, all became a bit more clear. Shane woke up that morning feeling hungry. Why bother with a typical breakfast when you can consume the rest of your purchase from the night before? Despite his constitution of a dozen oxen, the cake took its toll on him. Still, he ended up on the front page of one of the Netherlands' main newspapers the next day. Job done, I guess.

John Myers, Shane MacGowan And The Popes

RAMONES, LONDON 1995

Astoria, June 28th

Having developed a healthy obsession with the da Bruddas' unique style and their ruthless dedication to not evolve and remain integral to their roots, I paid my annual homage to see the Ramones.

On this occasion it was a two-night salvo at the Astoria in Tottenham Court Road. Having returned from a trip to Singapore and Malaysia, organised for dates that did not interfere with these Ramones dates, I took the 250-mile trip to London from Blackpool. The weather was surprisingly hotter than that on the other side of the world.

As a self-confessed introvert I can relate to the Pixies approach of just getting on with the gig accompanied by no verbal exchange in-between songs whatsoever. It was the same with The Ramones due to the old "One-two-three-four" introduction.

At most gigs, I'm the "stand away from the mosh pit" kind of guy, but close enough for full volume and energy from the band. On the second night of these dates, I went for it and cut loose for bloody once.

Seven songs in and the adrenaline was pumping with the band relentless and up-tempo as usual. I'd never experienced fainting and thought it was for girls awaiting the arrival of Take That or David Cassidy perhaps.

Sure enough, the legs buckled as the head-spins began. Thankfully people nearby helped out and off I went, dehydrated, for a pint of corporation pop courtesy of the gents loo, only to return to the pit with composure reassembled.

This was the night I realised how enhanced a concert can be with audience participation and how important the necessity of water is to the human body. For good measure, I crowd-surfed to the last song, "Beat on the Brat", with the intention of gate crashing the stage. The friendly security guy put paid to that, but I managed to acquire one of Cjay's plectrums as he threw them post-gig.

It was a one-off for me, as my normal conservative approach at live music events quickly returned. However, I unleashed my inner psycho, stared into the eyes of Joey through his glass lenses during "Chinese Rocks" and picked up that souvenir that I used to strum with in my own band for the next couple of years.

Stuart Diggle, Litterbug

VARIOUS, 1990s ON, MYRTLEVILLE, CORK

With a large window view that looked straight out to sea to where the Titanic was once parked, Pine Lodge Myrtleville in Co Cork became a haven for underground gigs at the start of the early noughties til 2016. So many punk rock gig flashbacks stand out. From Jeffrey Lewis playing his "Williamsburg Will Oldham Horror" song for the first time live as an encore (to a standing ovation), to Subhumans finishing a UK/Irish tour there (with a party on the beach afterwards). From to Mike Watt (Minutemen/The Stooges) and band (who featured a member of The Screamers) hiding behind the infamous stage curtain after their punk rock opera, to Fleshies front man lying in the middle of the floor with the locals dancing around him in a circle, arms around shoulders. From The Apes doing a (nobody expected this type of exceptional performance) full-on bizarre pysch-garage rock show on a quite cold winter night to Eddie Spaghetti and Ron Heathman from The Supersuckers (acoustic) getting the grandmothers out waltzing. From Cáit O'Riordan (The Pogues) singing "Haunted" (to be heard across Myrtleville due to windows opened) with Sean Wheeler and Zander Schloss (The Weirdos/Circle Jerks) plus Derwood Andrews (Generation X) was also an addition to the bill to XBXRX bouncing off the couch, walls and tables. From Kid Congo and The Pink Monkey Birds blasting a loud groove sound to an energetic crowd on a Sunday afternoon to a member of OVO getting crackly sounds from her extremely long dreadlocks with a fiddle bow.

These shows were only a brief touch of the memories in this unique juke joint venue. Many bands also stayed here (in the upstairs area) after city shows like NoMeansNo, The Ex, Cobra Killer, Citizen Fish and Acid Mothers Temple who even had the police follow them down to Myrtleville from Cork city (the police turned around and sped off once they saw the band members get out of the van).

Emmet Greene, promoter, Cork

THE HEADSTONES, TORONTO 1990s

Back in the 1990s, my club Ultrasound on Queen W in Toronto was a bit of a hot spot for talent spotting by the music industry and I am proud to say, that I really loved finding that new talent. One day, a cameraman, Tony, from our neighbours at Much Music TV station came in to see me with a spiky-haired guy in a chewed-up sweater and a tape of his band, The Headstones. I just loved the songs, they were a gritty, raw-sounding indie rock band so I immediately tried to find them a club spot.

A Monday night cancellation came up, so I called everyone I knew to come out and see them. Luckily, I was really trusted by the Toronto music industry as a bit of a tastemaker for my musical tips and so the club filled up to see this band I was excited about. The band didn't disappoint: the singer was a star with a punk attitude, throwing the mic stand around and spitting on stage, much to the extreme annoyance of my sound tech! They certainly excited the "experts" in the audience.

They were raw talent, with great songs and major in-your-face charisma. After a short, sharp set, full of a fuck-you attitude, Hugh the singer got off the stage, strode towards me and quietly whispered an apology for his behaviour and also for spitting. He told me he'd pay for any damage. That made me laugh and I knew right then that I loved them!

They landed themselves a manager, an agent and a Universal Records recording deal after that show.

Yvonne Matsell, promoter, Toronto

TADANOSHIN, NEW YORK 1998

In 1998, I formed a noise punk funk orchestra called Tadanoshin with my favorite punk rockers from Lower East Side NYC. We performed at places like Brownies, The Cooler, Coney Island High, CBGB's, Baby Jupiter, Rubulad party in Williamsburg, Black Cat in DC, etc. Sharing stages with a unique variety of acts like Von Lmo, Gogol Bordello, Mono Puff, Eszter Balint, Skeleton Key, etc. Every show was packed full of hipsters and we played some out-there music that couldn't fit any genre really. It was punk, it was funk, it was a big band and it was experimental.

I had some amazing personalities and talents in this big band. Because that's what I wanted. I wanted musicians with not only chops but big personalities. I wanted music to be exploded like you have never experienced before. I also had a bigger-the-better mentality for this particular music. So the band always consisted of eight people at least but not limited to that number, sometimes we had more percussion and horn players.

Let me introduce you some of the guys who played in the 1990s for this band.

Sissi Schulmeister – bass (Alice Donut); Dan Joeright – drums (Sulfer/Jim White/El Vez/etc); Garry "G Man" Sullivan – drums (Cro-Mags/Bernie Worrell/Nnek/etc); Genji Siraisi – drums (Nastyfacts/Groove Collective/etc); Stephen Moses – trombone/drums (Alice Donut/Rasputin/Percy Jones/etc); Paula Henderson – bari sax (James Chance & Contortions/Burnt Sugar Arkestra/Melvin Van Peebles/TV On the Radio/etc); Arron Johnson – trombone (Antibalas/Sharon Jones/etc); Ursula Wiskoski – cello (Rebecca Moore/Gamma Rays/etc); Yoshi Takemasa – percussions (Akoya Afrobeat Ensemble/Antibalas/Chin Chin/etc); Tamaki Ui – percussions/drums (New Kingdom/Brown Rice Family/American Pop/etc); Mars – samples/noise (E-Trance/Blue Whales/etc); me – vocals/drums/keys/conducting (Blonde Redhead/Ultra Bide/Russel Simins Band/Cibo Matto/etc).

Just imagine what these guys can offer musically… insanely powerful and colorful!

AUDIENCE

It was very interesting time in music scene in LES at the end of late 90s. There were still a lot of hipsters from late 80s who became somewhat successful (having record deals & touring) by the end of 90s hanging out, and there were also a lot of hungry new faces moving into city and started exciting new bands and stuff. So I would see guys from JSBX, SWANS, Foetus, THE THE who is already kind of legend, and I would also see up-and-coming guys like Eugene from Gogol Bordello, Torbitt Schwartz(Producer of Run the Jewels, House band for Mike Myers Gong Show), Jaleel Bunton and Tunde Adebimpe(TV On the Radio) started hanging out with us. During the set when I jump into audience with my drums for jams, those new hipsters would totally join me and bang on drums together. Now they do that to their audience!!!

MUSIC

Heavy, Gnarly & roovy bass was definitely the main thing I had set in my head. I always liked the sound of Lemmy from Mötörhead, Rob Wright from NoMeansNo, David Wm Sims from Jesus Lizard and Steve Harris from Iron Maiden. I also liked electro-music bass sound like The Chemical Brothers. At the same time I am a huge funk, soul, R&B fan. Good bass was a MUST; a weakass bass was a NO-NO for me. So I decided to have no electric guitars at all for this big band, so we can feature bass up front! To match that, I definitely needed a heavyweight drummer. So I had to get the best drummers in town. And, to unique things up more, I included electric cello, percussions and horn sections. Music totally became an epic "noise punk funk orchestra" indeed.

Each gig was totally high energy and insane as you can imagine. I had all these larger-than-life musicians behind me, with each of whom I was a friend and also a fan. It was so much fun conducting this monster band and such an honour to know these amazing individual human beings and perform epic music together. Every single Tadanoshinshow was an end of the 20th century extravaganza! Hope to reunite and perform again in a future.

Tada aka Tadanoshin

WEAKERTHANS, LONDON 2000

My gigging days started in 1974 when I cajoled my dear mum to take me to Blackpool Winter Gardens to see the then chart-topping Slade and continued recently in the same location watching oodles of bands on the many different Rebellion stages. I was only nine when I was whisked off to see Slade and remember her imploring me to stop jumping up and down on my seat. I even still have the gig programme buried among my zine collection and remember Noddy

Holders' opening salvo which he grinned to the crowd in a rich Black Country accent, the likes of which I had never heard before: "Bluddy 'ell – well yow've got a graite football team –four-nil!" Others that still resonate for various reasons are Billy Bragg at the Young Socialists' Conference (we weren't delegates, we nicked in), Fugazi at the Boardwalk, Cock Sparrer at Jillys, The Enablers, Hüsker Dü a couple of times at the International in Manchester.

But if I have to plug for one it would be The Weakerthans' first gig in London. I choose this for reasons. First I had picked up on The Weakerthans courtesy of Alan's Records in Wigan. He had recommended their second album ("Left and Leaving", 2000) which on first listening (rather like the time I heard Great St Louis's first demo) was one of those wow moments. All the songs were good, all the songs were different, from the full-on A-side to the mournful "Left and Leaving", the musicianship was amazing and the beautiful harmonies were something to die for. Once I devoured the lyrics I was not only drawn in but overcome. It's a good job CDs don't wear out.

I started researching the band and found out they were visiting the UK to play the Garage in Islington. At the time I was doing a few interviews and reports for Dave Monk's Fracture zine and decided to contact them. Once the arrangements were in place I booked a "cheap" B&B and hotfooted it down to the smoke. I met the band in the afternoon. John was great to talk to and the discussion could have gone on for hours. As it was the first time for the band in the UK, they were uncertain as to what size of a crowd to expect. When I told them it had been sold out for weeks, they all looked aghast.

Later that night the gig was amazing. Just before their set I remember bumping into Alan (Alan's Records) who said "I thought you would be here". We talked and I said I knew he liked the band but didn't think he liked them so much to make the big expedition down south. He flashed a Noddy Holder grin and said "As you were raving about their album so much I gave it a few more listens… They are the best band in the world." Rare praise indeed from the great record shop owner himself! To cap it all, it turned out that the band were also in the same B&B so we ended up sharing a couple of post-gig relaxing cans I had in my room as everywhere was closed and they didn't have any money.

Andy Higgins, Just Say No To Government Music

THE ATARIS/FABULOUS DISASTER/DOUGLAS, NEWPORT 2001

TJ's

One of the best ever: 350 kids packed into this small place, when Fab D was on, kids stage dove and hung off of the rafters and pipes, the walls were pouring with sweat and we were mobbed by fans. I hung out all night, I felt like I knew everyone. Being part-Welsh, I felt like I finally fit in with "the people" lol. Such a great night!! I got a Welsh dragon tattoo shortly after.

Lynda Mandolin, Inside Out

FUN-DA-MENTAL, NOVI SAD 2002

Being on the receiving end of lyrics, the music, the spectacle, the presence of being was good enough for me: I never had any drive to be in a band. It was during my first DJ stint in London that I met Aki Nawaz, who had recently co-founded Nation Records with Kath Canoville. He introduced himself by giving me some of their releases and then disappeared into the night as I cued up the next record.

Their ethos was to give a platform to a new generation of musicians armed with the record collections of their parents and the accessible new technology of samplers and computers. Sons and daughters of immigrants and native Brits had an infinite space to create and explore beyond borders. Club music was entering a new era, giving rise to bands such as Joi, Headspace, Hustlers HC, TransGlobal Underground, Loop Guru, Talvin Singh and Zuvuya among them. Fun-da-mental as this time was the only concept that Aki wanted Talvin Singh to be a part of.

Wilf Walker had been involved with the British arm of the Black Panthers in the 1960s. Now he was working as a promoter and was part of the Notting Hill Carnival organisation. At his request and with five days' notice, Aki, rapper Amir aka BadSha Lallaman, percussionist/vocalist Inder Goldfinger and DJ Obeah worked rapidly to assemble a seven-song set for the 1991 carnival.

Prior to returning to London in the summer of 1988, I was being informed by the UK music press, eagerly awaiting the arrival of the NME and the Melody Maker at the Record Peddler, a record shop in downtown Toronto. Here is where I got my fix. They imported the latest releases from the UK shores: Killing Joke, The

Redskins, Cabaret Voltaire, PIL, On-U Sound, The Three Johns and The Mekons found a home with me and it was these records among others that I relayed to Torontonians via my radio programme at CKLN, "Well Up and Bubble".

The reason I moved back to London from Toronto was the vibrant music scene there. You could catch a concert every day of the week. From Acklam Hall aka Subterrania in Ladbroke Grove, to the Mean Fiddler, which was five minutes' walk from my new home in Harlesden. The beer-drenched sticky floor of the Astoria, the Brixton Academy, the spacious Town & Country Club and the intimate Bull & Gate in Kentish Town, the George Robey in Finchley Road, the Hammersmith Odeon, the legendary Marquee and more, gave audiences a good run for our money. Sometimes I'd head out of town driving to Manchester, Brighton, Nottingham to catch a show, then hurry back on a deserted orange-lit motorway to get a few hours' sleep before starting work the next morning at Virgin Records.

The first Gulf War had come and gone, but the political residue was still present. Tones of western imperialism were at the forefront once again with the UK media doing their bit to uphold the establishment's perceived right to all resources and dispersing "British and western values" to all corners. Islam, "a religion of others", immigration, the society split among class, colour and cultural lines helped form Fun-da-mental's rhetoric.

They were now into their second year of existence. I'd seen a few shows around town and liked their edge and presentation, reminiscent of seeing Public Enemy's first appearance in Toronto. The provocative honesty of Lallaman's patois-influenced slang among snippets of Malcolm X waking up his people and images of female Iranian revolutionaries lighting up the backdrop as the band brought a new consciousness to those in the audience. Their politics spoke to me and resonated within.

I suggested to a colleague that worked in the A&R dept at Virgin that she should check them out with a mind to sign the band. Two weeks later, my occasional DJ partner Angus aka Pineapple Head, told me that Aki asked him if he could suggest anyone to replace DJ Obeah, who was giving up his slot in the band due to marriage commitments.

Within six months of me joining, there was some internal conflict and Lallaman and Goldfinger left the band soon after we returned from filming the "Countryman" video in Pakistan. Aki and I continued as a duo, and it was in live form where I took hold of the microphone for the first time. New vocalists in Hot Dog Dennis and

Mushtaq Uddin came into the fold and with them we delivered our debut album, "Seize the Time", the name taken from the book of the same name by Bobby Seale, one of the founders of the Black Panther Party for Self-Defence.

We confronted the issues of racism, sexism, the abuse of religious and political doctrines. There were a few instances of bomb threats at venues and threats of violence from white nationalist groups such as Combat 18, whose name references Adolf Hitler with A being the first letter in the alphabet and H the eighth.

On our co-heading tour with the group Blaggers ITA, they had several baseball bats within easy reach behind the drum kit should anything untoward happened.

In Norway, we performed at a squat club and a tall pale lover of the Aryan movement kept doing a Nazi salute in front of Aki. I kept a close eye on him and my hand on a massive MagLite torch until he ended up getting thrown out for fighting with his friend.

In approaching festivals in the UK for a slot, we often met with the following response, "We already have an 'Asian' band on the bill." With this in mind we were amped to return to the Exit Festival in Serbia with Asian Dub Foundation and Nation label-mates Charged. The setting was ripe for a forceful exhibition of who we were collectively – and as individual groups.

Our line-up now consisted of four vocalists including myself. I'd start the set and then Shamil, Nawazish and Lloyd took their respective turns. For my second or third turn as lead vocalist, I emerged from behind my turntable and mixer, took the mic and proceeded to deliver my lyrics. Barely into the first verse, an unidentified flying object struck my forehead, just above my eye. The microphone fell from my grip, it and myself hitting the stage in time with the driving beat that was coming out of the speaker stacks.

A few seconds later, I recovered and saw an empty beer bottle to my right. I didn't recall ordering a drink while onstage, but somebody delivered that beer bottle with precision. I was about to cut the night short, however I decided to return to the stage and pick up where I left off, delivering the lyrics to Bob Marley's "War" with anger and rage at the forefront as one can imagine.

As we descended the stairs from the stage at the end of the concert, a man was being held by two security personnel and the festival organiser Gigi told me this was the man responsible for throwing the bottle at me. I asked the alleged bottle-thrower, whose jacket was adorned with far-right badges, what was his game and why did he do it. He responded sneeringly in his native tongue. At this point, an agitated Gigi stepped before me, spoke to the man and once again the response was a middle-finger sneer. Gigi landed a lightning strike of a head-butt to his nose. His legs buckled instantly as mine had 30 minutes beforehand. The blood rushed down his face.

The security men of the festival were the type of people that bench-pressed a Mercedes-Benz for breakfast, and they dragged him away. I thought they were going to eject him from the festival. They did, but not before unleashing a severe punishment upon him. The beating was so bad that Shamil said he felt sorry for him. I seriously doubt he tried that move again. As I went out front to catch ADF's set, Gigi assigned two members of his security staff to watch my back. And all further drinks were delivered hand to hand.

Dave Watts, Fun-Da-Mental

NEW MODEL ARMY, US 2000s

Growing up in a small southern town in North Carolina, we didn't have much in the way of "influences" when it came to politics and music. Rocky Mount, North Carolina was the centre of the southeastern industrial railroad line at the turn of the 20th century, a prime stop, exactly half-way between New York City and Miami, along the eastern seaboard. A very conservative, old tobacco money and segregated town.

It's ironic that jazz legend Thelonious Monk was born there too and Jack Kerouac resided in Rocky Mount off and on with his family and referred to the town in his influential writing in On The Road. Not a community you would correlate with two of the greatest beat generation poets of our time.

At the end of 1985, I was reeling from the sudden passing of my father from a heart attack, one week after my 16th birthday (and two weeks before Christmas). I was a bit of a lost soul, wandering the halls of my school, feeling out of place and holding onto the one thing I loved and understood. Music.

By this time, I was in deep, especially gravitating towards music with a social and political message. It was the antithesis of the culture I grew up with. I was not doing it to rebel, I was drawn to it because I knew something was not right. The energy around me was toxic and suffocating. A friend had a show on Wake Forest University's radio station and would tape his shows for me and I would listen to them religiously. One day he played a song called "51ˢᵗ State" by a band called New Model Army. It knocked me off my seat. I wanted more.

I never had a chance to see them live but I kept following the band for years and, in 1990, while attending NC State University, I got a job at the premier record store in the area, Schoolkids Records. One of my co-workers was a huge fan, so I was at home. I was willing to travel to NYC or Washington DC to see them if it came down to it. There was a new record out but still no US tour dates. I soon found out the band's visas were denied by US immigration due to having "no musical merit". This was clearly censorship as the band had a major label deal – the decision had to be based on their political stance. The US was in the middle of the Gulf War so any anti-war stance was not looked upon fondly by the powers that be. This just deepened my resolve to support their cause. They responded in the 1990s by starting their own label, Attack Attack Records and their future albums were not available through domestic distribution. However, we specialised in imports so I was able to get them and follow the band's progress despite the limitations. In the public eye, the band's profile started to diminish due to no profile in the States.

In 2002 I was hired as the sales and marketing director at Redeye Distribution and was trying to obtain a copy of Justin Sullivan's solo record "Navigating by the Stars". I went to Schoolkids to order it, knowing it would be an import and was surprised that it was not available. The import market was starting to dry up. Frustrated, I then thought, "Wait a minute. I work for a distributor!"

I reached out to a mutual friend, Jack Rabid who runs the Big Takeover magazine, and was delighted to be introduced to NMA's manager, Tommy Tee. We immediately hit it off. Tommy said the band wanted to get back to the States and tour and needed distribution, so it was a perfect marriage. I offered them a US distribution deal and, for the first time in years, New Model Army was coming back to the States. Not only would I finally have my chance to see them live, I was directly responsible for opening the door.

Over the next few years, I remained close with Tommy, Justin and the band and would see them live several times. In late 2008, just a few days after Christmas, I received a call out of the blue from Justin with the shocking news that Tommy had passed away. The band was in total shock and lost. About to head into the studio to record their next album and planning a 30ᵗʰ anniversary tour, they needed help. Tommy had done everything for the band and I knew what I needed to do. I stepped in to be their temporary US manager and helped put together two incredible 30th anniversary shows in New York City. It remains the only two shows the band have played in the United States since Tommy passed. I could not be prouder being a part of those two glorious evenings.

The energy of their shows was overwhelming. The only words to describe the environment is that it is a euphoric celebration. Fans get up on top of shoulders and open their arms as if they were opening up to the heavens and letting their music into their soul for nourishment. It's a loving environment and an incredible experience with lots of singing, energy and love. It's family.

After 32 years working in the music business, I owe everything to New Model Army. I now own Schoolkids Records and see kids that remind me of myself coming in on a daily basis and provide that place for them to find their souls. Today, NMA remain true pioneers of their craft. You either know them and are a passionate fan and devoted loyal member of the Army or you are not. There is no in-between.

Anytime I see someone wearing a NMA shirt, hat or tattoo, or come across another fan, there is an immediate connection. We can hug it out, look each other in the eye and know we are family. How powerful is that? To have music bring so many people together, from so many different backgrounds, cultures, generations and from all across the world and create a family. That is special.

In today's time, we need a band like New Model Army more than ever, to move that needle back to where we prioritise social justice, human rights and our values as human beings. I do my little part every single day to provide that outlet for my community but New Model Army has and continues to be music that binds us all together.

Stephen Judge, Schoolkids Records, Chapel Hill, NC

SLEATER KINNEY, NEW YORK 2003

We spent the day battling the cops in the streets of New York City. Upwards of one million people turned out to protest against the coming war on Iraq. Many millions more protested around the world on the same day. In New York, we couldn't even get over to where the main speakers addressed the marchers – the cops blocked access so we couldn't get past Lexington Avenue in some places, Third Avenue in others. Eventually we made it to Third, where we found protesters filling the sidewalks (the mayor wouldn't grant a permit to march in the streets). It was still an amazing sight. Then, at some point, the cops – who were everywhere – let us fill Third Avenue, somewhere in the 50s. It seemed like they'd finally seen the wisdom of letting us get on with the protest. And on such a frigidly cold day, it was comforting to fill the block side-by-side with so many other people, a whole city, it seemed, turning out in solidarity. Until it wasn't comfortable.

Soon we realised that the cops had penned us in and wouldn't let us advance. Steadily, the street filled as more and more people kept marching northward toward the police barricade. And then they appeared: a line of cops on horseback. We figured they were there to just hold the line, but after about 15 minutes, they plunged forward in phalanx, splitting the crowd, pushing us on the icy, slippery streets toward the sidewalks again. I saw elderly people falling down and parents trying to protect children in strollers as the horses nervously tried to avoid stepping all over us. It was insane. The police eventually forced us to the sidewalks, where many of us sat down and were threatened with arrest. We had no plan, no prior expectation of this confrontation, so most cleared out, unwilling to go to jail for holding a meaningless piece of city sidewalk.

But it felt like a defeat, like we'd been strong-armed (which, of course, we had been). We repaired to a bar, Jimmy's Corner on 44th Street, to lick our wounds. We had bought tickets to see Sleater Kinney weeks in advance, but I was hardly in the mood now. Still, a bunch of us went ahead and were thrilled at the sight of the band coming on stage wearing the same anti-war paraphernalia – buttons and arm bands – and weary looks that we wore. I'm sure not everyone in that crowd had been in the streets that day, but because the band had marched with us and came out to talk about it, it felt like we all had.

When they played a scorching version of "Combat Rock" – one of the best musical critiques to date on that ugly era – I started to feel like we could go back out and take it to the cops again. It was a politically desperate time, and we needed an astutely political band. That night we had one. We emerged from the show soaked with sweat and buoyed by a sense that music and the artists who create it can prop us back up and help push us forward. I'll never forget that day.

Michael Stewart Foley, writer, Dead Kennedys' Fresh Fruit for Rotting Vegetables, Front Porch Politics – The Forgotten Heyday of American Activism in the 1970s and 1980s

SUZY & LOS QUATTRO, JAPAN 2005

Did a few home demos with girlfriend early 2002. Anniversary came close and we decided to record those songs in a proper studio, have a laugh, put them on the shelf. Record label friend pops up while we're at it, says he loves it, it could "do well in Japan". Now we're having a laugh! Long story made short, after those recordings came out, a few singles were done and with our first album, we get the call from the label asking how would we like to do a few shows in Japan. Yeah, we're in. Worst-case scenario, we get to visit a far away country and cover a fraction of the costs. Our average audience here is 60 to 150 so we think we'll be lucky if 30 people show up on our first tour there.

Land in Tokyo, Oct 29th, 2005. Jet-lagged as fuck, straight to soundcheck. Everything feels unreal like we landed on a different planet, but the icing on the cake of weirdness is hearing the show is sold out. We play with four more bands so someone must be very popular.

Set up the merch post and we have a queue of over 10 guys and girls ready to spend a fortune on all our stuff. They know everything about us, the recordings we've made, the bands we've played on since we picked up a guitar.

Four amazing bands play before us to a polite audience who don't seem to be much into them. Get in our stage clothes, play the intro, pop my head out a bit and it's packed to the rafters and people are screaming. The band goes on stage and you can feel there's a totally different electricity to the place. I take my stage right side and am greeted by a bunch of guys calling my name. I can see the rest of the band is getting the same from different people. They seem to have picked their favourites, but when Suzy comes in, the place literally erupts. We've been told a few things to say in Japanese but Suzy is so shocked to see the reaction of the crowd she says everything perfectly, just in the wrong order. The audience laughs, we count the first song in and it's fucking Beatlemania all over us. They know all the songs, they know all the obscure covers we play. They never stop jumping and dancing and stage diving and we're there looking at each other like what the fuck is going on?

When the show ends, we go back to the merch post and sign lots of stuff. Suddenly I hear a girl is crying and screaming and my drummer is standing beside her and I go "What the fuck did you do?" and he goes "I did nothing, I promise." She's just having some kind of fan freakout so I go there and she screams even more, and I try to hold her hand saying "It's okay! Don't panic!" but every time I touch her, she goes mental. So I go get Suzy to do more orgasmic screaming and she gives her a hug (right! just what we needed!) and the girl almost faints while her boyfriend is laughing his ass off. Suzy presented her with the belt she used that night during the set and she's looking at it like she's holding the Holy Grail.

This is just a fraction of what happened that night, let alone the whole tour. A rock'n'roll fantasy!

BB Quattro, Suzy & Los Quattro, TV Smith & The Bored Teenagers

REBELLION FESTIVAL, MORECAMBE 2005

If it's August it's Rebellion, and that means a visit to Blackpool. Each year the faithful return to the Wintergardens, as if directed homeward by the punk-nesting instinct embedded in their DNA.

But it was nearby Morecambe, way back in 2005, that was our first visit to the legendary festival. It was surprisingly our first show ever in the UK. We had been featured on No Future compilations and even had records released on the Brit label on the early 1980s. Interestingly enough, a lot of people still think we are an old school UK band due to those releases.

But we never really had the chance to play in England until we were invited by Darren to play at the then-titled Wasted fest.

We had spent the night before in Liverpool, doing all those touristy Beatles things of course. Drinking far too much as we toasted each other again and again for finally making it over, "Penny Lane" blasting in the background.

Friday, we sat in a noisy rail car with a crowd of other punkers, staring out at the gloomy countryside while nursing our hangovers with warm Carlsbergs and exotic cheese and onion sandwiches. It all seemed exciting, to be so far from home yet surrounded by our tribe. We talked with these people in the same language, yet not able to understand what they were saying due to northern accents and inebriated slurring. No matter, we were all on a jolly rail trip to a proper punk festival goddammit!

When we got to the gates of the festival, we checked in with Jennie. She gave us passes and beer tickets, directed us to the backstage trailer we could use for a bit before and after the set. We quickly dropped off guitars and went scurrying through the fest like children let loose in Disneyland on the first day of summer vacation.

UK Subs, Rezillos, 999! We were amazed to see all these bands playing, thought we would never see them again to be honest. It was as if our teenage record collections had come to life and gathered solely for our enjoyment. We stood in the humid Quonset hut before a set by Sham 69 – Sham, for god sake! – and were taken by the happy solidarity of the crowd. The band was late getting to stage, but no matter. The crowd simply entertained themselves with football chants and another chorus of "If the Kids are United".

A playful beer fight sends foam flying through the air, baptising us into this joyous family. We reluctantly made our way back to the trailer to get ready for our set. Lars from Rancid poked his spiky head in to wish us break a leg. It seemed all too wondrous, this day of our lives, and we hadn't yet hit the stage.

Of course, it all went by too quickly – it seemed like we'd only got up there and started before the stage manager was giving us the one more song signal from the wings.

We had started the set with "I Got a Gun", relying on an oldie for those old enough to remember us. But as we announced our thank-you and good night, a crew in front of the stage shouted out for the song once again.

Nowadays of course, we act like jaded international travellers on tours, complaining about the backstage pasta or the hectic routing favoured by sadistic booking agents. We've played Rebellion so many times we just leave guitars in the office of the Metropole Hotel. But whenever we meet back again on those northern shores, we are reminded of that first visit.

We stood on stage, not wanting to leave, as the growing crowd yelled louder for the song. So we looked at one another and grinned, pointed to the top of the set list and counted it off once again.

We gave them what they wanted; we had all we could ask for.

Mike Magrann, CH3

THIS BAND IS A BIKE BOMB/OTHERS, WICKLOW 2006

Paddy's Hall, Greystones, Co Wicklow, Feb 11th

Paddy's Hall was a semi-abandoned, former parochial hall in the sleepy coastal town of Greystones about 30km south of the Dublin metropolis. In the mid-2000s, the building was set to be demolished to make way for a shiny new apartment block. As it lay temporarily idle, the property developers gave the go-ahead to a group of local, music-hungry kids to put on gigs there. The Basta Youth Collective (BYC), as they were known, were idealistic teenagers who espoused community DIY politics. Their ethos would fit comfortably alongside Critical Mass, Food Not Bombs, community gardening and zine culture. Its core membership came principally from Bray, Greystones and Kilcoole with a smattering of others dotted around Dublin.

From October 2004 to March 2006, Paddy's Hall became Basta's de facto HQ and hosted about a dozen gigs with local and touring punk bands. They mainly took place on Saturday afternoon and were always all-ages – a rare thing in Dublin. Even more exceptional was that they were run by teenagers themselves. This was a marked contrast to most of the all-ages gigs in Dublin at that time. One regular gig in particular frequently faced justified criticism as their organisers were middle-aged, business-minded rogues of questionable moral values.

Paddy's Hall was the anthesis. Everyone involved was driven by not-for-profit principles. Entrance was always affordable. Facilities were basic. Alcohol was not for sale nor was it allowed on the premises. The crowd policed themselves and there was very little trouble. Gig details, and later reviews and photographs, were circulated on internet forums like Eirecore and PunkForIt. Facebook and Twitter hadn't taken off yet.

A motley crew of like-minded underage punky and scene kids travelled from all over Dubin on the Dart train to attend the Paddy's Hall gigs. I was slightly too young to make the first shows but was lucky to make it to three or four of the last ones. In my head, I associate every one of those trips with hot summer weather but that's probably a false memory as the gig that stands out most for me took place in early February 2006. I was a few months shy of my 16th birthday. Five bands took to the stage on that Saturday afternoon over a marathon six-hour session. Entry was just a fiver which is incredible thinking back as there were three touring bands from the States. Two particularly blew my mind that day. This Bike Is A Pipe Bomb from Florida played snappy, toe-tapping folk-punk with layered vocals and angsty lyrics seemingly all about train-hopping and teenage adventure. But they were political too and formed part of the same scene and sound as Against Me!, Defiance, Ohio and Ghost Mice. Criminal Class USA from Alabama, on the other hand, were more in-your-face and fired out melodic streetpunk with anger and grit. I bought their T-shirt and a CD of their album "Echos in the Street" which was played frequently from that day onwards. It seemed to fit in well with other favourites of mine at the time like Pennywise and Strike Anywhere! and some of the better British oi! Bands like Cock Sparrer and The Angelic Upstarts.

After the gig, we piled out of Paddy's Hall sweaty and happy. With the music still ringing in our ears, we grabbed chips for the train journey home and talked all the way back about our favourite band of the day and when the next gig would be. Nothing beats the excitement and freedom of those first years of seeing live music with your friends as a teenager. Many of those from the Basta Youth Collective are still active in the cultural sphere today as well-respected musicians, promoters, artists, photographers and recording engineers. I expect, like myself, they look back at those gigs in Paddy's Hall fondly.

Sam McGrath, author, co-founder of the Come Here To Me! history blog and occasional DJ

THE BOYS, TOKYO 2009

My good friend Peter Jones, English guitarist of Paranoid Visions who sounds more Irish than the lovechild of Dave Allen and Terry Wogan, asked me to write a couple of paragraphs about my favourite ever gig memory for this highly commendable book.

Now Peter is one of Bono's greatest fans so I thought I might regale him about the time I was wandering along the seafront in Cannes at midnight when I heard someone playing U2. "Wow, they've got that record on loud," I thought as I wandered unsteadily from the evening's merriment back to my hotel. But my next thought, as I raised my view from the pavement I was trying my best not to fall off was, "F*ck me, it is U2", as I saw the four of them playing an unannounced live set in front of the famous Film Festival Palais where their 3D film had just premiered. To be fair they were very good and the sound rocked. But then I was very, very drunk to borrow from Paul Whitehouse and I had once declared an undying love for Kool and the Gang while in a similar state.

My favourite gig experience, though, was not exactly a gig. I was with The Boys on tour in Japan. We had played our show and were enjoying the delights of Shinjuku on a Saturday night. This is a historic warren of tiny bars, so minute that if six people gather in some of them you spill into the tiny alley ways outside. In one of these was a Samurai warrior in full regalia including armour, head guard and, of most relevance, a bloody great sword sheathed at his side. To cap this off our pugilist had a guitar and was trying his hand at "Wild Thing" by The Troggs. Such is everyday life in Japan.

He was awful.

So awful in fact that we clamoured for him to lend his guitar to our Honest John Plain to have a sing song. Now Honest, so named because of his idiosyncratic relationship with the truth while loudly declaring "I didn't do it, honest!", is a world-class balladeer. Honest gave us "Dead Flowers" by The Stones, his own brilliant "Where Have All the Good Girls Gone" and various other classics. By the third song, a crowd had gathered, struggling to get in to hear our man to a bar which could only accommodate 10 of them.

But the Samurai was not happy. His glowering was steadily on its way up to Chernobyl levels. Worse was to come as Honest launched into "Wild Thing", a song the Samurai considered his own, which was received in rapture by the crowd in the alley outside, while our armoured man's version had been ignored. This was just too much as he exploded with a roar from the corner, sword raised high above his head, pushing through the bodies headed straight for John. Everything was abandoned including the acoustic guitar and a number of very expensive, half-drunk beers as we dived out the door and ran into the crowd, pursued by an armed opponent thankfully weighed down by body armour.

I can honestly say the evening was right up there with that chance encounter with Peter Jones's heroes in France. It included similar elements such as spontaneity, conviviality and a relationship with alcohol but pipped it at the post by having a unique element: the excitement of a near-visit to eternity.

Duncan Reid, The Boys, Duncan Reid and the Big Heads

'THE PARTY', NEW YORK 2010

A year after Willy Deville's death, members of his various incarnations of Mink DeVille and Willy's solo career got together to play a tribute show to him at BB King's Times Square location in New York. We played Willy's songs to a packed house of his fans, which included people who travelled far and wide from European countries where Willy's popularity far outweighed his US counterparts. But I digress. Although it was a fun, emotional, feelgood show as tribute shows involving people who worked with their deceased comrades usually are, the most fun in my 50 years of playing gigs was a private party that came about directly from the Willy Deville tribute show. A very well-known and well-connected music mogul who had been a fan of Willy's was in attendance. After the show, he approached a few of us and asked if it would be possible to hire a band of ex-Minks to perform some of Willy's songs along with whatever else we'd like to play at a party at his home in The Hamptons area of Long Island in a few weeks. We would just need to bring our instruments, as a sound company had been hired for the event. We accepted his offer.

The day of the party arrived. We had a band of ex-Minks including Thommy Price, Joe Vasta Jr., David J Keyes, Seth Farber, Boris Kinberg, Crispin Cioe, Mark Newman and myself. My wife, Elise, reminded me there would probably be some musical and other celebrities there. She told me Paul McCartney had a summer house in that area, was friends with the host and not on tour. When we arrived at the house, we were instructed to set up on a portion of the backyard. It was a gorgeous day to be in The Hamptons.

We began our first set. The sound system was good. The guests remained in their seats as we dove into Willy's songs, finishing each to the sound of one hand clapping. I figured it would be one of those gigs where we would basically be background music. Around the middle of the first set I picked up the accordion and we launched into a few zydeco favorites. As we played, I saw a couple get up and walk towards us. Our first dancers? As they got closer I could have plotzed. It was none other than Sir Paul and his future wife, Nancy Shevell. They began to dance and, after they broke the ice, others joined in dancing. Paul and Nancy seemed to be thoroughly enjoying the music. The Beatles were the reason I began to play and here was one dancing to our band 10 feet away! The last song of the set was "Bad Boy", the Clarence Palmer & The Jive Bombers pre-rock'n'roll R&B midtempo song that Willy covered on "Le Chat Bleu", my first album with Willy.

We announced we were taking a break and, soon after, Paul approached us and asked about the origins of the last song we played with "the Fats Domino 6/8 feel". I told him the title and artist adding that The Beatles also covered a different "Bad Boy". "Yes, the Larry Williams song," Paul said. I said "You guys seemed to like Williams. You covered his 'Slow Down' and 'Dizzy Miss Lizzie' as well." My nine-year-old self was in heaven from this conversation. Sir Paul congratulated the band on a "Well-played, fun set!" My 55-year-old self was in heaven!

Kenny Margolis, The Minks (Mink DeVille), Lucky Seven, Cracker

ARTICLES OF FAITH, CHICAGO 2010

Being a musician is a process of discovery. First you discover how to play an instrument. Then you discover how to play with other musicians. Then you discover how to play with the audience. Every step of the path entails a more nuanced and subtle set of skills. By the time you learn how to play with the audience, you have to really master the skill of listening, because that's what playing with the audience entails. You have to listen to them, even more closely than they are listening to you, in order to be truly rewarded.

The best gig I ever played was the last show Articles of Faith will ever play, and it was the best show I ever played because the audience made that show. It was deafening and wonderful. The show was October 9th, 2010, at some pick-up club in Wicker Park, Chicago. It was supposed to be a "surprise" show after AoF's one and only US reunion gig for Riot Fest that year. The fact that we were asked to play Riot Fest meant a lot to us. Riot Fest had been in business almost 10 years, and was a celebration of punk music in the city. Given AoF's role in the original US hardcore scene, it was an honour that we were asked to play, 25 years after we broke up, for the hometown crowd.

It took some work. I lived in Seattle, and one guitarist, Joe Scurderi, lived in San Francisco. The rest of the guys lived in Chicago, so we worked separately all summer, practising the old songs by ourselves. We had to get past step one, and relearn the instruments themselves – no easy thing to do if you were playing hyper-speed thrash that wore you down when you were in your 20s; in your 50s, it was brutal, especially for our drummer, Virus X. But if we were going to make a new record, it had to be good; if we were going to play a new gig, it had to be great. We set aside two full weeks for rehearsal before the show and recording, and Joe and I flew in from the west coast to Chicago.

Step two was getting back the groove we had as a group. The record helped a lot. We had to collaborate to get "that" sound, and pretty quickly it felt like we had never stopped playing together. It felt natural. Then our bassist, Dave, hurt his back at work – so bad that he ultimately had to have surgery. He could barely stand in practice, but he bore down and made it work.

The gig itself was the day after our formal show at Riot Fest. It wasn't really a club. It was more like a small warehouse that had been converted to playing shows. The PA was oversized for the space, and everything seemed kind of thrown together. It was very punk rock. But the small size worked to our advantage. The energy was trapped in that space and bouncing off the walls. People were crammed in, and they were ardent fans. People had flown in from Europe and the west coast for the show. The music meant a lot to them. That meant a lot to us. We picked up on the vibe right away. People were bouncing, moshing and singing along. We started surfing that wave.

We blew the PA circuits twice. The first time, we stopped and started the song over. But the second time we just kept playing – the crowd led and sang all the parts. We followed them. It was exhausting and glorious. By the time we finished – with a Johnny Cash song, I think – Dave couldn't even stand up. Everyone was spent and laughing. Afterwards, we talked about keeping AoF together and doing more shows. But when I went back to Seattle, I thought better of it. I don't think we could ever top that show, and it didn't feel right to try. It was better that we exit this way and wrap up that chapter of our lives.

Articles of Faith was an amazing experience to be part of. But to be part of that audience that night – with people who had grown up with that music and made it a part of them – you could never recreate that. So, we won't. And our best gig will always be our last.

Vic Bondi, Articles of Faith

LAST SUPPER, LONDON 2011

The Cravats have existed since 1977 but playing live was not a favourite pastime of mine in the early days due to finding it near impossible to sing and play bass at the same time. Since Svor Naan (Cravats sax behemoth) and I recruited new members and reformed for the Rebellion Punk Festival in 2009, I have loved doing the darned things and playing the final, Last Supper Steve Ignorant/Crass gig at Shepherd's Bush O2 on November 19th, 2011, was a particular highlight in the Cravats journey.

When we were asked to appear as special guests, I was somewhat surprised. The Cravats had never really slotted with ease in to the Crass roster of bands. We were silly, jazzy and peculiar but Penny Rimbaud had always been a huge supporter of the band and had, almost single-handedly, mauled our sound into what it had become. Although well-rehearsed, I think it was on the drive up to London from Brighton that the "fear" set in. What if the sold-out crowd decided we weren't suitable entertainment for this final Last Supper show and hurled abuse from our opening chord to the final feed-back racket of "I Hate the Universe"? Or worse still, stayed in the bar?

After Andy T and Paranoid Visions had shown how it should be done, we walked out onto the lovely old theatre stage of the O2. It was ruddy packed to the gills and I could see from the smiles that it was unlikely we were going to be machine-gunned by indignant punks that night. Never had I witnessed a reaction so glorious to our noise but it was a special night and there was a lot of Crass love in the air. Folk were happy and felt a part of the unique channel that Crass had created all those years ago. Our actual performance passed in a fuzzy, joyous cartoon blast that left us all shattered and chuffed. We went down a storm and still had the pleasure of seeing Penny and Eve do their stuff followed by Steve Ignorant and friends. Those Crass songs had meant so much to so many for so long. Top night.

The Shend, The Cravats, The Very Things

PUBLIC IMAGE LIMITED, DUBLIN 2011

Tripod, June

Public Image Limited are always an exhilarating live experience. Mr Lydon's menacing bravado and eerie caterwauling mixed with unsettling warped melodies and of course those thundering basslines are an intoxicating sonic compound. Their June 2011 Tripod show was particularly hotly anticipated. The band reformed after a 17-year break in 2009 and played a superlative set at Electric Picnic the following year, so the chance to see a headline show had caused quite a commotion among devotees.

The line-up – as it was then and is now – comprised the mercurial Mr Lydon, Pop Group co-founder Bruce Smith on drums, Scott Firth on bass and the inscrutable Lu Edmonds on guitar and various esoteric stringed instruments. Myself and Hot Press colleague Stuart Clark repaired to a nearby hostelry before the show to right the world's wrongs over several invigorating beverages. On arrival at the venue we took a prime vantage spot on the balcony. I remember several members of local stalwarts Paranoid Visions were present in addition to a considerable sector of the Dublin punk community.

The band trailed onto the stage, followed by Lydon ambling mischievously. The otherworldly "Home is where the Heart is" (an allusion to his heritage perhaps?) ushered in proceedings in quite an understated fashion. "This is Not a Love Song" was quite a different proposition altogether, all unadulterated squalling and bombast.

The personnel coalesced seamlessly. One couldn't help but be captivated by Lu Edmonds's somewhat demonic demeanour and dizzying array of instruments. On "Flowers of Romance" he cast a spell, playing an electric banjo he teased and tormented with a bow.

But the spirit of Jah Wobble loomed over the proceedings. His spectral figure watched from the side of stage. Even though his tenure with the band was shortlived, it was a formative period and his distinctive bass stylings are the foundation for so much of what we recognise as the sound of Public Image Limited.

Over the course of his career Wobble has remained more loyal to the punk spirit than Lydon, never afraid to plough his own furrow, whether it be dub, electronica, jazz or world stylings, regardless of commercial success. His Memoirs of a Geezer are so devoid of ego the experience is more akin to shooting the breeze with a friend over a pint than reading a rock star's memoir.

Over the years I have interviewed Wobble (real name John Wardle) several times, including a public interview at Louder Than Words in Manchester. His humility, politeness and affability never cease to amaze me. We struck up a friendship of sorts and I put him in touch with Irish promoters when he wanted to bring his Invaders of the Heart to these shores. Much to my surprise, he contacted me a couple of years ago to ask a favour. He needed a letter of recommendation for his passport application and he asked would I write one.

So, in a pinch-me moment to end all pinch-me moments, I found myself typing up a testament to John Wardle's suitability for passport ownership on Hot Press-headed paper, referring to our working relationship and friendship over the years. A few months passed before an excited John called to convey the news his new travel document had arrived.

The last time I met him was at the Vinyl Festival in Dún Laoghaire where I chaired an interview. He was as enthusiastic and engaging as ever. I brought a friend who was an ardent fan and John made every effort to chat and give him as much time as possible. As he did with everyone who approached him. What a Geezer he is. A total gent.

Punk memories don't get any better than these.

Roisin Dwyer, writer

PHAROAH OVERLORD, BIRMINGHAM 2011

Pharoah Overlord's set at Supersonic festival in 2011 was massively inspiring. They basically played the one riff for what seemed like their entire set while slowly morphing into and finishing in a pentagram-esque shape. It was ecstatic, meditative and utterly spellbinding. Repeating something till it loses all meaning then reforms into something new entirely.

Cormac MacDiarmada, Lankum

HENRY CLUNEY, BLACKPOOL 2012

Best gigs always throw up questions for me. Do I talk about the best gig I've been to or the best one I've done? The answer lately is the best one I've done… for specific reasons!

Blackpool, Rebellion, 2012. I knew about the festival but had never been. Then I was booked to play the Almost Acoustic room. I had been doing solo gigs since 2009 when I was support to The Damned and The Alarm. I had been playing in cover bands in America for 15 years and had more or less not thought of original music.

The gig was simply magic! Big crowd of SLF fans who helped me sing every song… though they got some lyrics wrong (or was that me? Lol.) The feeling of just being with people with the same musical outlook was just so good. I loved walking round the Winter Gardens and seeing bands, meeting people and just soaking in the whole experience.

I've done the same gig five or six times now but that first one will always be special as, a few months later, I had a brain tumour removed. I knew nothing about it that August except for some long headaches.

So 2012 will always be the year I remember for basically getting my life back and also for a gig like Rebellion!

Thanks to everyone involved... the people there and my surgeons in the US. It was the worst of times, it was the best of times.

Henry Cluney, Stiff Little Fingers, X-SLF

STEVE IGNORANT, NORFOLK 2012

June 9th

A few months previous to this event I'd been headlining at Shepherd's Bush Empire, my name stuck up in big letters over the entrance and over two thousand people cheering us on. Now came reality like a smack in the face: Carol, Pete and me in a quiet village in Norfolk doing our first gig as an acoustic outfit in a pub.

No PA, no stage, just a fag-end-singed carpet where the pool table usually stood, and maybe 20 people – some of them sitting on straight-back chairs so close my knees brushed theirs – looking at me in silence. They knew me but not my history, only a few had liked punk, and to say I was nervous would be a massive understatement. Every eye watching every movement: come on, entertain us.

And we played and I found myself actually singing for the first time in front of an audience, not shouting but singing, and there in the motes of dust swirling in the shafts of sunlight in that dingy room I felt a new confidence and a new strength inside of me, bolstered by the two people behind me. Just us, ourselves and our instruments, nowhere to hide, no drums, just us and a belief in what we were doing. The bare bones of what was to become Slice of Life.

That first gig was so important.

This is where you start.

This is where you spill your heart.

I remember saying to Carol and Pete after the set: "If we can do that, we can do anything." And we are.

Steve Ignorant, Crass, Slice of Life, author

VICE SQUAD, ALTAVOZ FESTIVAL, COLOMBIA 2012

I don't actually have a favourite gig of all time but one of the most memorable ones I played was the Altavoz Festival in Medellin, Colombia. Our guitarist Lumpy doesn't like flying so he got some Diazepam from the doctor to calm his nerves but the doctor didn't warn him that you're not supposed to mix alcohol with Diazepam. On the day of the flight we got to the airport about 7am and Lumpy was in the bar having a drink by 8am. We boarded a couple of hours later for a seven-hour flight to Miami where we were to get a connecting flight to Medellin. By the time the plane was ready to land in Miami there were 13 small empty red wine bottles in the pouch in front of Lumpy's seat, and he was most insistent that he didn't need to fill in an immigration form to pass through US customs. The bassist, drummer and me all filled in customs forms and after queueing for about 40 minutes passed through US immigration and got ready to catch our connecting flight.

Of course, after queuing for some time Lumpy had been turned away by a customs officer and told to fill in the form but was confounded by the fact that it was written in Spanish and being off his head he didn't think to turn the page over to the English side! We were panicking as there was no sign of him and we had to catch our connecting flight so we went through security and asked the flight attendant on the Medellin flight to delay the plane because one of the band members was missing.

At this point we didn't even know if Lumpy was still in the airport as he was in such a state we expected US customs to refuse him entry and send him back to the UK. I thought we'd be doing the gig as a three-piece and that I'd be practising very heavily for the next few days as I'd be playing lead guitar!

Eventually a staggering Lumpy appeared and he boarded the plane, berating the rest of us for not bringing his bag through security (you can't bring someone else's bag through airport security but try explaining that to a Yorkshireman who's mixed a large quantity of wine, lager and spirits with Diazepam at high altitude). The flight to Medellin lasted about three hours and when we landed we were filmed coming through the gates by Colombian TV.

We were taken to a five-star hotel and, for the next four days, we were wined, dined and expected to promote the show, which was fine except for the fact that Lumpy's bag hadn't turned up so he was wearing the same clothes for five days! A local tattoo artist took pity on him and gave him a t-shirt, but apart from that everything he wore was five days old and Medellin is very humid so he was somewhat "ripe".

We did various interviews for TV which was quite weird as we were used to being ignored in the UK and so found the Colombians' interest in us rather strange but very flattering. We did a secret press conference and were escorted by police with handguns into the theatre and we were amazed that it was packed full of people wanting to see us. It was like a surreal version of a chat show with the audience made up of punks.

There were more people at the press conference than at some of the gigs we played in England. The people we met were awesome and it was very, very humbling to learn that our first album had inspired so many of them to get into punk. Some had even built their own guitars, now that's DIY!

There is a lot of poverty in Colombia so punk is a lifeline for many people. You couldn't overestimate its importance. Every day a great guy called Roman would collect us from the hotel and take us out for lunch followed by promo. Roman had won the Colombian version of "Big Brother" so he was a bit of a celebrity and a real character.

We looked round a toy shop in a shopping centre and all the staff knew who we were because we'd been on TV, so we had to pose for photos. We also did the "sightseeing tour" – you have to do it because the mayor arranges it specially for the visiting bands. So there we were at the back of the bus with a Polish metal band like naughty school kids.

We visited the university and met some of the students and the whole day was filmed and televised. We were even filmed when we were eating. We'd never done so much promo before and were relieved to get back to the hotel thinking we would get a break from the cameras, but there was another TV presenter with cameras waiting for us in reception. Like I said before, we're accustomed to being ignored so all the attention and media interest was quite overwhelming.

The gig itself was amazing, we played in a stadium to an audience of 30,000 people and the show was televised live. I'm used to having the audience up close and not having much space but the stage was huge and I had to cover a lot of ground to get to the front to commune with the crowd. We were the most tired we'd ever been after the show, partly because of the altitude and partly from having been on the piss for five days, but being typical musos Lumpy, Wayne (bass) and me went out to a bar after the show rather than doing the sensible thing and going back to the hotel for a kip.

The return journey was quite arduous as the connecting flight from Miami to London was delayed so we hung round the airport bar for about five hours and were pretty out of it by the time we caught the London flight. A day later we were back in the UK playing some small club gigs up north. Business as usual!

Beki Bondage, Vice Squad

REVELATION RECORDS 25ᵀᴴ ANNIVERSARY SHOW, POMONA 2012

In 1987 I had a crush on a boy called Sam Cook. He had four T-shirts that he always wore and eventually my curiosity fuelled four record purchases: Minor Threat, Youth of Today, Black Flag and The Descendents. My introduction to hardcore and punk exploded and I was never the same again. I developed a lifelong passion for this music and my life became enveloped within a subculture and community that shared so many of my politics and values. Eventually I had my own zine and label, booking shows and touring with bands extensively. I visited the east coast of the US on many trips for months at a time. Developing strong bonds with the friends I'd previously been writing to and attending many shows with them. Like the first Dayton Festival in 1993. Where I cried like a baby holding SevaPriya's hand watching Into Another for the first time. So many shows, so many happy tears. How to pick just one to share in the pages of this book is such a challenge.

But I think it has to be the Revelation Records anniversary shows in the summer of 2012. Seventeen years ago, I took a job at Revelation Records and I've been living in California ever since. I'm the person who processes all the orders that ship to Europe. I'm the person who orders represses of Bold's records and orders the shirts to make the Quicksand merch – examples of a few of my daily tasks. Sometimes it still amazes me, as I'm picking the colour to press the Inside Out 7-inches on next. I can't believe that this is my life and I get to do this. My life is not defined by my work, but it's a huge component of it. And I sometimes wonder what would have happened if I'd never had a crush on Sam. Life-changing.

In the summer of 2012, Sam came to visit for the 25th anniversary weekend for Revelation Records. I introduced him to people as the reason that they knew me. We watched all the old Rev bands along with my friends of 20 years and more. That weekend was incredibly special to me. So many friends in town, from near and far. So many bands I'd seen before, like Sensefield and Quicksand, playing their hearts out. The feelings that flowed back as though it had just been a few years and not decades. Standing in a room of 800 people that knew every word. Who never thought they'd get to sing along to those words live again. Magical.

As was Into Another. Made all the more so because my Into Another partner of 19 years ago was by my side. SevaPriya and I once again held hands and cried. The emotions of hearing the songs that got me through some terrible times caused more tears than normal. Seeing and hearing the band get emotional also caused more tears. So much emotion for so many people, the energy in the room so strong and intense. Everyone feeling so much more than they expected.

I mean, seriously, who expects to cry watching Crippled Youth? I didn't expect it, but I certainly cried. Seeing your favourite straight-edge record played after all these years was actually possibly the best moment, for me, of the entire weekend with regards to bands on the stage. It's very likely I'm the only person that felt like that. But that's what makes an event like this so magical: each band means something different to someone else. And everyone has different favourites and different amazing moments. A large part of my weekend was spent getting people to sign the book I'd orchestrated for Jordan [the owner of Revelation Records] as a gift. I'd had many past employees, band members and friends write articles about when they met Jordan and memories of Revelation Records. It was all laid out in a little hardback book with tons of photos. I spent a large part of the weekend sneaking around behind Jordan's back and getting all the band members who I either hadn't had contact information for [or who missed the deadline] to sign Jordan's copy of the book. I had to be subtle about this and I somehow managed to do it without him seeing.

At the pinnacle of the show, just before Quicksand went on stage, I gave it to Jordan. It seemed to mean the world to him, and everyone got a little emotional. I'm so glad that we have this keepsake that reminds us why we do this. Why our lives revolve around shows and music and records and books and politics and community. Because we are fucking so lucky to have fallen down this particular rabbit hole. To be part of this community. One that shares stories about what they love about music and the scene. That pulls together to make something happen when people need our help. Benefit shows and benefit books and doing things for other people is a real way of life. It's 25 years of shows for me. Of knowing the people that I started this journey with. That I would hope will be right next to me for the Revelation Records 30th anniversary. And on and on.

I leave you with a picture of myself sandwiched between Sam Cook and SevaPriya. This was taken by the amazing Chrissy Piper. Could the three of us look any happier? The two of them hadn't met before this weekend but you'd never have known it. We were just about to watch Underdog I think. We went from one band to the next, one show to the next, in a daze of happiness that seemed surreal. But, as amazing as the bands were, it's the community of my friends that is the real tearjerker when I reminisce. The quick catch-ups and the long hugs. The meals snatched and laughing 'til we cried. The creation of a whole lexicon of new inside jokes within that weekend. The avoidance of the exes and the flirting with the crushes. The same stuff that I've been lucky enough to have experienced at so many shows. And possibly the best memory of all? Sharing thoughts and feelings on the drive home with Sam. Verbal diarrhea of excitement and happiness from us both. Smiling so widely our faces hurt. The best weekend of shows ever.

Vique Simba, Revelation Records, Simba Fanzine

THE DAMNED/SHAM 69/999/UK SUBS/SPLODGENESSABOUNDS/ THE AVENGERS/CHELSEA/THE VIBRATORS/TV SMITH/HAZEL O'CONNOR, LONDON 2012

I'm sure you've heard the old adage "If you remember the 60s, you really weren't there!" Well, turn it up to 11 then apply it to my life of gigging and ligging since the age of 12 my first two gigs being Hawkwind (with Lemmy on Vox) at Southend's Kursaal, followed by Bowie at the Marquee (don't ask).

Luckily for me, having been a music journalist for my entire adulthood (starting with zines, then scribing professionally for Sounds, Noise and numerous publications worldwide), I know that I've been in attendance at thousands of seminal and brilliant gigs because it's recorded in print. (And yes – I was at the original Two-Day Punk Special at the 100 Club with The Pistols et al in 1976 and the rebooted follow-up Second 100 Club Punk Festival headlined by Buzzcocks in 1997!)

Whatever failed to be noted for musical posterity comes in oh so many mostly fond flashbacks from the early days of punk – but also a few awful memories of having to run for one's life en route home being pursued by gangs of Teds, fascist skins or whatever the tribe of "punk haters" was around at the time.

I've always found it a nightmare to pick a favourite of anything – records, bands, venues – (well, okay, the 100 Club for venue!) and gigs particularly. But as this is for such a wonderful cause, I'm picking a fairly recent one (recent in my almost 50 years of gigging): the Xmas Wasted Festival at the now sadly defunct Astoria venue on London's Charing Cross Road, on December 12th, 2004.

The line-up was a corker, including (in no particular headline order) The Damned, Sham 69, 999, UK Subs, Splodgenessabounds, The Avengers, Chelsea, The Vibrators, TV Smith… and Hazel O'Connor!

After an initial hiccup of blagging only one "AAA pass" (which resulted in a mad dash to the nearby newsagents to make a dodgy – yet passable – photocopy of the same for my other half), the night transpired into a blinder of a gig, not least because it seemed every mucker that I knew from our scene was crammed into this den of punk iniquity, be they actually playing, ligging or as a punter – such an eclectic community of misfits under one roof!

But as well as the usual brilliant sets from all, it was the night's crass backstage antics than ensure this particular gig sticks in my addled memory banks forever. It all kicked off when my dear old pal and erstwhile partner-in-crime Max Splodge and I realised we'd necked all of Splodgenessabounds' rider way too fast and were out of booze. The horror, the horror.

So as Hazel O'Connor took to the stage for her set, we snuck into her dressing room where we proceeded to "borrow" (ahem!) anything drinkable that wasn't nailed down! We did leave a "thank-you" note of sorts – by scrawling "You've been splodged" in enormous letters on the wall in my red lippy! Sorry Hazel – our need was far greater than yours, of that I'm certain. I don't recall too much else after that – but one thing I can guarantee about any punk gig… It'll all end in BEERS!

Bev Elliott, (aka The Punk Queen of Soho) writer, Sounds, Noise etc

BOB MOULD LONDON 2012, OUT OF SPITE FESTIVALS, PODSTOCK 2015 AND MORE

My most favourite gig of recent times? After so many years it takes something very special to move me these days. This is the easiest one for me to choose. By a mile, it is Bob Mould playing "Copper Blue" at Shepherd's Bush Empire in 2012. It was the 20th anniversary of that album and he decided to do some gigs playing the whole album from start to finish with a few extras at the end.

Bob Mould is a huge influence on me and my guitar playing, and "Copper Blue" is up there with my all-time favourite albums. I did see him on the Copper Blue tour back in 1992 but this for me was a massive trip down nostalgia street. He and his band played every song beautifully and it was so nice to hear all of those songs played live again. Bob himself seemed very into the moment as well and had a massive smile on his face from start to finish. There was a whole bunch of old friends at the gig and we all walked out of there thinking that we had watched something special. I think it'll be some time before I see anything to top that.

Most favourite gig I've ever played? Now that is an impossible one to answer as some gigs are enjoyable for different reasons. The only thing I can do is talk about gigs that stood out for different reasons. The ones that do stand out are the great times we had at the Out of Spite festivals in Leeds. These are great memories not just because of the great gigs but the awesome people and friends at these gigs. The actual playing was a small part of the whole weekend but these do hold very special memories for me.

Another one that stands out is the time that we played at the LA2 in London in 2002. It was a joint promotion with Deck Cheese, Household Name and Jamdown Records I think. Basically this was a gig with a line-up full of UK punk bands and we sold it out. It was a great day. The European tour we did with MU330 was sooo much fun as well.

I have to mention as well Podstock this year. It was Vanilla Pod's 20th birthday in 2015 and we decided to put on a two-day party with all our mates playing at the Owl Sanctuary in Norwich. The venue is a 150-capacity and it sold out within 12 hours of tickets going on sale. We couldn't really believe how quickly they went. We were lucky enough to have the likes of Snuff, Capdown, Consumed, The Great Cynics, Random Hand, Wonk Unit and many, many others of our friend agree to come along and play.

Everybody who came to the gig had the right sprit of exactly what we wanted and it was full from the first band to the last band. Us playing was a very small part of this but it really made me proud of what we had achieved over the years. It was a truly memorable weekend and it's really nice to be able to put one of my favourite gigs as being one in very recent times.

Steve Pod, Vanilla Pod, Menshevik

THE GODFATHERS, PARIS 2014

This saga begins in March 2014 at a gig in Paris playing drums with The Godfathers. Tensions were always high in this band and this jaunt was no exception.

The gig in Paris was in La Java, an old basement music hall kind of place, which had apparently hosted Edith Piaf and Maurice Chevalier in bygone days, walls dripping with history. The following day was to be an early start with a long drive (450 miles) to the next gig in Montpellier in the south of France. This was going to be a tough few days on the road, seeing as the day after that, we had to set off on a killer 18-hour drive back up to Glasgow to start a 17-date run around the UK with Stiff Little Fingers. Half the band wanted to reschedule the Montpellier show because of this gruelling leg (which was endured in a splitter-van, not a luxury tour bus) but due to internal pressure we agreed to do it, albeit under much duress. In fact, tensions ran so high on that journey up to Glasgow, that a punch was thrown in the van while we were travelling up the M6. A bit hairy indeed, as the recipient was driving at the time! The writing was on the wall for me at that stage.

Arriving in Glasgow on St Patrick's Day at about 4pm, the air was cold and hazy and as we loaded into Barrowland, the nostalgia and history of the venue quickly replaced jaded feelings with excitement and reminded me of all the reasons I got into rock'n'roll. We went down really well that night, the band performing at full tilt, tensions being converted into pure energy which was the fuel The Godfathers usually ran on. It was exhausting and exhilarating all at the same time. I loved playing with this line-up.

Anyway, at the end of Godfathers shows, I used to jump down off the drum riser to say hello and shake a few hands with people at the front. On this night in Glasgow though (and Barrowland had filled up to near-capacity during our set), as I skipped towards the front of the stage, I was greeted with a Glasgow chorus of… Fuck off! I was humbled, terms of endearment come in many guises... I guess. I met some great people in Glasgow that night, including the prolific Glasgow poet Fred McNeill. Fred wrote some beautiful "in memorandum" pieces for my late mum and dad and for my late great mate John Brady who played bass with a version of the Irish Skid Row. John tragically died in a car accident in 1993.

I dedicate this piece to John Nicholas, Mary Elizabeth Nicholas and John Brady. Not forgetting the late Frank Murray, who was a huge influence on me.

Grant Nicholas, The Godfathers, The Citizens of Nowhere

CONCERT LOG 2014

Too numerous to mention. I've been giving this some thought, but unfortunately haven't got very far. It's such a daunting question having played and attended so many. I always cite NoMeansNo, Alice Donut and Melvins as my favourite live bands, and have seen them all so many times I couldn't even choose one gig from those three bands. So many great hardcore shows in the 1980s with seven or more amazing bands in one night! Thankfully I grew up in a time and place where a lot of different things were happening, and I was interested in everything. Coincidentally, I just started going through my ticket stubs and made a concert log. This doesn't account for 90 per cent of the shows I've been to or even all the concerts. But it's a fairly diverse cross-section of music. Your whole life is spent curating one big festival!

Concert Log

1980: Van Halen

1981: Rush

1982: The Police, Devo, Van Halen

1983: Police/Madness/Oingo Boingo, Butthole Surfers/Dicks/Dead Kennedys, Fear

1984: Grateful Dead, X, The Pretenders, Scorpions, Psychedelic Furs, PIL, Black Flag

1985: Metallica, Violent Femmes, Motorhead/Exodus/Wendy O Williams

1986: NoMeansNo, Aerosmith, Red Hot Chili Peppers, Sonic Youth/fIREHOSE

1987: Stevie Ray Vaughan, Scratch Acid, Grateful Dead, Melvins

1988: UB40, Metallica, Primus, Mr Bungle, Grateful Dead

1989: Robert Fripp, Jane's Addiction, Animal Logic, Soundgarden, The Who

1990: Nirvana, Rush, Santana, Eugene Chadbourne, Jesus Lizard

1991: Blue Oyster Cult, Lollapalooza, Lynyrd Skynyrd, Metallica, Smashing Pumpkins

1992: Beastie Boys, Fishbone, Public Enemy, Rush, Jonathan Richman

1993: Lollapalooza

1994: Rolling Stones, Weezer, Pavement, Bjork

1995: Boredoms, Bjork, Lollapalooza, Melt Banana

1996: Toy Dolls, Kiss, Turbonegro

1997: Residents, Rolling Stones, Ween

1998: Shellac, Phish

1999: Ween, Gamelan Sekar Jaya, Diamanda Galas, ZZ Top, Fantomas, KRS-One

2000: Steely Dan, Queens of the Stone Age, The Cramps, Kiss

2001: Willie Nelson, U2, Spinal Tap, Shellac/Neurosis/Oxbow

2002: Public Enemy, Beck, The Coup, Willie Nelson

2003: Hedwig and the Angry Inch, Ween, Patti Smith

2004: Judas Priest/Slayer, The Black Rider

2005: Gang of Four, Pixies

2006: Zappa Plays Zappa, Flaming Lips/Ween, Touch and Go 25th, Pogues

2007: The Stooges, Mastodon, Bjork, The Police, Moonchild

2008: Jonathan Richman

2009: Ornette Coleman

2010: Paul McCartney, Tool, John Zorn, Grinderman, Zappa Plays Zappa

2011: Ween, Steve Ignorant

2012: Roger Waters

2013: Nick Cave & the Bad Seeds, Beck

2014: Judas Priest

Larry Boothroyd, Victims Family, Jello Biafra and the Guantanamo School of Medicine

RABIES BABIES, LA VALETTE 2014

France, September

I go to so many gigs, probably too many. I love hearing music live. I spent too much time thinking about which is my favourite gig. Eventually I came down to a list of favourite gigs, and realised that a favourite gig isn't only about the band – a favourite gig has good sound, a good band, a good venue and, most importantly, a good audience. All of these parts are needed for an outstanding gig.

In my mind, this is the best show that my band Rabies Babies have played. I was talking with Screw our drummer last week and he says our best show was one we played in Czech this summer. I suppose that is what "favourite" is. Everyone's "favourite" is different. This one is my favourite. The La Valette show was at the end of a French tour. Laura our guitarist was six months pregnant and showed off her baby bump beautifully in a bumblebee costume. I dressed for the tour as a superhero and our drummer did one gig naked and the other shows dressed as a bear.

Laura wasn't drinking alcohol, so I decided to do the tour sober too. Sober touring is so much easier. No hangovers! No regretful mornings! We travelled by National Express coach and trains mostly, with a couple of lifts from friends to places that were impossible to reach by public transport and had some adventures along the way. La Valette is a tiny village hidden in the mountains of southern France. It is a free-thinking community of many nationalities who live, eat and work communally.

The village venue is really small, and the stage is low, so you play more or less in the audience. We have played there many times before but this night the place was packed. People were swinging from the rafters, jumping off the drum kit, crowd surfing and dancing on the bar. Everyone was going really mental. The atmosphere was electric. It was sweltering hot and all the guys had taken their shirts off.

Halfway through the gig all the girls took their shirts off too. I threw glitter over the crowd, so everyone was sparkling and naked. After our set there was a big dance party and we danced till the sun came up. We spent the following day relaxing in the sunshine in the village and the following day our friend Joe drove us to Montpellier to take the train to Paris. We got hit by flash floods and ended the tour on Laura's birthday, stranded by floods in Montpellier train station wrapped in gold foil blankets, being interviewed for French TV and eating food parcels from the Red Cross.

Lorna Tiefholz, Rabies Babies

THE MOCKERS, CATALUNYA 2015

A few years ago while we were touring Spain, we rolled into Sant Feliu de Guíxols, a small Catalunya seaside town north of Barcelona. We'd never played in this town before, and it was a Tuesday night, so we didn't know what to expect.

Our expectations sank further when we found out from the club manager (it was community-owned) that the night before the town had experienced the worst thunderstorms in 40 years. Many homes in Sant Feliu were completely flooded, as well as the club itself, which also lost most of its gear.

When we arrived, the electricity was still out. They were going to cancel the gig, but in the end, they borrowed a small PA, and a generator of some sort.

We played the show, and it seemed as if half the town was there. The lights flickered most of the night, but we kept on playing. We even did a few songs acappella when the electricity went off for a bit.

At the end of the show, they all started yelling "A LA CALLE!!!!" (To the street). We had no idea what they meant until they literally jumped up on stage, picked us all up on their shoulders and carried us out of the club cheering. We found out later it's an old tradition where they'd carry bullfighters out of the ring if they were particularly impressive.

The next day, the club manager wrote this on Facebook: "The day after the worst storms of the last 40 years, where a lot of our friends lost everything, The Mockers came to play at Atzavara Club. And they appeared like the bright light of the sun, bringing hope, and for two hours, incredible happiness."

For me, every time you get onstage, you hope for moments like this, and a chance, for at least a few hours, to bring joy and help someone forget their problems.

Seth Gordon, The Mockers

WRECKLESS ERIC, TORONTO 2015

"And why would someone know to book you to play in Toronto?"

"Because I'm famous – I wrote the tune they use in the McDonalds commercial."

"Really." (flat voice)

"What sort of music do you play?"

I could hardly say rock music, just me sitting there alone, posing as an old buffer in a Buick Le Sabre, so I said the first thing that came into my head:

"It's bubblegum," and added "with dementia" by way of explanation and justification. She handed back the paperwork, and threw my US Green Card at me as an afterthought.

"Enjoy your stay in Canada."

I'm sure I'm going to. I've been pretty nervous about this show, the Toronto NXNE Festival. Everyone else on the bill seems so young, so vibrant, fresh, up and coming, exciting and positively *now*. And then there's me – feeling in comparison like a man in his 60s – a has-been, assuming of course that I ever even was.

I haven't played live for months. I've been busy making a new album. Now the album's due for release and it's time to start touring again. I'm nervous, full of misgivings: what if I can't do this anymore? And why would anybody want to hear me doing it anyway?

In the weeks leading up to this engagement I've been anguishing about what songs I should play, what order I should put them in. I've written lists and then written them out again in a slightly different order. I've half-heartedly tried a few things out and promised myself that closer to the time I'll have at least one full rehearsal of the chosen set list. I've assured myself that the set list will eventually come together, and then got on with attending to a few welcome distractions.

And now here I am in Toronto, still desperately trying to compile a set list. I forget about songs, lose faith in the ones that bubble into my consciousness – I've made lists of every song I've ever written on every album I've ever made. The list bewilders me so I look for another distraction and try to convince myself that a set list will somehow magically occur.

It doesn't.

In my room at the Hyatt Regency Hotel I'm experiencing a crisis of confidence. I put a post on Facebook:

Slowly losing my mind in a hotel room in Toronto.

People post helpful suggestions – "Toronto's a cool town, go out and explore."

No chance of that, not before the execution – the show that is. No rewards, just constant low-level anxiety and a feeling of anguish.

And still no set list.

I often wish I could start again, come at playing music fresh, fully formed but without the baggage. As much as I try to reinvent myself, to move forward, there's still the baggage – a sense of obligation, as in people come to see me because of things I've done, like "Whole Wide World", or "Reconnez Cherie", or "Take The Cash". Like it or not, you get known after a while for certain things, though I really don't mind playing "Whole Wide World". Fuck it – I love playing "Whole Wide World"! It's every boy's dream after all – it's a hit! If I get a bit jaded (and I can honestly say I don't), the audience's enthusiasm for the song lifts me up and turns it into a glorious moment. But how can I put it in the context of something new without doing something lumpy and embarrassing like singing it acapella or performing it in a drone style, or worse, as a rap number?

I don't think I'm going to do that.

I force myself to eat and that makes me feel a bit better about everything. Then I go to the venue. The organisers, the crew, they're all kids. The stage manager is barely 20. She's never done this before. They seem really pleased that I've actually showed up. A crew of teenage boys help me load in my equipment – two guitars, one case with leads and pedals in it, and a Guild Superstar amplifier that none of them can lift. They take it all very seriously and put everything in a corner of the tiny, grimy backstage. They want to make sure it's going to be safe. They discuss putting some kind of tape around it as a sort of cordon but I dissuade them of that idea.

There's no soundcheck so I have a quick discussion with the sound engineer. He's a bit older than the others. He tells me not to expect too much of the monitors, I tell him I've already figured that out, that I'll be using an electric guitar, no acoustic guitar, so all I'll need in the monitors is my vocal and electrified harmonica. I warn him that I'll probably be playing quite loud and he says that's fine, he likes volume coming off the stage. This surprises me, I've never heard that from a sound engineer before.

Then there's time to kill. I have to get away from the venue which appears to be filling up with young people who are obviously not going to want to hear someone like me. I stroll through a residential neighbourhood thinking about the elusive and by this time bigger-than-I-am set list until it's time to meet up with a woman called Claire who's taking photos of me for some sort of online magazine. I can never understand why anyone would want to take a photo of me because in the end I just look like a bloke – *here I am standing in front of a tree… propping up a lamp post… loitering outside a shop…* She's very nice, good company. We talk about the nature of creativity and she takes photos with a real camera, one with film in it.

I've never seen the photos.

Suddenly it's time to play. I still haven't written a set list so I go on with a notebook open at the page where I last desperately tried to concoct a set list, and then I play a completely unrelated set of songs. The anxiety falls away, I'm here in the moment, playing a few tunes for a crowd of people who seem so happy to see me. Someone shouts for one of my songs and I excuse myself from playing it. "I'm sorry," I say, "I just don't feel like playing that one tonight, here's another one…"

After my alloted 40 minutes I leave the stage to great applause. It went well. I have no idea what tunes I played. I love all the other acts on the bill and it seems they love me. It's a great night. I don't know what I was worrying about.

Rush are also playing in Toronto tonight. Back at the hotel the lobby is full of successful-looking middle-aged men: lawyers and businessmen looking just slightly not quite comfortable in their various eras of Rush T-shirts. Together they present an inspiring tableau, the history of Rush in faded T-shirts. There's an abundance of mullets. I talk to a mulleted and T-shirted man in the elevator – he tells me he's seen Rush 92 times. Tonight will be show number 93. He's excited, and for a moment I'm too, but I think I'd rather be *Bubblegum With Dementia* than *Mullet Rock*.

Eric Goulden, Wreckless Eric

VISHWA MOHAN BHATT, SYDNEY 2016

I love Indian classical music, ragas etc.

Seeing and hearing Vishwa Mohan Bhatt in a small room at the Sydney Opera House very close to the stage with only about 40 people was something else. I had seen Partho Sarothy, Gundecha Brothers and other masters previously and any one of those could have been the greatest sublime experience. However I guess as a guitar player this one was it for what he could do. His dynamics, tone and control of his instrument were a lesson in mastery and I love getting lost in sound so ragas appeal to that. We were close enough to hear the ambient sound as well as amplified. This show was wacky as it was a Sunday afternoon: he played two sets, quite long but never enough.

From what we could gather he had been flown out for a wedding as there were no other shows anywhere, and gratefully the father sprung for the cost of renting the room at the opera house (not cheap even small ones) and somehow I and a couple of friends found out and got there for a small entry. The father took a decent hit so we could bliss out on a master of his craft. The way the classical musicians play and interact with each other and create a journey of sound and transcendence is amazing, and I do not understand the intricacies of the tradition but I certainly get the effect. Everything that music can be was there that day: the quality, the randomness of how it happened, and the physical and esoteric effects of the beauty of sound done with passion and heart.

Kent Steedman, Celibate Rifles

CYANIDE PILLS, WERMELKERCHEN 2016

My name is Paul North. I drive bands. In fact I drive, do merch, tour manage, throw people off stage, collect money, load the van, drive to repair shops, deal with police and customs, book flights and ferries. The beat goes on.

So when someone comes up and says you are the driver? I usually list the above or answer yes I'm the fucking driver! I manage a band called The Cyanide Pills, a band locked in a time capsule of 1978 punk and power pop. They are very good but of course have a limited appeal. However, in Germany and Spain we can draw a quorum every now and again. On this occasion, we are at one of our favourite places, the AJZ in the long-lost city of Wermelkerchen. It's a celebration of the venue and the organiser and friend of the band, Toto, has paid us handsomely, fed us wonderful food (three courses) and a beer fridge that is never empty. And a band flat upstairs, rudimentary but clean and no driving, get in!

Lots of various types of punk rock bands play. It runs like clockwork. Sound and lights are perfect. It holds 250-ish and it's pretty full. The Pills race through their set 21 songs, 31 and a half minutes. We are well-received get on and off stage on time. The crowd have had a good drink, there's a punch-up at front. Handbags really, but funny, just added to the gig. These gigs are on YouTube if you want to get an idea.

The headliners play. We all get into the drink while selling some crap. A friend of mine brings vodka so it's all good! The singer Phil Privilege has warmed up with his stage drink of brandy followed by beer he's not supposed to drink (gluten) and finished off with a red wine chaser (bottle). I notice he's gone awol. I get the call. Paul!! Phil's collapsed in the bog, there's claret everywhere! I finish my drink, sell a T-shirt and rush to the bog. There is indeed claret everywhere. Phil's once-white biker jacket is now red and brown. He looks in a coma. Chris Wrist drummer pops his head in, shrugs his shoulders "It's what he would have wanted" and fucks off to the bar. I say "Toto we need an ambulance. He looks worse than usual." His reply: "No chance, it's Saturday night. They don't come here."

I'm concerned. Then this American wobbles in and says "I'll save him!" He picks up said singer and shakes him like a rag doll. I think to myself if he's not dead yet he soon will be! PHIL PHIL! The American screams at Phil while shaking him. His eyes open, he smiles. We throw him in the bunk face down. Toto mops up the blood. I return to the bar. The others have not moved.

The following morning – still in jacket – he rolls in for breakfast (another culinary triumph). Looks at the blood and dirt on the jacket. "Looks good," he says.

Touring is hell!

Paul North, tour manager to the stars

ANGELIC UPSTARTS, THUN 2016

As guitarist for Angelic Upstarts, I have toured many countries and played many memorable shows, everything from big festivals down to shoe cupboards but one of my fondest memories of gigging and touring was of playing at a venue in the Swiss town of Thun called Café Bar Mokka. To anyone not familiar with the venue, it was run by the wonderfully exotic and eccentric Padu Anliker (RIP) who very sadly died in 2016.

From the moment you arrived at Café Bar Mokka, you intuitively knew you were going to be in for an incredibly special experience. Everything about the place is wonderfully alternative, kitsch, cheesy, cool, surreal and wacky. From the couple in the boat floating above the driveway to the Velociraptor which greets you at the front entrance to the venue and even the dressing room, which was a scene in itself. The main stage/bar area followed the same décor, lots of 1950s and 1960s Americana and even an ET, wearing a tinsel garland. Then there was Padu Anliker himself, a true one-off, once met never forgotten character. Features-wise, he appeared to sit somewhere between Bill Bailey and Keith Lemon, but his cool, aloof, eccentric mannerisms put him out there (way out there) driving his own silver lame machine. I thought he and his venue were class from the first moment of arriving then meeting him.

The show itself went down well in front of a busy and appreciative audience but my abiding memory of the gig will be of Padu, dressed in a bright yellow satin shirt, full eyeliner on, arranging flowers at the end of the bar (his day job was a florist) and giving us all stickers carrying the music venue's name "Café Bar Mokka Thun" with the message underneath reading "Musik ist Scheisse" ("Music is Shit")! What a venue, what a guy, what a memory.

Neil 'Newts' Newton, Angelic Upstarts

THE PUKES, LONDON 2016

Right from the off, being in The Pukes has meant playing gigs in strange, random, non-comfort zone places. We've embraced the weird and wonderful gigs with much gusto and it's taken us to amazing spaces such as the Tate Modern, Somerset House, Stoke Newington Library, Wanstead Tennis Club, on boats, in houses and even being chased out of London Fields by a park keeper who said he had a gun in his shed.

One memorable day in 2016 we had been invited to perform at the Queen Elizabeth Olympic Park in London for Sport Relief. Sport Relief is a bit like Comic Relief but, as it turns out, not funny at all. We jumped at the chance of playing the stadium – we would be a punk rock Spice Girls: they had played there a few years before at the Olympic Games closing ceremony to 66,000 people. Excellent! We couldn't wait!

The event organisers' plan was to have various entertainers positioned at different spots around the park throughout the day. We were given an itinerary, which included turning up at 8.30am on a cold Sunday morning in March, armed with 10 ukuleles and a bunch of practice amps. What we hadn't realised was that our only audience would be families taking part in various sponsored sporting activities. There was no crowd, six people would have been fuckin' amazing, let alone 66,000. Our first spot was in the middle of the outdoor cycle track. We set up and started our set in a windy and shambolic manner, playing to no one except a couple of nice boyfriends who had come along for the ride. Then every five minutes or so a couple of families of cyclists would come pedalling past, aghast and bemused at the sight of a gang of punks strumming ukuleles and belting out "Sheena is a Punk Rocker" and other classics. They went round a few times, catching 20 seconds of a song each time they lapped the circular track. One poor child was so busy trying to work out what the hell we were playing at that she took her eyes off the road and fell off her bike!

And it pretty much went downhill from there. We trudged around in the rain to the points set out the itinerary, repeating the set to no one in particular, hungry and cold, and at one point getting drowned out by a marching brass band, until one of us said, "Fuck this, let's find a pub" and the day improved considerably thereafter. Still, it's nice to have Queen Elizabeth Olympic Park on our CV, and if it's good enough for the Spice Girls, it's good enough for The Pukes! Let's just hope they raised plenty of cash for good causes and that they never ask us to do it again.

Debs and Clara Puke

NICK CAVE, LOS ANGELES 2018

Nick Cave cures all known forms of jet lag.

I had arrived home in LA after an 11-hour flight and seven weeks on the road in Europe with my band Black Star Riders. I was met at the airport by my wife who excitedly told me that we had tickets to see Nick Cave that night at the Greek Theatre. Now I love Nick Cave... but having not slept at all on the flight, I was loving the idea of getting into my bed and sleeping for a couple of days or even more.

Obviously this was not going to go down well with my wife. So for the good of love, peace and understanding, I acquiesced.

I don't even remember the Uber ride to the venue. We had great seats but all I wanted to do was curl up and sleep in mine. I felt like crap and was in a foul mood. Then...

Nick Cave took the stage. The sound was unbelievable as were his band... and I was suddenly awake, very awake. I felt euphoric in fact. The connection that he had with the audience, the pure raw soul of those wonderful songs was inspirational and made me forget what time zone I was in or where I was. I left the concert on high. Nick Cave has cured my jet lag!

When we got home, my wife had a glass of wine, and we talked for hours about how amazing the show was. Then I went to bed and slept for two days.

Ricky Warwick, The Almighty, New Model Army, Thin Lizzy, Black Star Riders

THE RISING SUN, REBELLION, BLACKPOOL 2018

It's a strange phenomenon at Rebellion Festival that whatever time you intend on going to bed, you always seem to be coming back to the hotel as the sun's coming up. You miss breakfast (again) after not eating properly the day before.

After five or six years of this routine, I decided last year to get home while the night was relatively young. Still… gig done, I did need to chill out with a beer or something somewhere. "Come round to our hotel" said Tom, singer of The Professionals, so off we went.

So there I was, sitting outside chatting to one Paul Cook (yes, he of The Sex Pistols fame) about our upcoming Crack 40 tour and other things. "Last orders," shouted one of the barmen. It was 3.30am. "I've managed it!" I thought. A relatively early night. But "Rambo's on the phone," said Chris McCormack the Prof's guitarist. "John wants a few people back to his hotel – he needs cheering up – don't bring any idiots!"

So Chris said to me and girlfriend Tara Rez, "Come on you two, you're not idiots." "Jesus," I said. Was he talking about John Lydon? Yes he was! Cookie said that he wasn't gonna go and I said that there was no way I was going to meet John Lydon, pissed, at 3.30 in the morning! I'm just about ready for my early night.

So Cookie left and then as we were starting off on our walk back to our safe haven, I got a text with the hotel address. "Weeell… maybe we'll go... just for a little while. So we jumped a cab – the hotel was a way away and we had to get met at the gates by a security man who escorted us in. We walk into the outside area and there was Mr Lydon with a few friends/band members and Cookie had turned up in the end. So I walk up to introduce myself to John Lydon.

"Hello Mr Lydon, I'm Segs from The Ruts. Last time I saw you was in 1979 – you were looking at our album cover ("The Crack")."

To explain: We had just entered the press room at Virgin Records that day and proudly seen *the* Johnny Rotten holding up our up first LP. "Then," I told him with a smile on my face, "You said 'Bunch of faggots!'"

He just said, "I deny it! I deny anything that I've ever been accused of." He shook my hand warmly and told us that the bar was open "Get yourselves a drink and come and join us."

So there I was chatting away to John Lydon. He was actually really friendly to everyone! We rolled him a "cigarette" and sat down – the conversations were pretty deep. I even had the Dutch courage to sing him a couple of lyrics from "Music Must Destroy!" (Ruts DC's last album), What was happening? After an hour or so – the evening drew naturally to a close. He said he had to go and take care of a few things – and next minute he was gone. We said our goodbyes and got in a taxi… you guessed it. As our driver transported us along Blackpool's well-trodden promenade, the sky was well into its morning. The land of the rising sun indeed.

Segs, Ruts/RutsDC

SLEAFORD MODS, DUBLIN 2019

My most memorable gigging experience as both a musician and a punter was when my band Vulpynes supported Sleaford Mods for three dates in Ireland in February 2019. At that stage we had encountered our fair share of rude bands, artist managers, tour managers, roadies, you name it. Myself and Kaz would smirk at the "big international acts" who seemed to think they had made it because they were playing a small capacity venue on a Monday night in Dublin that wasn't sold out. If you got a gratuitous nod from their tour manager, you were doing well.

Our first date with the Sleaford Mods was in the Academy in Dublin. It was sold out and I was feeling apprehensive. I respected Sleaford Mods and I considered myself a fan. I wondered if I would I get a chance to talk to them, if they would have a big crew or if they would be locked away in the private dressing room that support bands dare not venture into.

The reality was they didn't have a big crew (I think there was four of them in total, including the band) and they offered to share their dressing room. That was a first. After the Dublin gig, Jason caught me rolling up our Vulpynes back drop in the hallway backstage and came over to shake my hand and thanked us for playing with them. That simple gesture meant a lot to me, because in person, they were as authentic as their music. They were complete gents throughout the rest of our mini tour. As a fledgling musician, it was a pivotal milestone. It was proof that you can navigate the music industry by simply being real. No frills. No fuss. No attitudes, no egos. Sleaford Mods are the real deal.

Molly, Vulpynes

SEBADOH, NEW YORK 2019

My name is Catonia Whalen and I've been a music industry professional and DJ for over 20 years. In 1996, I had the pleasure of working with the lo-fi indie rock band Sebadoh while handling marketing in Canada for their album Harmacy on Sub Pop Records. The band came to Toronto that October to perform tracks from the new album at the Phoenix Concert Theatre. Plus, they did an in-store at Tower Records that same day before the show.

It was then that I got to meet Lou Barlow for the first time, the founding member of Sebadoh, Dinosaur Jr. and Folk Implosion. Lou was hands down one of the sweetest indie rockers I've ever met. He gave me his phone number and said to call if I was ever in Los Angeles. Fast forward about three years to late July 1999.

I was in LA on a work trip since I had just started a job working for Universal Music Canada and was training with both Interscope Records and MCA Records. Since I was there for two weeks and had a bit of spare time on my hands, I called Lou to let him know that I was in town. He graciously invited me over for a BBQ. I asked if I could bring a friend and brought my pal Cecil along.

When we got to his house, I was expecting a large number of people but it turned out to be only about eight of us there including me, Cecil, Lou, his wife Kathleen, singer-songwriter Elliott Smith and musician Steven Drozd of The Flaming Lips. It turned out that Sebadoh were playing with The Flaming Lips the following night at the Palace in LA so I ended up going to that concert as well as the intimate BBQ at Lou's house. That night, at the BBQ, my pal Cecil got to jam in Lou's kitchen with him and Elliott.

I also ran into Elliott Smith a couple of nights later at the Silverlake Lounge. I said hello and bought him a drink for his birthday, which was the next day. It turns out that he was a fellow Leo. Elliott was another super kind soul, who would end up passing away just four short years after my LA trip.

Fast forward again to 2017 and I was visiting Toronto on a work trip to attend the Canadian Music Week conference. Sebadoh were doing a showcase at the legendary Horseshoe Tavern. My friend Rob Higgins from Canadian rock band Dearly Beloved was there and he happened to mention my name to Lou Barlow before the show. Lou actually remembered me and asked Rob to bring me backstage after the show.

I couldn't believe he remembered me after all those years! It was so nice to catch up with him. But that wouldn't be the last time I saw him.

I've been living in New York City for the past 19 years, working for a few music business companies: Koch Records, Virgin Records/EMI and now The Orchard/Sony Music. I've also been DJing, under the name DJ Catskillz, all of that time at music industry events, private parties, and more importantly at amazing rock venues and dive bars around NYC.

In 2019, I started DJing at the Bowery Ballroom after the bands would perform. I was excited that I got booked to DJ an afterparty following an upcoming Sebadoh concert on July 26th. When I got there to set up that night, Lou was at the merch table selling T-shirts and vinyl. I waited for him to finish with a fan so I could say hello. Lou turned towards me and said "Hi Catonia" without skipping a beat. I explained that I was going to DJ some indie rock, lo-fi, post-punk and new wave after his gig. He was happy to hear that and came by to check out some of my DJ set after he played. I loved that we got to hang again that night pretty much 20 years later.

Catonia Whalen, DJ Catskills

THE PSYCHEDELIC FURS, NEWCASTLE 2019

I've seen a lot of gigs and I've done a lot of gigs. It's hard to look beyond The Clash and Richard Hell and The Voidoids at the King's Hall, Derby, on November 3rd, 1977; The Adverts at the same venue in early 1978; or The Cramps at Derby Ajanta Theatre in 1980. I know these were life-changing events and I feel incredibly lucky to have been there.

There are little elements of all three that I could write about but, in reality, they are now too far away to remember in any great detail. I was 17 at that Clash gig – I am now 60. I have seen a lot of stuff in the years between, although not much has hit those high standards. All generations think they lived through the best period of music in their formative years, and I am no exception. However, the objectivity that comes with age makes you wonder whether this was really true.

The first Psychedelic Furs album was released on March 7th, 1980. It was a good album, but it was merely part of a massive wave of brilliant and diverse music that was coming through at that time, powered by the paradigm shift of punk. We played it a lot, saw them support Iggy Pop in Birmingham, bought the "Dumb Waiters" single with the flexidisc on the cover and enjoyed them as just one of the many great artists producing stuff around the turn of the decade. For example, the Pauline Murray and The Invisible Girls album was released in September 1980. Both albums looked ahead to a new kind of pop.

On Wednesday, October 9th, 2019, at the O2 Academy, in Newcastle, I saw The Psychedelic Furs again. It takes a lot now for me to lose myself in the beauty of music the way I did as a teenager, but they were able to give me that experience. They transcended the blandness of the O2 (I've played a lot of O2s, they're mostly horrible) and put on a performance that was authentic, exciting, majestic and cool. They made me realise that they were even better than I thought they were all those years ago. Nostalgia had nothing to do with it.

It's a lot harder to do this than you would imagine, but I'd like to think that Penetration are one of the bands that can. In the end, it's the music that fans first fell in love with and it's the music that they continually return to. It's your job and your duty to play the music in the way The Furs played it that night. If you can do that, it is incredibly life-affirming for both the performer and the listener. It will create a bond forever.

Paul Harvey, Penetration

THE MENSTRUAL CRAMPS, BRISTOL 2020

Emilia – In January 2020 we played at our lovely, favourite local venue, it was packed out, WAY above capacity, and some people at the front were moshing and smashed microphones into our mouths, and smashed pints onto the floor, so then half-way through a song I pulled out a massive chunk of glass out my foot, but no staff could get to the front of the pub to do anything about it! hahaha

AJ – They did put their coats on the ground for you to stand on after though! (Also filled with studs and safety pins.)

Emilia – Hahaha. I loved that gig! Someone at the front tried to give me their own shoes off their own feet for me to wear! They were like 12 sizes too big for me 'cus I have child's-size feet, but what a lovely gesture!

AJ – And someone smashed the toilet in half!

Emilia – After they had menstruated in the toilet!!! Hahahaha that was great! That was one of my favourite gigs, I loved it!

AJ – HAHA! You have to go to the Chelsea Inn to experience a true Bristol punk gig. It's something special.

Emilia, AJ, The Menstrual Cramps

PLAYING ON ENEMY TERRITORY

"As you all know, rock 'n'roll is played on enemy territory… and that's where we all are tonight!" On February 1st,1984, a frustrated Joe Strummer yelled out to a restless crowd at a sold-out Clash gig at San Diego's Fox Theatre. He was attempting to face down uncomprehending fire marshals and venue management over an unwanted barrier at the front of the stage.

For the authorities, the barrier was a safety device, standard operating procedure. For Strummer, the barrier represented a betrayal of the promises of punk culture. If audience and band weren't mashed together, intermingled, staring each other in the face, a critical message would be lost: audience and performer are essentially the same, caught up in something transformative that they could only create together.

Strummer's words were a nod to an idealistic concept of rock – briefly in vogue during the late 1960s and early 1970s – that set that culture against showbiz formulas and big money men. In this, Strummer was perhaps showing his age, for this lofty image of rock as somehow at odds with the Establishment had largely ceased to be real by the mid-1970s. Indeed, for younger firebrands, the term "rock 'n'roll" itself had become an epithet loaded with connotations of compromise and cliché.

This surrender to industry convention and commercial convenience helped to spark the punk insurrection The Clash were so central to – and much of the drama of that band's history came from its passionate yet quixotic effort to simultaneously pursue rock stardom and punk revolution.

Nonetheless, Strummer's idea has lasting relevance for any attempt to build something that does not simply kowtow to the blind, grasping money god that too often rules our world.

We are born and live in "enemy territory" in this sense. Yet we have nowhere else to stand, at least at the outset, till we generate our own communities of resistance and invention – so our hope must be that we can be in this ugly world, but not of it. We can begin to build a new world in the shell of the old, as Dorothy Day and Peter Maurin, founders of the radical Catholic Worker Movement, often used to say.

In Washington DC, this meant that kids who generally disdained alcohol – and the age limits that it often imposed on live music – would come into bars and make them their own. For two hours, three hours, four hours, the rules that governed business as usual would be suspended, and punks would create a liberated zone, where anything was possible, and the only barrier was your imagination.

This did not in itself change the world, except in the hearts of those who took part, learning that this experience has eternal relevance. Everywhere could be a venue for authentic expression or reinvention of reality, on whatever humble or grand scale, pressing "what is" toward a more supple, compassionate and truly human form: "what could be".

Such shows in enemy territory became my passion, and bands willing to push that envelope became my inspirations, confronting fear and expectation, making the moments pulse with life, sometimes danger, but always possibility.

The Clash busking through the north of the UK after the defeat of the miners' strike, playing for free to anyone who turned up or passed by.

Fugazi in the freezing cold at the White House, protesting the Persian Gulf War, picking up on the thunder of the punk percussion protest that had preceded them.

Johnny Cash at Folsom Prison, playing with warmth and dignity for those regarded by so many as the scum of the earth.

Steve Earle interrupting his fast and vigil on the sidewalk of the Supreme Court, to play a set protesting the death penalty.

Bad Brains rocking the feared Valley Green public housing complex in south-east DC, making "Rock Against Racism" real in their hometown.

The MC5 and Phil Ochs playing in Lincoln Park in the 1968 Democratic convention, racing to retrieve their gear as the tear gas closes in and the police begin to riot.

The Evens playing not from on stage, but from amidst the audience at the 9:30 Club 30th Anniversary celebration, confusing some but inspiring others.

Woody Guthrie playing for farm labourers, hobos and immigrants in ragged camps, warmed by campfires during the Great Depression.

Bikini Kill playing before a boy-heavy hardcore crowd, lead singer Kathleen Hanna facing down the hostile crowd with equal parts ferocity and vulnerability.

Mission Impossible at the Burke Virginia country club, with a gaffer tape line on the floor jokingly dividing stage from audience.

Rage Against the Machine playing inside a cop-built cage in a protest at the Democratic National Convention, 2,000 riot police at the ready.

The SNCC Freedom Singers in a church in the deep south during a bloody voter registration drive, knowing the police and Ku Klux Klan were waiting outside.

Dead Kennedys at the Lincoln Memorial surrounded by cops, Biafra describing the monument as the "great eternal Klansman with his two flashing red eyes".

Chilean Victor Jara in the Santiago Stadium with guitar and hands broken by brutal guards, nonetheless leading prisoners in song until he is finally shot and killed.

I wasn't at most of these shows. In fact, I was a kid lost in rural Montana, USA, when several of them happened, and not alive for at least one of them.

But whether I was there or not, these actions sparked deep things in me, a sense of immense possibility, of the freedom that comes from a willingness to risk it all, to put your life on the line. Sometimes quite literally.

And, finally, these moments gave me a belief that if we are willing to invade enemy territory with our wits and our souls and our strength and our dreams, we can somehow redeem not only ourselves, but that land as well. We can, in the end, not only survive on that terrain, but make it our own.

What it takes, however, is people together, sharing a spirit, a transparent moment when the truth transcends and takes flight, lifted to the heavens on some chords, beats and breath.

In that instant of people finding power together at one time with one heart, something shifts, snaps into place... and somehow we find ourselves beyond defeat. Who can say? This revelation might only last for one moment, in one place. But if we have courage to stay with its call, maybe – just maybe – it is for always, it is for everywhere.

Mark Andersen, Positive Force

TEN COMMANDMENTS OF GIG

I have gigged. Sometimes very little, sometimes way too much. I began doing this as a confrontation with the general public, some 40 years ago. I hope you won't mind, then, if I put forth my lifetime findings, the Ten Commandments of Gig.

1. The Act and the Audience: they won't always love one another

Evidence: Jackie Leven, quietly facing down a hostile Doll By Doll "audience" in Cork in 1980. All it took was a few unfaltering and simple words. Beneath a giant backdrop of Antonin Artaud's head and shoulders, and accompanied by Jackie's immanent staring eyes. Resulting in a silence – tense, but silent all the same. In contrast with my own fate as a performer on various occasions, handled with far less composure and, indeed, success.

2. The Act: always have transportation, with fuel on board

Evidence, the first: Microdisney, including me, in its second month of existence, travelling the 160 miles to play in our nation's capital city of Dublin. Extreme shortage of petrol and rail strike. Meaning overnight travel, on deserted roads where fuel usage could be regulated. Witnessing various possible roadside mirages of (others') inebriation and nudity on the unlit single carriageway. Six of us then settling down to an in-vehicle pre-dawn snooze, under the obelisk in Dublin's Phoenix Park. Worth it.

Evidence, the second: some eight years afterwards, on a shoestring UK tour with The Fatima Mansions, inching along an office park driveway, just before lunchtime, somewhere in the English Midlands. The engine of the hired vehicle was roaring and rattling at giant volume, perhaps due to the fact that none of its ever-rotating cast of troubled custodians had favoured it with supplements of oil and water, or, indeed, any form of scrutiny at all. For weeks. The suddenly turning heads, and repulsed faces, of business-dressed people through the floor-to-ceiling office windows gave our tableau the air of a menacing Jacques Tati movie. Not worth it, but hilarious.

3. The Audience: proximity to livestock makes them sleepy

Evidence: again in the English Midlands, The Fatima Mansions. Huge steel doors, for access to a working cattle market, were located just alongside the stage. The audience was very tranquil indeed. Which might have been the force-field of primeval animal trading, or perhaps full stomachs from the apparent barbeques which had produced those blackened tinfoil pieces on the floors of the venue's toilets?

4. The Audience: rugby makes them talkative

Evidence: at Warrington, the proprietor preceded our soundcheck by soliciting reverence for his venue, "the Anfield of Rugby League" (sic). Our dressing room was a rather cluttered and dusty directors' box. The audience didn't give a monkeys, either way. It was Saturday night, and human roaring would be unconfined, all of it directed at one's mates.

5. The Venue: Americans – they like to have fun at work, and this is all work to them

I've quite often had reason to observe, both as a performer and as a punter, that venue and stage crews in the US tend (with notable psychotic exceptions) to exude a sense of fun, even joy, as they go about their work. This stands in contrast to the passive aggression and clinical depression more usually exhibited in equivalent situations on this side of the Atlantic. Must be the lack of affordable healthcare.

6. The Act: don't play in car showrooms

Yeah, this is a big one, don't do it. Once happened in Foggia, Italia, with Microdisney. We played on one of the several podia, and the 1985 Datsun range commanded the remainder. One guy, out of his mind, kept screaming at me to, I quote, "take [my] fucking clothes off". While not meant to be taken literally, it nonetheless grew tiresome.

7. The Act: don't play L-shaped rooms with two PAs and two sound crews

Bad. Also happened, mid-afternoon in Lodz, Poland. If asked, suggest Venue hires a second Act and makes it into a proper soundclash. Or blues jam.

8. The Act: check there's a venue

It's the year 2000 – I'm back from oblivion, rejuvenated! The Grand Necropolitan Quartet and I were booked to play a reputable medium-sized venue in central London. Just before the soundcheck, word arrived that the venue would be shutting down immediately, having lost its licence. Hilarity ensued.

9. The Act: don't expect your hometown to love you

Evidence: New Year's Eve, 2018/2019, Rocket From the Crypt, playing a big venue in San Diego, where they reside. Rattling the floorboards with wild rockin' noise and charisma. Full house, no takers.

10. Acts & Audiences: this ain't El Dorado, at least not the way they say

I get downcast when I hear people say things like, "live work is where the living is earned", or threadbare censorious stuff to that effect. True for some, but a mirage for most, and after the Covid time of writing this, who knows what will persist? So where's the magic? It exists, and I've felt it most recently at shows in Dalston by Sean O'Hagan, Brigid Mae Power, Kenny Process Team and Daniel O'Sullivan's Dream Lion Ensemble, and at the final show in Deptford by the stellar revival known as This Is Not This Heat. Nights when energy and good feeling seem to palpably flow off the stage, to move around the room for a while and then flow back onto the stage, and on, in continuous exchange. Just as happened at shows in Cork by The Only Ones and Planxty, all those years ago. For that, perhaps we can all muddle through somehow.

Cathal Coughlan, Microdisney, The Fatima Mansions

DIY SCENES 2020

Our story is less of a specific gig memory and more of a love letter to the love of our lives, the cream in our bun, the Helta to our Skelta, the Sydney punk and DIY community. In the scheme of things, we haven't been around long. Our contribution to the Sydney DIY community is a drop in a very big, very deep ocean. It's probably true that our modern-day DIY scene in Sydney pales in comparison to the wild, coming-of-age years in the 1970s to 1990s scenes. And while there is probably less blood and tears, the heart of the thing has remained the same and the path laid by our musical heroes has only been strengthened by also becoming an inclusive safe space for minorities. Even through crippling lockout laws during the 2010s and subsequent venue shutdowns, the DIY scene continued. People seem to always find a way and a place to express themselves, and unusual gig spaces always show up vacant when they're most needed. We've seen great bands play in laneways on the back of a truck, in gutted warehouses and in inner-west living rooms. Sometimes the sound is shit, sometimes the venue is so hot it's a fire hazard, and sometimes it's impossible to categorise what you're seeing. But what a beautiful thing to behold. A timeless and self-sufficient idea. Creativity at its purest. We want to thank everyone across the world and through all time who has contributed to the DIY/punk world. Don't ever stop. We're honoured and inspired by your work every day. Long live.

Jonathan and Kirsty, Party Dozen